AN ILLUSTRATED HISTORY OF
DUKE BASKETBALL

An Illustrated History of
Duke Basketball
A Legacy of Achievement

Bill Brill

with Ben Cohen and Duke University
Foreword by Mike Krzyzewski

SPORTS PUBLISHING

Sports Publishing books may be purchased in bulk at special discounts for sales promotion, corporate gifts, fund-raising, or educational purposes. Special editions can also be created to specifications. For details, contact the Special Sales Department, Sports Publishing, 307 West 36th Street, 11th Floor, New York, NY 10018 or sportspubbooks@skyhorsepublishing.com.

Sports Publishing® is a registered trademark of Skyhorse Publishing, Inc.®, a Delaware corporation.

Visit our website at www.sportspubbooks.com

10 9 8 7 6 5 4 3 2 1

Library of Congress Cataloging-in-Publication Data

Brill, Bill.
An illustrated history of Duke basketball : a legacy of achievement / Bill
Brill with Ben Cohen ; foreword by Mike Krzyzewski.
p. cm.
Includes bibliographical references and index.
ISBN 978-1-61321-000-0 (alk. paper)
1. Duke University--Basketball--History--Pictorial works. 2. Duke Blue
Devils (Basketball team)--History--Pictorial works. I. Cohen, Ben. II.
Title.
GV885.43.D85B74 2011
796.323'6309756563--dc23
                                  2011041096
Printed in China

Photos courtesy of Duke Photography, Duke Archives, Duke Sports
Information Archives, Jon Gardiner, Jeffrey A. Camarati, Chris Hildreth,
Matt Barton, Ned Hinshaw, Robert Crawford, Chuck Liddy, Jim Bounds, Bob
Donnan, Bruce Feeley, Michael Hirsch, Bob Rosato, Jay Anderson, Jim Wallace,
and the *Durham Herald-Sun*.

All photos were pulled from Duke University's Sports Information Department archives.

Thanks to Duke Sports Information Director Jon Jackson and Basketball Legacy Fund Director Mike Cragg for their advice and editing.

An Illustrated History of
Duke Basketball

Contents

100 SEASONS OF DUKE BASKETBALL

Just writing those words brings an incredible flood of great memories for me. So many recollections of games won, games lost, great players, outstanding competition, and playing in the greatest venues in all of sports help shape my thoughts. I also think of the absolute privilege of coaching at Duke University and in the Atlantic Coast Conference.

Most importantly, the relationships that develop as a result of being part of something bigger than one's self are what make me emotional. The smiles, the tears, the hugs, the confident faces of accomplishment on and off the court mean so much more to me and to our Duke program than championships, game-winning baskets or won-loss records.

No matter how many of those tangible things we accomplish—and that body of work has been sizeable in our first 99 years—the measure of achievement for our program will be determined by molding young men of whom we can be proud as representatives of Duke in the world, no matter what their chosen profession.

Throughout my career, I've learned that coaching and teaching is best served at a place you love, at a place in which you believe, at a place that is in your heart. Duke. It has always been about Duke, for me, for our players, for everyone associated with our program, for the Cameron Crazies who provide us with the best home court advantage in the country, for the hundreds of thousands of Duke fans who support us every season.

In celebration of the 100th season of Duke Basketball, I hope that we reconnect with the values that have made our program—OUR program—special: caring, collective responsibility, communication, trust and pride. It is that FIST of values—of five fingers—coming together as one that has made our program great—before my time and will no doubt continue past my time here.

It was once written that D-U-K-E is the most feared four-letter word in college basketball. Whether or not that is true I don't know. I do believe that the name Duke has become synonymous with consistent excellence. We truly have a Tradition of Excellence that goes hand-in-hand with our great University.

The multitude of great coaches—Eddie Cameron, Vic Bubas, Bill Foster to name a few—and players like Bill Werber, Bill Mock, Ed Koffenberger, Dick Groat, Art Heyman, Jeff Mullins, Jack Marin, Bob Verga, Mike Lewis, Randy Denton, Jim Spanarkel and Mike Gminski set the foundation for future stars. I've had the good fortune to coach the likes of Gene Banks, Johnny Dawkins, Mark Alarie, Tommy Amaker, Danny Ferry, Christian Laettner, Bobby Hurley, Grant Hill, Roshown McLeod, Trajan Langdon, Elton Brand, Chris Carrawell, Shane Battier, Jason Williams, Carlos Boozer, Mike Dunleavy, Chris Duhon, J.J. Redick and Shelden Willams—all All-America selections who've carried the torch in keeping Duke among the elite programs in the nation.

Some of the achievements by Duke through the years are staggering: three national championships, 14 Final Four appearances (second all-time behind only UCLA's 15), 1,731 victories all-time, 14 ACC championships, five Southern Conference championships, 25 final top 10 rankings, 96 weeks ranked as the nation's No. 1 team, eight National Players of the Year (six since 1986), five National Defensive Players of the Year, 31 All-Americas and nine Academic All-Americas.

But you know what is better than all those numbers? It is the sense of family that I feel and I hope every single player, coach and fan feels when Duke takes to the court. I know I feel a connection to the first players wearing the Trinity College uniforms as well as the coaches and players of every decade.

Now entering my 25th year at Duke, I am truly honored to be a small part of Duke's rich history. It is a history we should all cherish and appreciate as we move forward. And it is one that future Blue Devil teams will try to uphold.

What follows is a chronicle of the highlights from our first 99 years. I hope you enjoy it and are as proud of Duke's accomplishments as I am.

Mike Krzyzewski

August 2004

CHAPTER

1

THE CENTENNIAL SEASON

On a dreary, cold, rainy May morning in 2004, there is a lone figure working in empty Cameron Indoor Stadium. Luol Deng, a Duke freshman, second-team All-ACC, is practicing moves that he's taking to the NBA.

Five floors above, at the top of the Schwartz-Butters building, Mike Krzyzewski sits with a visitor. He is not happy. Only 90 minutes before, he had learned that his top recruit, slender point guard Shaun Livingston, called to say that he—like Deng—was placing his name in the 2004 NBA Draft.

While neither player had hired an agent, and thus was eligible to play for Duke next year, the nation's leading college coach did not expect to have either of them on his squad. It is possible that Duke, which just a month before had gone to its 10th Final Four in the previous 19 years, would play in a loaded ACC in 2005 with eight scholarship players.

For years, including the dominating stretch from 1986-94, the Blue Devils were immune to attrition to the pros. That changed dramatical-ly in 1999, when NCAA-finalist Duke lost two sophomores and a freshman to the NBA.

Three years later, three juniors left school early. Jason Williams did so with a degree. Carlos Boozer was within a few classes of becoming a Duke graduate. Mike Dunleavy, who left unexpectedly, had a year of school left and already had been named a co-captain for the 2002-03 team.

But these latest defections were the most telling. In the summer of 2003, recruit Kris Humphries was released from his commitment to Duke after he and his father sought assurances from Coach K that the incoming freshman would be guaranteed playing time. He went to Minnesota and averaged 21.7 points and 10.1 rebounds—and left after one year for the NBA.

Thus, the scholarship senior class of 2007 at Duke, which would have been Deng and Humphries, was gone. And the leading recruit, Livingston, didn't play in college. The school which only six years before had never lost a player early to the NBA only got one year (Deng) out of a possible 12 from the trio.

9

"It is not a good time for the collegiate game," Krzyzewski said. "There are no borders. The NBA people, they have no rules. The pros can talk to the kids, the colleges can't. All they see is the NBA."

Later that month, a tournament run by Bob Gibbons played games in Cameron. The pro scouts were on hand. No college coaches were permitted to see the players perform. "It is not good for the NBA or us," he said. "The pro game has become a culture. All the kids see are the names and colors of the pros. They know about the money. It's intoxicating."

The colleges, he said, "have to keep adjusting. To try to maintain what we've done, it's difficult. It's a very precarious route."

Krzyzewski remained aware of the temptations. "There is something about now. We have to be able to resist now. This is a changing environment, and it's eroding our game."

He was concerned about the lack of communication. "You recruit guys and you're not going to get them. In the college game, there's now lots of attrition, and there is no desire to right that."

Since the NCAA went to an expanded 64-team tournament field in 1985, no school has dominated the way Duke has. There have been the 11 Final Fours—Krzyzewski is 10-1 in regional finals—and four national championships since 1991. Duke also had a legitimate chance to win four more titles, in '86, '94, '99 and '04.

There is no telling how successful the Blue Devils might have been had their leader always been healthy. Krzyzewski missed most of the '95 season following back surgery and exhaustion. He had hip replacements immediately after the '99 and '02 seasons, having coached both in extreme pain.

DANIEL EWING IS ONE OF TWO SENIORS ON DUKE'S 2004-05 TEAM.

But he has produced teams that regularly have finished the season ranked No. 1, captured an unthinkable five consecutive championships in the highly competitive ACC, and began the 2005 season—the 100th for Duke basketball and his 25th as the coach of the Blue Devils—with a string of 148 consecutive weeks being rated in the Top 25.

Despite the premature loss of players, Krzyzewski was not changing his recruiting procedures. "We'll still go after the best kids, good students who want to go to college. Not every player wants college, but the ones we go after will graduate if they come and remain for four years. We'll maintain our principles. We won't deviate from the things we do."

Just how this plays out is yet to be determined. Krzyzewski is aware that there is no sympathy for Duke. "Football is different," he said. "There are (far) fewer schools, and half of them believe they have a chance to win a national championship. In basketball there are over 300 schools, and most of them don't have the goals we have. If we lose players to the NBA, they have no reason to care."

Duke had the same goals for 2005 that it had every year—win the NCAA, with winning the ACC as a byproduct. This team featured several excellent players, among them senior Daniel Ewing, juniors J.J.

SEAN DOCKERY SLAPS THE FLOOR IN DUKE'S TRADEMARK DEFENSIVE POSITION.

Redick, Shelden Williams, Shavlik Randolph and Sean Dockery, and freshman DeMarcus Nelson. There were no scholarship sophomores.

Half a decade later, Duke's status as the nation's top program is indisputable. ESPN.com's Joe Lunardi compared what Duke has achieved under Krzyzewski to the UCLA dynasty of John Wooden, which occurred during the days when only league champs appeared in a 23-25 team field, all games were dictated by geography, and two wins put you in the Final Four.

"Again, with all due respect to UCLA," Lunardi wrote, "there are no Drakes (in the Final Four) on Duke's list. My point is that there are ways to dominate in an era that transcend winning the last game. And what the Blue Devils have done under Mike Krzyzewski has been every bit as dominant as what the Bruins did under John Wooden." In the dozen years that UCLA went to the Final Four, Wooden beat 15 different schools. In his 10 appearances, Coach K has beaten 34.

The Duke numbers since the Age of Duke began in '86 are revealing:

In that time, as Duke has gone to 11 Final Fours, so has the entire Southeastern Conference. The Big East has gone to seven; the Pac-10 six. The Blue Devils have been to more Final Fours than Conference USA, Atlantic 10, WAC and 22 other leagues combined. The other members of the ACC collectively have been as many times as Duke.

In his 30 years, Coach K has coached teams that were ranked No. 1 in 163 games (144-19). He has coached unranked teams in 139 games, many in the first three years.

Overall, Duke has been in 15 Final Fours and won 1,877 games, fourth all-time behind Kentucky, UNC and Kansas. After a century of basketball evolution, the school's record of 81-25 in NCAA play was the nation's best. There were eight National Players of the Year (six under Coach K); five National Defensive Players

NO K IN L.A.: KRZYZEWSKI STAYS AT DUKE

From July 1, 2004, when the news broke, until July 5 when the situation was resolved, there were a lot of nervous people in Blue Devil Nation.

Mike Krzyzewski was talking with the Los Angeles Lakers, who were offering enough money to make him the highest paid coach ever in all of sports. And it wasn't just the reported $40 million for five years, but also the team presidency and an ownership percentage of the club.

But early on the morning of July 5, after making his decision late the evening before, Coach K called Lakers' general manager Mitch Kupchak and informed him he was staying at Duke for his 25th season. Then he called the school's new president, Richard Brodhead, whose first official day on the job coincided with the job offer to the university's highest-profile employee.

Later, at a news conference with athletic director Joe Alleva and Krzyzewski that was televised across the nation, Brodhead said, "I have the happy news of saying that Mike Krzyzewski, the famous Coach K, is going to be staying on at Duke. I am so delighted that you decided that your real place was in the world of college basketball."

Krzyzewski first heard from the Lakers prior to the NBA Draft, and thought before returning the call it would be about the status of freshman Luol Deng and recruit Shaun Livingston, who eventually were selected seventh and fourth overall. "I talked with Mitch Kupchak at a time when I was taking inventory (of his own situation). I said, 'I'm 57, maybe I should just look.' As it went on, I took a closer and closer look. As I looked at this and myself, I found that I wanted to lead.

"Your heart has to be in whatever you lead. It became apparent that this decision was somewhat easier to make because you have to follow your heart and lead with it. Duke has always taken my whole heart. I didn't make this decision because of tangibles. I made this decision because of intangibles, and the intangibles were, as they always have been, so much here."

Coach K said that he wanted to coach for a long time. "The allure of coaching in college has no price. To me, it was what was going to give me the most happiness, and I've been really happy at Duke and really fulfilled at Duke."

of the Year (for seven years); and 31 All-Americans (19 under Krzyzewski).

Krzyzewski had been National Coach of the Year nine times and had won 64 NCAA games, one behind Dean Smith's record. Overall he had won 694 games, including at Army, and was sixth on the list of active coaches. All the others were at least seven years older.

Despite the defections, Duke looked ahead to the 2005 season. In the season past, Duke recorded its eighth 30-victory season, all under Coach K. Seven of them have come since 1991 and a record four times ('99-02) the Blue Devils finished ranked No. 1.

The 2004 season began with a struggling 67-56 win over Detroit, after which the second-ranked Blue Devils played in the Alaska Shootout. They were unimpressive in beating Pacific and Liberty and fell apart in the second half of the championship game against Purdue. Leading 39-33 at halftime, Duke was outscored 16-2 starting the last period and never led again. The Devils shot 38 percent and just five for 22 on three-pointers as the Boilermakers, behind Kenneth Lowe's 22 points, won convincingly, 78-68. It was something of a trend for the season; only three of Duke's losses came in games in which it trailed at halftime.

The next game was at No. 5 Michigan State, and Krzyzewski addressed two critical areas—defense and rebounding. The Blue Devils did well in both. Duke shot better than 59 percent, dominated the boards, and won going away, 72-50. It was MSU's worst home loss since Coach Tom Izzo had lifted his program to elite status. Not a single Spartan scored more than eight points.

That win got the Blue Devils back on track. They went on to win the next 17 games, most of them blowouts. Included was an 89-61 win over '03 Final Four contestant Texas in Duke's "home" game in Madison Square Garden. A sellout crowd of predominantly Duke fans watched in a game

in which the Blue Devils handled the tickets. It was a financial bonanza as well as one of the best performances of the season, in which the veteran Longhorns (four returning starters) trailed by 19 at halftime as Duke shot 62 percent for the period and 57 percent for the game. J.J. Redick's 20 points led six players in double figures.

THE CAMERON CRAZIES CELEBRATE ANOTHER J.J. REDICK THREE-POINT FIELD GOAL.

Duke's entry into ACC play included romps against Clemson (19 points), Virginia (22), N.C. State (19) and Wake Forest (12). In each case, the Blue Devils opened up significant halftime leads and won with ease. After going three for nine on threes against Clemson, Redick heated up in the next three league games to make 12 of 19 from beyond the arc.

Playing at College Park, Duke won 68-60 over Maryland in the lowest-scoring game in the rivalry in 22 years. Redick was the offensive star again, getting 26 points, including five of six three-pointers. He also made all nine free throws, including four in the final minute after the Terps had rallied to within three points. The Blue Devils had

SHELDEN WILLIAMS SHOWS WHY HE IS KNOWN AS "THE LANDLORD."

AFTER GOING COAST TO COAST, CHRIS DUHON MAKES THE WINNING LAYUP AT NORTH CAROLINA.

their most dominating rebounding game, 49-34, including as many offensive boards (24) as Maryland had on defense.

Duke remained in the nation's capital and crunched Georgetown, 85-66, three days later before the first sellout the Hoyas have had at the MCI Center. Again, there were a lot of Duke fans on hand. The shooting remained hot (56 percent) and Shelden Williams had his most dominant game with a career-high 26 points.

Returning home, Duke needed a critical three-pointer by Chris Duhon in the final 36 seconds to subdue stubborn Florida State, 56-49. Only Redick seemed able to score, getting 24 points. FSU sagged its defense around Williams, who did not take a single shot. The Seminoles dominated on the backboards, which would prove to be a trouble area for Duke in the last half of the season.

In the first meeting with North Carolina, at Chapel Hill, the Blue Devils survived in overtime when Duhon went the length of the floor to score on a reverse layup with 6.5 seconds left for an 83-81 win. UNC tied it at the end of regulation on a three by Jawad Williams and again in the extra period on a three by Rashad McCants with 13 seconds left.

After Duhon went end to end for the winner, UNC coach Roy Williams blamed a defensive mistake for letting the Duke captain go all the way. It was the first meeting between Williams and Krzyzewski since the former took the Carolina coaching job and left Kansas, which had ended Duke's season in the Sweet 16 in 2003.

Wins over Clemson and Virginia in Cameron ran the winning streak to 18 games before the Blue Devils stumbled against N.C. State at the raucous RBC Center. State made 12 straight free throws in the final 1:10 for the upset. The 'Pack got superior performances from Marcus Melvin and Ilian Evtimov, a 6-7 sophomore who played the high post on offense and consistently drove around Williams for easy shots. State led by 10 points at halftime and controlled the tempo throughout. Redick (28 points) and Duhon (17) were the only offensive threats for the nation's No. 1 team.

In the next game, at Wake Forest, Redick went scoreless from the floor for the first time in his career. The team's leading scorer had just two free throws as the Deacons won, 90-84, behind the play of freshman guard Chris Paul. In the final five minutes, Paul had a dozen of his 23 points. The Blue Devils led by 13 points in the last half, but faded badly down the stretch.

"They were just better than we were," Gary Williams said, after Duke ended its losing ways with an 86-63 defeat of Maryland in Cameron. Redick rebounded from his subpar effort with 20 points and Williams added 18 points and 11 boards. The only problem, however, was rebounding. The Terps led 38-35 in

LUOL DENG SCORES AGAINST NORTH CAROLINA'S SEAN MAY.

what was becoming a trouble spot. In the next game, a 97-73 blitzing on Valparaiso, the Devils were outrebounded by six.

Opponents actually got more rebounds in eight consecutive games, or until the semifinals of the ACC Tournament. In a couple of situations, it proved critical. Georgia Tech came into Cameron having lost 15 games in a row to Duke, and shocked the Blue Devils, 76-68, ending a 41-game home winning streak, longest in the nation. Tech blocked 11 shots and held Duke to 34 percent shooting.

In the regular-season finale at home against North Carolina, Duke rallied behind freshman Deng, who came off the bench to score 25 points on 12-for-16 shooting. Duhon did a great job on defense in the second half against McCants, who had led the Tar Heels to a 33-30 intermission lead. With Duke ahead by three points in the closing seconds, Redick stole the ball when McCants lost it and clinched the win with two free throws with 2.7 seconds left to make it 70-65.

The Devils headed to Greensboro seeking their sixth straight ACC Tournament crown. Behind the sensational play of Williams, they advanced to the finals by beating Virginia and Georgia Tech. Williams scored 47 points on 14-17 shooting and claimed 31 rebounds, including 18 offensive.

In the finals against Maryland, Duke appeared well on its way to another championship, forcing Gary Williams to take two timeouts within 20 seconds as the Devils led 77-65 with 4:58 left. They never scored another point in regulation. With guard John Gilchrist going wild, the Terps went on a 12-0 run. The tying point on a free throw with 20 seconds left came as Williams fouled out. Maryland led all the way in the extra period for the stunning 95-87 victory and G. Williams's first ACC championship.

The loss was costly although Duke was seeded No. 1, but placed in the Atlanta Region, rather than the East Rutherford Region, and meant the Devils were bracketed with Connecticut. Kentucky was the overall No. 1 seed and Duke was No. 2.

The first two games were at Raleigh, where Duke blitzed Alabama State 95-61 and Seton Hall 90-62. Advancing to their seventh straight Sweet 16 in Atlanta, the Blue Devils faced Big Ten regular season champ Illinois. The question mark was Duhon's ribs, banged up badly when he rammed into a camera support in the ACC Tournament. But Duhon was sensational on defense, shutting down Illini star Deron Williams, and leading his team with a career-high 10 rebounds. It didn't matter that he took just one shot; he handed out eight assists, and he showed disregard for his body by diving out of bounds for a loose ball. Duke won, 72-62.

Duke became the only No. 1 seed to advance to the Final Four by edging Xavier, 66-63. It was the school's 14th Regional triumph, and the 10th for Krzyzewski against only a loss in 1998 to Kentucky. Two key plays by Deng produced the victory. With the score tied at 56, he rebounded a missed shot and passed to Redick, who hit a three that gave the Devils the lead for good. With 1:55 remaining, the fresh-

MIKE KRZYZEWSKI CELEBRATES HIS 10TH REGIONAL CHAMPIONSHIP IN 2004.

CHRIS DUHON GETS TREATMENT FROM TRAINER DAVE ENGELHARDT.

man tapped in a Duhon miss to create a five-point lead.

"I was so excited to see Deng make a couple of plays (on his own)," Krzyzewski said. "He's only a freshman, and we've been creating plays for him, but those he did on his own." Deng scored 19 points and was voted Most Outstanding Player in the Regional.

SHAVLIK RANDOLPH ENDED AN OUTSTANDING NCAA TOURNAMENT WITH A STRONG GAME AGAINST CONNECTICUT.

At the Alamodome in San Antonio, the Duke-UConn game was considered the championship battle, even though it came in the semifinal. The Huskies, who beat Duke for the title in '99, were led by Emeka Okafor, the nation's most dominant player, and guard Ben Gordon.

The most important people turned out to be the officials, who constantly blew their whistles, and virtually every play in the post was called a foul. Okafor got two personals in the first 3:09 and sat for the rest of the half. Krzyzewski left his big men, Williams and Shavlik Randolph, on the floor. They each collected a third foul before halftime.

Duke led 41-34 despite missing six layups, one of them a breakaway. The Blue Devils trailed 15-4 after six minutes, but outscored

AFTER EARNING AN ACC REGULAR-SEASON CHAMPIONSHIP, THE BLUE DEVILS REACHED THE SCHOOL'S 10TH FINAL FOUR IN THE PAST 19 YEARS.

UConn 37-19 the remainder of the period. In the second half, Okafor got just one more foul, while Williams and Randolph fouled out, which proved critical.

The Devils led by nine at 59-50, and were still on top 75-67 with 3:15 to play when Randolph, sensational on 6-6 shooting, got his fifth against Okafor. Williams (15 points) fouled out with 5:04 left and Duke ahead, 70-62.

With its two big men gone, Duke had nobody who could stop Okafor, although Nick Horvath fouled out trying. The three Blue Devil post defenders collected 15 fouls in 41 minutes.

The Huskies went on a 12-0 run to take a four-point lead before Duhon hit a 40-footer at the buzzer to leave Duke a 79-78 loser. In that span, Deng missed two three-pointers. With four minutes left, he missed a one and one, and Okafor blocked his layup try. The winning goal came after Okafor missed a jumper, then grabbed the rebound out of Deng's hands and made the layup for the 76-75 lead.

It was a bitter ending to a 31-6 season that easily could have been better. But the record itself demonstrated Duke's continuing Legacy of Achievement.

CHAPTER

2

THE PLAYERS

Following the scintillating overtime victory over North Carolina at Chapel Hill in the first coaching matchup against Roy Williams since his hiring as the Tar Heel coach, Mike Krzyzewski downplayed the coach versus coach theory prevalent among the media.

"This is not about the coaches," he said. "It is about the players. It is the players who make these programs, and we are fortunate enough to coach them."

Duke's dynastic program has featured some great coaches, notably Eddie Cameron, Vic Bubas, and now, for a quarter-century, Coach K. But it also has had an extraordinary list of superb players.

There are 13 jerseys hanging from the Cameron rafters. There is one unusual theme, a bond among almost all of them. With the exception of Art Heyman, whose final year at Duke was 1963, all of them either remain connected to basketball, or made the sport their career.

Consider the list:

DICK GROAT

Dick Groat was the first, a two-time All-American in basketball and baseball. Although he played professionally in baseball for 14 years, he always at heart was a basketball player. A native of Swissvale, Pennsylvania, a Pittsburgh suburb, he has remained in that area his entire life. Groat has been the analyst on the Pittsburgh basketball network for almost 30 years.

Jeff Mullins had Duke's most successful professional career, most of it with the Golden State

JEFF MULLINS

Warriors. Upon retirement, he spent a year in Duke sports administration, left to own an automobile firm in Cary, but returned to basketball as the coach at UNC-Charlotte. He remained there for 11 years, and, upon retirement, became an analyst on television.

MIKE GMINSKI

Mike Gminski played 14 years in the NBA, later worked for the Charlotte Hornets and was an analyst on their radio network. He now works as the TV analyst for Fox Sports, which produces the ACC's Sunday night games.

BOBBY HURLEY

Bobby Hurley's playing career ended after a devastating auto accident that nearly claimed his life. After recuperating, he returned to the NBA, but never recovered the quickness that had been his trademark. He became an owner of race horses, one of which ran in the 2002 Kentucky Derby. In 2003, Hurley got back into basketball, becoming a scout for the Philadelphia 76ers, whose president is another former Duke player, Billy King.

JASON WILLIAMS

Other Duke stars have been hampered in the pros by injury. Jason Williams missed the 2004 NBA season with the Chicago Bulls. He was fortunate to survive a motorcycle accident following his rookie campaign. Still recuperating, he hopes to return to the pros in the 2005 season.

GRANT HILL

Grant Hill, a five-time All-Star who has been Duke's greatest performer in the NBA, has missed virtually all of the previous three seasons because of a variety of ankle and foot injuries. Now with Orlando, he has just now fully recovered after yet another major surgery.

CHRISTIAN LAETTNER

Christian Laettner has been a pro since '92-93, but missed one season after tearing an Achilles' tendon during a workout at Duke.

Danny Ferry played two years in Europe after graduating from Duke in '89, then 14 years in the NBA. He was a member of the 2003 champion San Antonio Spurs and now works for the team's front office.

DANNY FERRY

Johnny Dawkins played nine years in the pros, then returned to Duke. After a year in administration, when

JOHNNY DAWKINS

he also served as analyst on the basketball network, he became an assistant coach. He is currently the associate head coach for the Blue Devils.

Shane Battier is now playing for the Memphis Grizzlies. Heyman, who played two years with the New York Knicks after being selected No. 1 in the '63 NBA draft, lives in New York and owns a restaurant. He never has had any connection with basketball since he retired as a player.

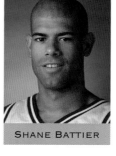

SHANE BATTIER

Groat was the first Duke player to have his jersey retired. Appropriately, it occurred on May 1, 1952, before a baseball game against UNC. He was a star shortstop for the Blue Devils, who were No. 1 during the regular season and who played in the College World Series.

J.J. REDICK

Groat, who never played a game in the minor leagues, had a 14-year career in which he won a batting title, was the National League MVP, and captained World Series champs Pittsburgh and St. Louis. Although he played only a handful of games for Fort Wayne in the NBA, he considers himself "a retired basketball player."

SHELDEN WILLIAMS

Groat is the lone member of the retired-jersey club who did not play in the Atlantic Coast Conference. He averaged 25.2 points in '51 and 26.0 the next season. His

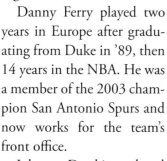

831 points as a junior stood as the school record until Jason Williams broke it in 2001. The national player of the year in 1952, he set a Duke scoring mark with 48 points against Carolina in his home finale. That record stood for 37 years.

ART HEYMAN LEADS DUKE IN CAREER SCORING AVERAGE (25.1PPG).

Dick has co-owned a golf course in Ligonier, Pennsylvania, with former Pirates teammate Jerry Lynch, for 37 years.

Heyman and Mullins were teammates during the Bubas era, when Duke went to its first Final Four. After initially committing to UNC, Heyman became the first Bubas recruit, one day after Vic had become the Blue Devils' coach in May, 1959. In his three seasons of varsity play, Heyman was the most consistent scorer ever. He averaged 25.2, 25.3 and 24.9 points. His overall average of 25.1 remains the school record.

Heyman led Duke to its initial Final Four in his senior season in 1963. He was the national player of the year, and in an extraordinary vote, was selected as the MVP of the Final Four even though Duke was defeated by Loyola of Chicago in the semifinals. At 6-5, he never was a great shooter, but he often retrieved his own missed shot for a basket. He averaged more than 10 rebounds every season, and is

MIKE GMINSKI WAS A THREE-TIME ALL-ACC SELECTION AND ACADEMIC ALL-AMERICAN.

JEFF MULLINS, A TWO-TIME ALL-AMERICAN, WENT ON TO A SUCCESSFUL NBA CAREER.

second—to Laettner—for the most free throw attempts (853) although he just had three seasons of eligibility. In his last home game, against UNC, Art had a career-high 40 points while collecting 24 rebounds.

Mullins, an inch shorter than Heyman, was a year behind him in school. He played in two Final Fours. He was a three-time All-ACC choice and twice made All-America. He won the ACC's McKevlin award in 1964 as the league's top athlete. Unlike his running mate, Mullins was a superb outside shooter, and his field goal percentage for his career was 51.5. He averaged more than 20 points every season, including 24.2 as a senior, when he led Duke to the NCAA championship game against UCLA.

His career scoring average of 21.9 is fourth all time. He scored 40 points in an NCAA game against Villanova, and played on the gold medal U.S. Olympic team in '64. As a pro, he was a five-time All-Star, led Golden State in scoring six of seven years, and was the first Duke player to be a member of an NBA champion when Golden State won in '75. Mullins had 13,017 points in the pros, most ever for a Duke player.

Gminski graduated from high school after his junior year, which was good news for Duke, whose coaches were aware of the possibility and began recruiting him early. Even as the youngest player in the ACC, barely 17, he shot 51.5 percent from the floor as a rookie while averaging 15.3 points and 10.7 rebounds. His sophomore season, he starred as a young Duke team went all the way to the championship game, where it lost to Kentucky. He became a three-time All-ACC selection, three-time Academic All-American and was an All-American in 1980.

Duke's third all-time leading scorer with 2,323 points, the 6-11 Gminski shot 53 percent from the field and 79.1 percent at the foul line during his career. He averaged 19 points. He still holds the school record for career rebounds with 1,242 and the record for blocked shots with 345. And he graduated from college when he was just 20.

Having lost a chance to recruit well because he was hired late after the 1980 season ended, Coach K did not figure out the process during his second year. He went after all the big names—and struck out. By the time 1982 came around, it was obvious that Duke needed to strike it rich, or the program, having just finished last in the ACC, would be in trouble. The staff reduced the number of prospects, and enhanced the intensity toward getting those it wanted.

The first to commit was Dawkins, a slender guard from the Washington, D.C., suburbs. It would turn out to be the most important catch of Krzyzewski's career. Four years later, the Blue Devils won an NCAA record 37 games, finished No. 1 in the polls, and reached the title game against Louisville. The leader was Dawkins.

He played that freshman year as a point guard. With four freshmen often starting, Duke again finished last and was trounced, 109-66,

JOHNNY DAWKINS IS DUKE'S ALL-TIME LEADING SCORER.

by Virginia in the opening round of the ACC Tournament. That was hardly the fault of the 6-2 Dawkins, who averaged 18.1 points while making half of his shots from the floor.

That was just the beginning. As a sophomore, Dawkins moved over to shooting guard as the point was handled by freshman Tommy Amaker. Johnny averaged 19.4 and, more importantly, Duke improved from 11-17 to 24-10 and gained Krzyzewski's initial NCAA bid. Except for 1995, when Coach K missed almost the entire ACC season because of a back problem and exhaustion, the Blue Devils have gone to the NCAAs every year.

The big win in '84 was over No. 1 UNC in the ACC semifinals. The following season, with Dawkins leading the way, the team was 23-8 and posted the first winning record in ACC play since 1979. As a senior, Dawkins was fabulous. He averaged 20.2 points, shooting 54.9 percent from the floor and 81.2 at the foul line. He made All-ACC, ACC tournament MVP, NCAA East region MVP and was named national player of the year. He was Duke's first two-time consensus All-American. He would finish his career with a school record 2,556 points, having led his team in scoring every season. Johnny scored in double figures in 129 of the 133 games in which he appeared.

Selected 10th in the NBA draft, he played nine years professionally. He just completed his seventh year on the coaching staff.

Ferry probably was the second most important re-

DANNY FERRY SCORED AN ACC-RECORD 58 POINTS AGAINST MIAMI.

cruit ever. The son of the general manager of the Washington Bullets, he was heavily recruited by North Carolina after a top prep career. Considered the No. 1 high school player in the nation, when he chose the Blue Devils, it validated Krzyzewski's recruiting capabilities.

After serving as a valuable backup for the senior-dominated '86 team (Ferry made the winning basket against Kansas in the Final Four), he became the team's leading scorer. He was second-team All-ACC as a sophomore, and in his junior year, he hiked his scoring average to 19.1 and made All-American while leading Duke to the Final Four.

His senior season was his finest. He averaged 22.6 points as Duke again went to the Final Four. Ferry was national player of the year, All-American and winner of the ACC's McKevlin award as top athlete. He established an ACC and school scoring record that still stands, making 23 of 26 shots at Miami en route to 58 points. Danny became the first player in ACC history to score more than 2,000 points, grab 1,000 rebounds and hand out 500 assists. His final totals were 2,155 points, 1,091 rebounds and 506 assists. Selected second in the pro draft, he played his first two years in Europe before joining the NBA. He retired after the 2003 season with the champion San Antonio Spurs.

Duke basketball was now in high gear. The Blue Devils won back-to-back national championships, the only school to achieve that accomplishment since the NCAA field was expanded to 64 teams. In '92, when Duke made it back to back, three of the starters eventually would have their jerseys retired. That year they

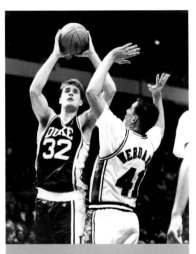

CHRISTIAN LAETTNER STARTED IN FOUR FINAL FOURS.

were senior Laettner, junior Hurley and sophomore Hill.

Laettner may have been the most hated player when Duke played on the road, but he also became the most successful performer in NCAA Tournament history. He started in four straight Final Fours. No other player in history ever has done that. What's more, he was a major contributor every time. He made more critical shots than anybody ever in the postseason and is still the all-time scoring leader in tournament annals.

As a freshman, Laettner thoroughly outplayed Georgetown's Alonzo Mourning in the NCAA East Regional finals. As a sophomore, he made a jumper at the buzzer after a called play by Krzyzewski, throwing the inbounds pass to roommate Brian Davis and getting it back to upset Connecticut in the East finals. After losing to UNLV in the NCAA championship game, Duke returned to the Final Four again in '91 to face the unbeaten Rebels in the semifinals. Laettner made two free throws, capping a Blue Devil rally that produced the stunning 79-77 victory. He scored 28 points in that game, and came back with 18 more against Kansas in the title clash as Duke won its first crown. He was the Final Four MVP.

In his senior year, Laettner was spectacular as the Blue Devils started the year No. 1 and never lost that position. He outplayed Shaquille O'Neal as Duke, without Hurley, beat LSU on the road to make it two straight over the Tigers and their mammoth center. Christian averaged 21.5 points, shot 57.5 percent and 81.5 percent from the foul line. He finished his career with 2,460 points and 1,149 rebounds, both second in school annals. He was a unanimous choice as national player and was the MVP of the ACC.

Laettner also scored the most famous basket in Duke history. Against Kentucky in the East Regional finals in Philadelphia, with the Wildcats leading 103-102 and 2.5 seconds left in overtime, he caught a 75-foot pass from Hill, spun and made the 18-foot jumper that sent the Blue

BOBBY HURLEY IS THE NCAA'S ALL-TIME ASSIST LEADER.

Devils to the Final Four in what is still considered by many as "the greatest game ever played." In that contest against UK, Laettner was a perfect 10 for 10 from the floor and also from the free throw line as he scored 31 points. The third player chosen in the NBA draft, he played in 2004 with the Washington Wizards.

Hurley was the ultimate gym rat. The son of one of the top high school coaches in the nation, Bob Hurley of St. Anthony's Prep in Jersey City, the scrawny point guard was installed as a starter in his first year at Duke, and he never gave up the position. His teams went to the NCAA finals in his rookie year and won it the next two.

The consummate playmaker, Hurley became the all-time NCAA leader in assists with 1,076. He set the school record that still stands with 289 assists in his sophomore season, and he has the top three single-season marks at Duke. He also increased his scoring every season, from 8.8 as a freshman to 17.0 as a senior, when injury-riddled Duke lost in the second round of the NCAAs despite 32 points from Hurley.

He made himself into a dangerous three-point shooter, and

GRANT HILL WAS NATIONAL DEFENSIVE PLAYER OF THE YEAR.

his gutsy three against UNLV in the '91 semifinals with Duke down five points in the closing minutes is considered among the most important baskets ever for the Blue Devils. He was a consensus All-American as a senior and All-ACC. He was named the MVP of the '91 Final Four. Chosen seventh in the NBA draft in '93, his pro career was cut short by a horrendous auto accident that almost killed him.

There's little doubt that Hill is the greatest athlete ever to play for Duke. As spectacular as he was as a Blue Devil, he was even better in the NBA until a series of injuries and ankle surgeries sidelined him virtually all of the past three seasons.

At 6-8, the son of football Hall of Famer Calvin Hill could jump out of the gym. His memorable dunk after an apparently overthrown lob from Hurley in the '91 NCAA finals against Kansas became a *Sports Illustrated* cover. There simply was nothing that Hill couldn't do, including play point guard after Hurley went down with a broken foot in '91.

Grant's numbers were fine, but not spectacular. He finished his career with 1,924 points while shooting 53.2 percent from the field and nearly 70 percent from the foul line. But it was his all-around play for which he will be mostly remembered. He was the first player in ACC history to have more than 1,900 points, 700 rebounds, 400 assists, 200 steals and 100 blocked shots. He won the Corinthian Award as the National Defensive Player of the Year in 1993.

Hill's most vital defensive contribution came in the NCAA South Regional final against top-seeded Purdue and its superstar and national player of the year, Glenn (Big Dog) Robinson in '94. He stifled the 6-8 Robinson at every turn while also serving as the primary ball handler from his point forward position. Duke won to advance to its seventh Final Four in nine years, 69-60. An All-American and Street & Smith's National Player of the Year, Hill was the third choice in the

SHANE BATTIER WAS A THREE-TIME WINNER OF THE NATIONAL DEFENSIVE PLAYER OF THE YEAR AWARD.

NBA draft by Detroit. Co-winner of the rookie of the year, Grant was a five-time All-Star before joining Orlando.

Battier was the consummate leader, the best ever under Krzyzewski's command. In his four years, Shane's teams won an all-time NCAA record 133 games and lost just 15. As a freshman, his team was ranked No. 1 most of the year and finished third in the final poll. It was No. 1 the next three years, in part because of Battier's all-around skills and leadership.

After his sophomore year, when Duke won 37 of its first 38 games before losing to Connecticut in the NCAA finals, three Blue Devils—national player of the year Elton Brand, sophomore Will Avery and freshman Corey Maggette, left for the NBA. They were the first pro defections for Duke. The Blue Devils began the next season with just three veterans—Battier, Chris Carrawell and Nate James—ranked 10th in the nation. After losing their first two games, they fell to 18th. With Battier and senior Carrawell as leaders, Duke won its next 18 and finished rated No. 1 in the polls.

Battier was not a prolific scorer until his junior year, when he averaged 17.4 points. He hiked that to 19.9 as a senior, when he was the consensus national player of the year and named top defender in the country for the third consecutive season. He led the team in charges taken and blocked shots. After Duke rallied from a 22-point deficit in the NCAA semifinals to defeat Maryland,

it was Battier's remarkable tap-in that sealed the victory against Arizona and provided the school with its third national championship in 11 years. A Dean's list student his entire career, Shane was the sixth pick in the NBA Draft. He plays for the Memphis Grizzlies.

Williams not only was the first Duke player ever to win national player awards in consecutive years, but he also graduated in three years, thanks to an accelerated academic schedule devised by the Duke staff after hearing the wishes of the player and his parents. In that short period, he started all 108 games that Duke played, was on three ACC championship squads and his team finished No. 1 every time.

The National Prep Player of the Year as a senior, Williams, a strong 6-2, proved his worth at point guard from the beginning. After a relatively modest beginning (14.5 points as a freshman),

JASON WILLIAMS HOLDS THE SINGLE-SEASON SCORING RECORD.

he broke the school record when he scored 841 points as a sophomore as Duke won the national championship. He was the NABC player of the year—the only one Battier didn't win—and a consensus national player in 2002, when he averaged 21.3 points. He finished a stellar career with 2,079 points, 644 assists, 313 three-pointers and 235 steals.

He scored the first eight of Duke's 10 points in the Miracle Minute at Maryland, when the Blue Devils rallied from a 90-80 deficit in the last 61 seconds and won in overtime. A fearless driver as well as a long-range sniper, Jason overpowered opponents inside as well as outside. He was the No. 2 pick in the NBA draft by the Chicago Bulls, behind 7-6 Yao Ming. In June, 2003, he was severely injured in a motorcycle wreck. He rehabilitated at Duke, where the numerous surgeries took place. His pro future is still uncertain.

Elton Brand's jersey was not retired at Duke, only because he stayed in school just two years. But the 6-8 New York native had an enormous impact in that short period, and he became the first Blue Devil ever to declare early for the NBA draft. Brand left with Coach K's blessing. Until then, every Duke player of significance had been a four-year man.

ELTON BRAND WAS NATIONAL PLAYER OF THE YEAR.

Brand actually played just 60 games for Duke. In his freshman year, he broke his foot in practice the day after Christmas, and was sidelined nearly two months. He returned in time to help the Blue Devils rally in Cameron to defeat North Carolina. His all-time record when he was in uniform was an astonishing 55-5.

As a sophomore, Brand was the dominant player in the nation. He was a unanimous choice as national player of the year as Duke finished with a 37-2 record, including a school-record 32 consecutive wins before the UConn loss in the title game.

Remarkably, Brand never played in a regular-season ACC loss. The team did lose to UNC in the ACC Tournament his freshman season. Counting the tournament, his record against league opponents was 24-1, including 19-0 in his sophomore season.

Elton became just the second Duke player to be chosen first in the NBA draft, by Chicago. Art Heyman was the other in 1963. In five years as a pro, Brand has become a perennial 20-10 performer in points and rebounds. The only Duke player who had better numbers as a professional was Grant Hill.

Duke has had seven winners of the national defensive player award since its inception in 1987. Battier became the lone three-time winner from '99-01. Hill won in 1993.

Amaker, who became an immediate starter at point guard as a freshman in '84, was the initial recipient of the honor in '87. Never a prolific scorer, he nevertheless wound up with 1,178 points and averaged 12.5 as a senior, when he made All-American.

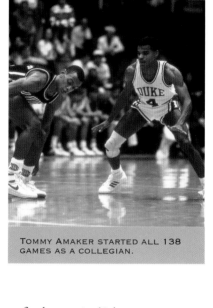

TOMMY AMAKER STARTED ALL 138 GAMES AS A COLLEGIAN.

The 6-1 Virginian started every one of the 138 games he played at Duke, which is one behind Hurley's record. He is third in steals (Battier, Chris Duhon) with 259, third in assists (Hurley, Duhon) with 708 and fourth in minutes played (Duhon, Hurley, Dawkins) with 4,666.

After serving as an assistant coach at Duke under Coach K, Amaker became the head coach at Seton Hall and is now at Michigan.

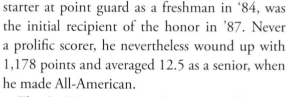

BILLY KING IS NOW THE PRESIDENT OF THE PHILADELPHIA 76ERS.

King never averaged more than 7.2 points ('87, junior year) for Duke, which came in his first of two seasons as a starter. But he was such an aggressive force that he was named the national defensive player in 1988.

CURRENT ASSISTANT COACH STEVE WOJCIECHOWSKI WAS A DEFENSIVE STOPPER.

His most impressive performance came in the NCAA East Regional finals that season against No. 1 Temple. In that game, King simply put a defensive blanket over Owls star Mark Macon as the Blue Devils pulled off the upset, 63-53, to advance again to the Final Four. Macon could do nothing and was reduced to tears in the Temple dressing room after the game.

King has made his mark in the NBA, where, still in his 30s, he became the president of the Philadelphia 76ers in 2003.

If there was a perfect match between coach and player, you would be hard-pressed to find anything stronger than the relationship between Krzyzewski and his present five-year assistant coach, Steve Wojciechowski. And that includes the difficulty in spelling their names.

Wojo was never a star. He was second-team All-ACC as a junior and third team as a senior. He never scored much, with his highest average being 6.9 as a junior in 1997. But he was the heart and soul of the team, and if ever awards were given for body burns, he would have had a room full.

His 82 steals in '97 was the second highest in school history. He ranks in Duke's top 10 career list in three-point field goal attempts (10th), steals (eighth) and assists (eighth). He also was named National Defensive Player of the Year in 1998.

Always a winner, the Blue Devils were 121-20 in his first four seasons as an assistant coach.

Bill Werber was Duke's first All-American and, like Groat a generation later, he played big-league baseball. But when he first showed up at Duke in the fall of 1926, as a recruit of rookie coach Eddie Cameron, Werber was being partly financed by the New York Yankees.

BILL WERBER WAS DUKE'S FIRST ALL-AMERICAN.

He got $2,000 from the Yankees and another $500 for his education in 1929, his junior year. He received an additional $500 as a senior.

Werber came to Duke from Washington, D.C., along with McKinley Tech teammate Harry Councilor. They then talked their center, Joe Croson, into attending Duke. At 6-4½, Croson was the big man that team needed.

Werber was All-Southern Conference in 1929 as a junior and made All-American the next year. During his baseball career, one highlight is that he was the first man to bat in the initial game ever televised. Now 96 and living in Charlotte, Werber had part of one leg amputated because of diabetes, but he still does 100 push-ups daily.

JACK MARIN, WHO LED THE BLUE DEVILS TO THE 1966 FINAL FOUR, HAD A DISTINGUISHED PRO CAREER.

Jack Marin was a star on the 1966 Duke team, which was ranked No. 2 in the nation behind Kentucky. The Blue Devils and Wildcats met in the Final Four semifinals at College Park, Maryland., but unfortunately, the other scoring leader, Bob Verga, had strep throat. Although Verga played, he scored just four points, 15 below his average, and Duke lost, 83-79.

Kentucky could not stop Marin, who had 29 points and seven rebounds in one of his best performances ever. Two years previously, Marin came off the Duke bench in the Final Four to score 16 points against UCLA, which won the first of its 10 NCAA titles for John Wooden.

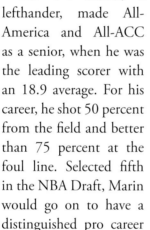
STEVE VACENDAK WAS THE ACC PLAYER OF THE YEAR.

The 6-6 Marin, a lefthander, made All-America and All-ACC as a senior, when he was the leading scorer with an 18.9 average. For his career, he shot 50 percent from the field and better than 75 percent at the foul line. Selected fifth in the NBA Draft, Marin would go on to have a distinguished pro career with the Baltimore Bullets and three other teams. A lawyer and a scratch golfer, he lives in Durham and has won events on the Celebrity Tour.

In 1966, Duke senior guard Steve Vacendak was voted the most valuable player in the ACC Tournament and also the player of the year.

What was most interesting about that vote was Vacendak wasn't selected as All-ACC. Teammates Marin and Verga were. Actually, the 6-2 guard was ninth on the all-conference voting list, which placed the Atlantic Coast Sportswriters and Sportscasters Association in a bind.

What had happened is that Vacendak had been a key player in Duke's 21-20 semifinal victory over North Carolina, when Dean Smith unveiled the four corners for the first time and held the ball throughout, and in the 71-66 victory over N.C. State for the league title. Vacendak led the scoring in the championship game with 18 points.

ACSWA (Atlantic Coast Sportswriters Association) changed its rule as a result of the POY voting. Previously, the All-ACC ballots were taken at the end of the regular season. The player of the year voting occurred after the tournament. Vacendak had a terrific year and played brilliantly in the Final Four against Kentucky. But his 13.3 scoring average was fourth on the team behind Marin, Verga and Mike Lewis.

Player of the year voting now can be made before the tournament, although writers have the authority to wait. Few do. Up to 90 percent of the voting is pretourney. And the All-ACC team is announced at that time. There is no way the Vacendak vote ever could be replicated.

Marin's teammate, Verga, would have greatly benefited had the three-point line been in effect during his career, which ended in '67. A jump-shooter with limitless range, there's no telling what he would have done had the trey been available. As it was, his average his senior year of 26.1 remains the all-time Duke record, just ahead of Groat's 26.0.

BOB VERGA'S 26.1 SCORING AVERAGE IS THE SINGLE-SEASON SCHOOL RECORD.

Like Marin, Verga was a consensus second-team All-American in his '66 season. In his final year, he was a consensus first-team selection. After a brief pro career, he became a tennis professional in his native New Jersey.

C.B. CLAIBORNE WAS THE FIRST AFRICAN-AMERICAN TO PLAY AT DUKE.

Integration came slowly in the ACC and the rest of the South. It was during the 'mid to late '60s that the schools initially brought in their first African-American athletes on scholarship. In most cases, the coaches tried to recruit a star immediately.

Duke's first African-American player, guard Claudius (C.B.) Claiborne did not fit that category. The 6-2 Claiborne, an outstanding student from Danville, Virginia, never was more than a role player for the Blue Devils during the last three seasons of Vic Bubas's coaching career.

In an era when freshmen couldn't play on the varsity, Claiborne participated in just 12 games as a sophomore, 19 as a junior and 22 (of 28) in his senior season in '69, which was the last for Bubas as a coach. For his career, he averaged 4.1 points while shooting 36.5 percent from the floor.

Duke's first high-profile African-American was 6-6 Don Blackman from New York. He was recruited by Bubas and played as a sophomore for Bucky Waters in '70, averaging 6.2 points. Then he transferred. Willie Hodge, who started in his

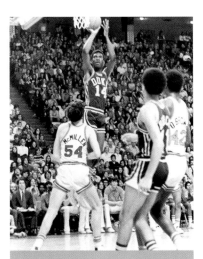

WILLIE HODGE STARTED HIS FINAL TWO YEARS AT DUKE.

final two seasons in '75 and '76, was the first African-American player ever to be a significant performer at Duke. In his senior season, he averaged 16.9 points, second on the team.

Jim Spanarkel, '79, was one of eight Duke players to score more than 2,000 points. He wound up a distinguished career as a two-time All-American with 2,012 points and a 17.6 average, both in the school's all-time top 10.

A 6-5 guard, Spanarkel posted amazing numbers during his career, which coincided with Duke's return to basketball power under coach Bill Foster. He never shot below 51.6 percent from the floor and wound up his career at 52.7. He also shot 80.6 percent from the foul line and when he graduated he was the school career leader in free throws and assists.

Duke won the '78 ACC title in a surprise, and went to its first Final Four since 1966. Spanarkel had 20 points in the semifinal victory over Notre Dame and 21 in the championship game loss to Kentucky. Another New Jersey native, he has been the television analyst for the New Jersey Nets. He was drafted in the NBA first round by Philadelphia in 1979.

JIM SPANARKEL SHOT 52.7 PERCENT FROM THE FLOOR DURING HIS CAREER.

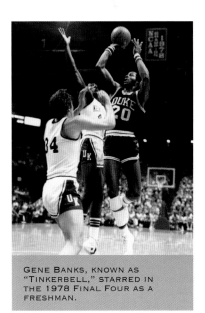

GENE BANKS, KNOWN AS "TINKERBELL," STARRED IN THE 1978 FINAL FOUR AS A FRESHMAN.

Gene Banks was one of the most important re-cruits in Duke history. Rated along with Albert King, who select-ed Maryland, as the top prep player in the nation, the 6-7 Philadelphian stunned most ex-perts when he committed early to Duke's Foster. He eventually led the revitalization of Blue Devil bas-ketball, which had been in a deep slump most of the '70s.

TRAJAN LANGDON IS COACH K'S ONLY THREE-TIME FIRST-TEAM ALL-ACC HONOREE.

"Tinkerbell" was one of the more flamboyant players in school history. In his final regular-season game in Cameron, he threw red roses to the crowd, then made the winning basket against favored North Carolina.

In his freshman year, playing on a team with All-Americans Spanarkel and Gminski, Banks was the third-leading scorer with a 17.1 aver-age as the Blue Devils came on strong to win the ACC Tournament and advance to the NCAA fi-nals, where they were beaten by No. 1 Kentucky. Banks, despite a death threat delivered during the Final Four, ignored that and scored 22 points in each game. He was the ACC rookie of the year.

Bull-strong at 6-7, he shot 53.1 percent for his career and was an excellent rebounder. He made some All-America teams as a sophomore and again as a senior. He was chosen in the second round of the draft in '81 and played professional-ly for six years. Now living in Greensboro, Banks has served as the coach at Bennett College.

Mark Alarie was a member of Krzyzewski's first great recruiting class in 1983. Dawkins was the highlight signing, but Alarie, a 6-8 resident of

Scottsdale, Arizona, would have a distinguished ca-reer and finished with 2,136 points, which remains fifth on the all-time Duke list. Other members of that class were forward David Henderson, now the coach at Delaware and a former Duke assistant, and ESPN TV analyst Jay Bilas, a Charlotte law-yer, who also was an assistant coach for Krzyzewski.

Alarie, a two-time All-ACC selection and an All-American his senior season in '86, was an amazing outside shoot-er despite his height. He shot 55 percent for his career, including 58.5 as a junior. He also made just under 80 percent at the foul line. He was picked in the first round of the NBA draft by Denver, but his career eventually was short-circuited because of in-juries.

MARK ALARIE SCORED 2,136 POINTS IN HIS CAREER.

Trajan Langdon, the Alaskan Assassin, is the only three-time All-ACC choice under Coach K. The former minor league baseball player, he was technically a recruited walk-on until his fifth year at Duke. The San Diego Padres paid his way for four years.

He had a career-high 17.3 average as a senior in 1999, when the Blue Devils lost just once—in Trajan's home town of Anchorage—in 38 games prior to the NCAA finals against UConn. He still holds the Duke record for three-pointers made and attempted, and is second in three-point percent-age. He also holds the career record in free throws at 86.2 percent, fourth all-time in the ACC.

A first-round NBA choice of Cleveland, he played three seasons for the Cavaliers, and the past two seasons he has played in Europe. He makes his permanent home near Washington, D.C.

CHRIS CARRAWELL WAS NAMED ACC PLAYER OF THE YEAR.

When Duke lost three underclassmen to the NBA following the '99 season, and another transferred, the Blue Devils were left with only three veterans, including sophomore Battier. The lone senior, Carrawell, led the group to Coach K's house, where the trio (including James) said they would make certain that Duke's fortunes didn't fade.

Carrawell more than did his part. He led a squad that included six freshmen to a 15-1 ACC record and 29-5 overall, rated first nationally in the final polls. The 6-6 Carrawell was the second leading scorer with a 16.9 average (behind Battier) and was the team's spiritual leader. He was named the ACC's player of the year and Chris was a consensus All-American. He continues to play pro basketball internationally.

In 2002, Carlos Boozer and Mike Dunleavy were the other two-thirds of the three-pronged Duke attack along with Jason Williams, the National Player of the Year. For the only time in ACC history, all three won first-team honors. Dunleavy was the third-leading vote-getter behind Williams and Maryland's Juan Dixon, while Boozer finished fifth, well ahead of the Terps' Lonny Baxter.

The 6-9 Boozer was the No. 2 scorer with an 18.2 average behind Williams. Dunleavy averaged 17.3 points. Boozer, who had announced prior to the season that he was going to leave early for the NBA, unaccountably fell to the second round in the draft. He was a steal for Cleveland, where in his second season he averaged better than 15 points and 10 rebounds. Dunleavy, selected third by Golden State behind Yao Ming and Williams, became a starter in his second year.

CHRIS DUHON ENDED HIS CAREER AS DUKE'S ALL-TIME STEALS AND MINUTES PLAYED LEADER.

Chris Duhon will be remembered more for his leadership than any statistics. Essentially a four-year starter at point guard in a stretch that included two Final Fours and a national title in 2001, Duhon ended his career as the only player in ACC history to have at least 1,000 points, 475 rebounds, 800 assists and 300 steals. He ended his Duke career as an All-American in 2004 and as the school's all-time leader in steals (300) and minutes played (4,183). He was part of 123 victories, the second-highest total in league history—behind only one-time teammate Battier's 131.

CHAPTER

3

CAP CARD

When Wilbur Wade Card arrived at Trinity College in 1895 from his home in Franklinton, N.C., he already was 21 years old and had significant prep school training. He planned to become a Methodist minister, but during his college days, he changed his mind and elected to go into athletics as a profession.

Because of the change in majors, it took him five years to graduate. As an athlete, he participated in baseball and track. There were no eligibility rules in those days, so Card played baseball all five years. He was elected captain in 1899, and, until his death in 1948, he was known only as "Cap."

Cap Card became the first basketball coach at Trinity, but before the first game ever played by the school, the coach had in-

CAP CARD WAS TRINITY'S FIRST BASKETBALL COACH.

troduced football, track and field, gymnastics, bowling, swimming, fencing and volleyball.

In late 1905, the basketball coach at Wake Forest, Richard "Red" Crozier, proposed that his team play a game against Trinity. Wake Forest, then located in Wake County not far from Durham, had a squad that played against various YMCA and club teams.

Trinity, of course, had no team, so Card organized one. In a front-page article on January 30, 1906, the school newspaper, the *Chronicle*, reported on the proposed new sport:

"It is well-nigh a certainty that Trinity is to have another game added to her list of athletic sports in the near future. The game in question is basketball, one of the most fascinating and intensely interesting indoor sports known today."

31

A century later, the Chronicle's article is still 100 percent accurate.

"Many preparations have been made within the last few days in the gymnasium with the view of starting practice as soon as examinations are over. Iron guards have been fastened around the electric globes and detachable goals have been constructed. Unlike baseball, the game is played most often at night."

Card's primary job was to assemble a squad. Although accounts of the team in the school paper suggest there were 16 students on the squad, a picture of the team showed only eight, plus the coach. Of those, just six played in the first game.

Card agreed to play Wake Forest at Trinity's Angier Duke gym, which had been built in 1898 on what is now Duke's East Campus. It still exists, and is known today as The Ark.

The gym might have been new, but it also was small. The playing floor was 50x32. A modern court is approximately three times larger at 94x60. It was actually possible to shoot the ball from one end of the court to the other.

THE ARK STILL EXISTS ON DUKE'S EAST CAMPUS TODAY.

One of the Trinity starters, Garland Greever, was a graduate student. Another player, reserve B.S. Womble, was in law school.

None of the team members had ever played the game, so Trinity had three weeks of practice before playing host to Wake Forest on March 2. By then, the visitors had played the first game ever in the state, against Guilford on February 6. Trinity-Wake Forest would become the initial contest ever played by two schools that would become part of the Big Four (with North Carolina and N.C. State).

Card was handicapped because several of the school's better athletes were playing on the baseball team. But he did his best, and Trinity took on the visitors with great anticipation.

Wake Forest won, 24-10. According to the *Chronicle*, "The game was an unusually clean one from start to finish. Very few fouls were called and roughness was rare." Perhaps that was because Crozier was the referee, as was the custom at the time.

Fifty years later, surviving members of the team were honored at a Duke-Wake Forest game. H.E. Spence, a substitute on the Trinity team, wrote, "Few fouls were called. In fact, the only fouls that were certain to be called were when two men ganged up on one, or when a man put both arms around the man he was guarding. Otherwise, he could hold, push and pull all he pleased. So with such persistent guarding, few goals were thrown. There were few fouls called for hacking, tripping, blocking, charging or even cross-hipping."

The goals were actually baskets, and the ball had to be pushed out by a broom after any successful score. Then play resumed with a center jump.

Wake Forest was in command for the first half, leading 18-3 as Trinity made just one basket. In the second half, the home team actually outscored the visitors, 7-6, making the final score 24-10. The *Chronicle* described the second half this way: "Trinity utilized the knowledge gained from the first half and held down the visitors, scoring one more point than they."

There was little dribbling and players passed the ball the same way they shot it—with two hands. Only one guard was permitted to cross the midcourt line to participate in the offense, which, considering the miniscule court size, was probably a good thing.

Wake Forest's star was Vanderbilt Couch, who personally outscored Trinity with 14 points. Trinity guard "Reddy" White led the home team

with four points. The rules of the day had a designated free-throw shooter for each team, and these two players shot all of the foul shots. The Trinity starters were White, Greever, C.R. Claywell, T.G. Stern and C.R. Pugh.

Two weeks later, Trinity took a train ride to Wake Forest for its first road game. The result was essentially the same. Wake Forest won, 15-5. The last three games of that initial season were against a YMCA team, Trinity Park. Trinity won the first and third to give Card a 2-3 record.

He remained as the coach for six more seasons, and most of the games were against YMCA teams. The 1909 team finished 8-1, losing only to Wake Forest, 30-5. In the previous game, Trinity had defeated Wake Forest, 22-14. Presumably, the second game was played on the road.

The team became much more proficient. One of the victories posted by the 6-1 squad in

AN OVERFLOW CROWD WATCHED THE FIRST GAME AGAINST WAKE FOREST.

1912, Card's last as the coach, was over Virginia Christian, 69-9. That year Trinity played only college teams, including two contests with N.C. State. Each team won one game.

Years later, Duke would name the building on West Campus where the games were played after Card. He lived long enough to see the team move from Card Gym next door to the Indoor Stadium, which eventually would become Cameron Indoor Stadium.

While Card was the father of Duke basketball, there was little stability for 15 years after he gave up the coaching position. Trinity was the first school in the state to win 20 games, going 20-4 in 1917, although the final victory is recorded as a forfeit over N.C. State, an outcome that State does not acknowledge.

During those 15 years, there were no less than 10 coaches. Only George Buckheit, the last on that list, coached more than two years. He was the coach from 1925 through 1928, as Trinity was making the transition to becoming Duke University. His record was 25-36 and only in his final season, '28, did he post a winning record (9-5).

Then came the coaching change that eventually would make Duke the basketball powerhouse that it remains today.

Eddie Cameron played football at Washington & Lee, graduating in 1924. He remained at his alma mater as an assistant coach for a season, then interviewed at Duke with university vice president William Wannamaker. Duke already had hired the W&L coach, Jimmie DeHart, although DeHart would remain in Lexington, Virginia, to fulfill the final year of his contract.

Wannamaker looked at the 23-year-old Cameron and asked, "You're too young to coach football, aren't you?" Ever candid, Cameron replied, "I don't know." So they agreed that Eddie would coach at Greenbrier Military in West Virginia for a year, where he took his team to the championship.

In 1926, Cameron became the freshman coach at Duke, and the following year he became the coach of the freshman basketball team. Two years later, he would become the head coach in basketball at the age of 26. At the same time, he was an assistant coach in football under the legendary Wallace Wade, who had been hired away from Alabama when Duke opened play in the football stadium that today bears Wade's name.

Cameron coached for 14 years, winning 226 games and losing just 99. He was Duke's winningest coach until Mike Krzyzewski began his quarter-century of success in 1980. It wasn't until

EDDIE CAMERON CONSIDERED BILL WERBER HIS FINEST PLAYER.

1990 that Coach K surpassed Cameron's victory total.

Cameron's teams won three Southern Conference championships. His first year at Duke coincided with the school becoming the 23rd member of the Southern. His last two teams were champions, including the '42 squad that finished 22-2, the best winning percentage in history until Coach K's first great team in '86 went 37-3.

Four other Cameron teams reached the finals of the Southern Conference tournament, and Duke qualified for the eight-team event every season.

Cameron's first season was only average—until tournament time. But it was special to the coach, not just because it was his initial year, but "because it was our first year in the Southern Conference. We went to the finals of the tournament. We beat Alabama, North Carolina and Georgia. Our five starters played almost every minute and, with four games in three days, were exhausted. We lost to N.C. State (43-35). We came back the next year to make the finals again. This time, Alabama won."

Led by Duke's first All-American, Bill Werber, the Blue Devils won 15 consecutive games after losing to Cameron's alma mater, W&L, in the fourth game of the season. The Alabama loss left the team with an 18-2 record.

Cameron had only one losing season, in '38-39, when his team was 10-12. Ironically, that was the same school year that the football team went unscored upon during the regular season before losing to Southern California, 7-3 in the final minute, in the Rose Bowl.

EDDIE CAMERON IS CONGRATULATED BY CHANCELLOR JOHN BLACKBURN AFTER DUKE STADIUM WAS RENAMED IN CAMERON'S HONOR.

It was the money from that football game that enabled Duke to build the basketball arena that today carries Cameron's name. He designed the building, at the time the largest facility in the south, on the back of a matchbook cover in 1935.

Cameron's final basketball team, in 1942—this time after Duke actually hosted the Rose Bowl less than four weeks after Pearl Harbor led to the start of World War II—was his finest.

That 22-2 team which won the Southern featured four players from Durham High who played only for tuition grants. The local quartet—Cedric and Garland Loftis, Bob Gantt and Gordon Carver—lived at home, "So they did not get room and board," Cameron said. It was a wonderful, if cheap, investment.

Cameron had to give up basketball because Wade went back into the army after the Rose Bowl game, which Duke lost to Oregon State. Cameron took on dual duties as football coach and athletic director.

Cameron coached football until Wade returned. His teams went 25-11-1, including a victory over Alabama in the Orange Bowl, 29-26 on January 1, 1945. Legendary sportswriter Grantland Rice called that contest "the greatest bowl game ever played."

Cameron remained as the athletic director until he retired in 1972 after 46 years of service to Duke. Just before his retirement, the basketball building was renamed Cameron Indoor Stadium. Eddie called that his "most cherished honor." Duke upset heavily favored North Carolina, 76-74, that night.

Cameron had been one of the leaders when seven schools left the Southern and formed the Atlantic Coast Conference in 1953. The primary reason was to help football scheduling, which was haphazard at best in the widespread, convoluted Southern.

"That is why the seven of us pulled out," Cameron said. "We hated to do it because we left

BLUE DEVILS

How did Duke wind up with a Blue Devil for a mascot and an athletic nickname? Curiously.

Following the end of World War I, the then-Trinity administration ended its 25-year ban on football. That first year the team was known either as the Blue and White or the Methodists—neighboring Wake Forest being the Baptists.

The student newspaper, the *Chronicle*, campaigned at the start of the 1921 season for the school to adopt "a catchy name, one of our own possession that would be instantly recognizable nationwide in songs, yells and publicity."

Among the nominations was Blue Devils, named after the Chasseurs Alpins (Blue Devils) of the wartime French army. They had become well known for their unique training and alpine knowledge and for their distinctive blue uniform with flowing cape and beret.

Irving Berlin even captured them in song as "strong and active, most attractive...those Devils, the Blue Devils of France."

The *Chronicle* then campaigned that a name choice be made from among Blue Titans, Blue Eagles, Polar Bears, Blue Devils, Royal Blues or Blue Warriors, each using the school's blue and white colors.

None of the nominations produced a decision. There was some criticism that Blue Devils might elicit some opposition on the Methodist campus for "obvious reasons." As a result, the football season passed without any selection of a name.

At the start of the '22-23 school year, the editors of the *Archive* and *Chanticleer* agreed that the newspaper staff should choose a name. So William B. Lander, editor in chief, and managing editor Mike Bradshaw began calling

the athletic teams the Blue Devils. They acknowledged that it was somewhat unpopular, but they thought it the best of the names nominated.

That first year, neither the press nor the cheerleaders used the name. The *Chanticleer* even made fun of it. But, much to the surprise of Lander and Bradshaw, no opposition materialized, not even from the administration.

So, the *Chronicle* staff continued to call the various teams the Blue Devils, and by repetition, the name eventually caught on.

The origin of the nickname is one of the most requested questions asked of the University Archives. Questioners almost always are surprised to discover the origin is more military and patriotic than religious.

some wonderful friends, but we felt it was a move we had to make."

The seven members of the new ACC—Duke, UNC, N.C. State, Wake Forest, Maryland, Clemson and South Carolina—would add independent Virginia within a few months. And Cameron's insistence that the league hold a postseason tournament created tremendous financial possibilities for the young conference.

At the time, the Southern was the only conference to hold a tournament and the ACC often was scorned by the national media for having its own event. But the ACC Tournament would eventually become such a financial bonanza that almost all of the other leagues finally staged their own. Now only the Ivy League does not hold a tournament. The ACC established the standard by which everybody else was judged wanting.

Although Cameron coached for a long time, he insisted that his finest player was the first man he ever recruited, Bill Werber. "He was the best player I ever had. If anything ever opened up between him and the basket, he'd drive like anything for it, knowing he'd either get fouled or score. He could jump and get a shot off in the air."

This was 1929 and 1930, when almost every shot taken in a game was a set shot when the player had both feet on the floor.

Werber wrote a book years after he left Duke, *Circling the Bases*, in which he described his early moments in college. He had come mainly as a baseball player, and the New York Yankees helped pay for his expenses.

He had been recruited by Duke primarily for baseball, after his brother's roommate, June Greene, sent word of Werber's abilities to his brother, Willie Greene, who was a football and baseball player at Duke. He arrived at Duke with his teammate from McKinley Tech in D.C., Harry Councillor. It signaled the beginning of Duke as a big winner in basketball that still exists nearly 80 years later.

"I was expecting to find a tranquil green oasis, magnolia trees and ivy walls," Werber wrote in his book. "Instead, Duke was a mess.

"It had changed its name from Trinity College to Duke University in 1924, when Duke tobacco money was received and a brand new institution was being developed. A railroad track ran up the middle of the quadrangle of the campus to be, and each night … railway cars disgorged their cargoes of brick. Dust was everywhere. When it rained, mud was six inches deep.

"Planking fastened to risers of blocks ran in all directions, and woe be the errant or hasty walker on a rainy day. His clothes spattered and wet, he suffered further misery by becoming mired in mud. Dormitory doors were innocent of hardware, so when the breeze blew at night, which it frequently did, those doors would bang, bang down one side of the corridor and up the other, never in unison. Sometimes this clatter would last all night long.

"The riveters would start on the steel work at the crack of dawn. All of this, plus the heat, dust, noise and confusion, was just too much. I almost decided to pack up and go home. Duke, in September, 1926, was a sorry-looking place."

But Werber elected to remain, and the Blue Devils began their surge in basketball. He and Councillor convinced DeHart, who was also the athletic director, that Duke should give a scholarship to Joe Croson in 1927. Croson would go on to become the first—and best—big man Cameron ever had, and that McKinley Tech trio would lead Duke to its 18-2 season in 1930 and consecutive seasons in the Southern Conference tournament finals.

That year, Werber not only became Duke's first All-American, but he and Councillor were All-Southern, and Croson made the second team and again in '31 after his two high school classmates had graduated.

CHAPTER 10

4

GERARD, GROAT AND BRADLEY

With Eddie Cameron having taken the Duke football job as Wallace Wade went off to the military, the school now needed a new basketball coach for the first time in 15 years.

Cameron promoted his assistant, Gerry Gerard, to that position.

Gerard's given name was Kenneth Carlyle Gerard, although he was never known by anything other than Gerry. He was a native of Mishawaka, Indiana, who had played football at Illinois. For the Illini, he was the backup for the immortal running back Red Grange, the Galloping Ghost. "I never played much," he said, "because Red never got tired."

GERRY GERARD WAS ALSO DUKE'S FIRST SOCCER COACH.

Gerard was hired at Duke in 1931 to run a new intramural athletic program. In 1935, he was the coach of the school's first soccer team. In 11 years, the Blue Devils posted a record of 40-23-9.

But this was during the Depression, and coaches didn't make the huge salaries they do today. Gerard worked as a football, basketball and track and field official. He also worked as a radio announcer for Atlantic Refining Co., doing play by play on basketball games.

In the summer, he would manage a resort in Virginia Beach, Viriginia, and throughout his career at Duke he was a teacher in the Physical Education Department.

In 1948-49, Gerard actually missed the opening game, a one-point loss to Hanes Hosiery, as well as the practice sessions leading up to the contest. He had taken a one-week sabbatical to officiate two football games, William and Mary-Arkansas and Clemson-Citadel. There was no media criticism and the absence had been approved.

In his eight years as coach, Gerard won two Southern Conference championships—it was a 19-team league—and four other times Duke reached the championship game, all of which were played in Raleigh. His overall record was 131-78.

Gerard's teams almost always featured some football players, including in 1945, when the Blue Devils defeated Alabama in the Sugar Bowl.

Basketball players Gordon Carver, Cliff Lewis and John Crowder also were on the football team. They missed the first nine games, of which Duke lost four.

Gerard's first team in 1943 won the regular-season title, but lost to George Washington in the tournament finals. Cedric Loftis, Bob Gantt and Bubba Seward were on the all-tourney team.

Wartime basketball was different. When Duke played host to Wake Forest on a Monday night, the Durham newspaper reported that the crowd in the indoor stadium was no more than 100. "It was fraternity meeting night and no-co-ed night, the feminine students being confined to quarters. These two factors combined to keep down the crowd." Other games had small crowds because of gas rationing.

EMPTY SEATS—AND NO GLASS BACKBOARD YET—SYMBOLIZED EARLY YEARS IN DUKE STADIUM.

The next year, Duke finished the regular season 10-13 but won its third Southern Conference championship in four years and the first under Gerard. The record was deceiving because most of the losses were against teams from military bases, who were loaded with pro and college stars.

One such team was Norfolk Navy, No. 1 in the nation, and led by eventual Knicks coach Red Holzman. The Blue Devils did defeat Fort Bragg, whose stars included Bones McKinney and Pvt. Cedric Loftis, who had played for Duke just the season before.

Military rules prohibited Navy personnel from being gone more than 48 hours, so William and Mary replaced South Carolina, which was forced to withdraw from the Southern tournament. Duke beat the Indians 68-25.

After defeating N.C. State in the semifinals, 40-32, the Blue Devils trounced UNC, 44-27, for the championship. Carolina had beaten Duke twice in three games during the season. The stars were Gordon Carver and Bill Wright, a transfer from Tennessee. Another transfer, Harry Harner from Washington & Lee, was the No. 3 scorer.

After that slow start in '45 because of the Sugar Bowl, Duke rallied to an 11-8 record and finished second behind South Carolina. Just as they had done the previous year, the Devils won twice in one day to reach the finals against North Carolina, which had to play just once on Friday.

The Tar Heels won 49-38. It was the sixth straight season that Duke had reached the championship game, a Southern Conference record.

The next season the war was over, and players returned to college. Some, like McKinney, switched, going from N.C. State to UNC. There he and another All-American, John "Hook" Dillon, led the Heels to a 30-5 record.

But it was Duke, with no starter taller than 6-2, which won the crown.

Seward, who played at Duke in '42 and '43, was liberated as a prisoner of war in April after 71 days in a concentration camp. Back in the U.S., he was discharged from the army on December 3, and headed back to Duke.

There Seward joined Duke's third All-American, Ed Koffenberger, to help the Blue Devils upset UNC at Chapel Hill, just one of two regular-season losses for the Heels.

In the Southern tournament, Duke blitzed Wake Forest 49-30 for the championship. It was the fourth in six years and would be the last for 14 more seasons. After losing their first two games, the Devils finished 21-6.

The next year, the team was 16-3 before losing at Carolina. That started a slump that didn't end. The Blue Devils would finish 19-8

At halftime of the consolation championship (fifth place) game in the Dixie Classic at Reynolds Coliseum in Raleigh, Duke trailed Tulane 56-27. Moments before the Green Wave had led by an astonishing 32 points.

Blue Devils star Dick Groat recalled in 2004 that Duke coach Hal Bradley told his team before sending them out for the second half, "Make it a little respectable."

Duke did more than that. In a comeback that is still in the NCAA record for the greatest rally, the Blue Devils staged a remarkable turnaround to win, 74-72.

Duke had gone more than six minutes without scoring before intermission until Groat finally made a basket. "But we never gave that much thought to winning the game," he said. "We never had played well in the Dixie Classic."

In the last half, Groat scored 26 of his game-high 32 points. At one stage during the rally, which had a capacity crowd of 12,200 roaring, he scored 10 consecutive points. He and Duke captain Scotty York were the primary heroes, but the Green Wave became flustered as the Blue Devils shut them down defensively.

Bob Reed led Tulane's scoring with 22 points, but his last basket came with more than 11 minutes left to play and, incredibly, the Green Wave did not score again.

Groat's basket with just over a minute left tied the score at 72, and the crowd reaction sounded as though this was the championship game.

Duke forced a Tulane turnover, and 6-7 center Dayton Allen made an uncontested layup with a minute left to cap the incredible surge and give the Blue Devils the unexpected victory.

Some 54 years later, this is still the greatest halftime comeback in NCAA history.

Most of the attention in '49 was paid to the freshman team, and superstar Dick Groat. He was among four scholarship players, the first that the school ever had given. The varsity did not do well. It finished 13-9, but just 5-7 in the league, and missed playing in the league tournament for the only time in history. Ironically, the event was played at Duke—where the players served as ushers.

Shortly after the season ended, Gerard became ill at a national tournament. He was rushed back to Durham and had surgery at Duke after being diagnosed with cancer. Given six months to live, Gerry staged a remarkable recovery, and when the 1949-50 season started, he was on the bench as the coach.

That team was leading the Southern Conference at the semester break, and Groat was averaging 14.5 points. But he and team captain Tommy Hughes were dismissed from school for an academic violation for a semester, and Duke fell apart. The team wound up 15-15.

after falling to South Carolina, 56-54, in the first round of the Southern tournament. The only consolation was that Koffenberger, a 6-2 forward, broke his school record with 416 points and again made All-America.

The '48 team was limping along with a 11-11 record but finished strong and reached the Southern finals. There Duke lost to powerhouse N.C. State, the nation's highest-scoring team, 58-50. The Blue Devils advanced to the finals for the eighth time in nine years.

DICK GROAT LED THE NATION IN SCORING AND ASSISTS.

Meanwhile, Gerard's cancer had returned.

Taking no chances, Cameron had hired Red Auerbach in the summer of '49. It was presumed that he would take the coaching job if Gerard couldn't go. But Auerbach, who had a tiny office in Card gym, stayed less than three months. "Gerry had cancer and nobody felt worse about it than me," Red said. "I didn't want to have to get a job that way."

While he was at Duke, Auerbach worked with Groat virtually every day. "I learned more in that time than I did in four years," Groat recalled in a 2004 interview.

"I loved Dick Groat," Auerbach said. "Believe me, he would have been a better basketball player than he was in baseball. He would have been an all-star, and I'm not shooting off my mouth. He would have paid the price. He was like Bill

Sharman, a great offensive player. I saw Celtic stuff in Groat."

More than 50 years later, Groat said he still considers himself "a retired basketball player" although he was in the major leagues for 14 seasons, winning a batting title and a National League MVP.

By November 1950, Gerard was too sick to continue coaching. He stepped down and was replaced by little-known Hal Bradley, 39, who was the coach at Hartwick. Nine years later, Bradley left for the Texas job, where he could have 20 scholarships, while Duke allotted a dozen. His record was 167-78, a 68.2 winning percentage that was just below Cameron's 69.5.

While Bradley never won a championship—Duke entered the Atlantic Coast Conference in his fourth year—he did win 20 or more games four times and also finished rated in the top 20 on four occasions, something that the Blue Devils never had done before. The three times that his teams played for the league crown, they lost to N.C. State at Reynolds Coliseum.

His teams never finished lower than third in the league and he was 14-11 against North Carolina, beating the Tar Heels at least once every season except in 1957, when they went undefeated and won the NCAA title.

Bradley's teams averaged better than 80 points for four straight years starting in 1953. They topped out with a school record of 85.2 in 1955. His squads scored more than 100 points 13 times, and his all-time record at home was 74-11, with four of the losses coming in the first season.

He did all this without ever having a superstar other than Groat, whom he had inherited. And, for the most part, his teams were small. But they were well balanced, and all the starters usually averaged in double figures.

Generally, the mild-mannered "gentleman coach" was unappreciated. That included the media. His '58 team was unbeaten at home and finished No. 10 in the AP poll, the highest ranking Duke had achieved. But the Devils didn't have a player on the All-ACC team and only Bucky Allen was on the second team. Case was named coach of the year, although Bradley beat him twice, including 17 points at Raleigh, and both lost in the semifinals.

In '56, when the Blue Devils finished 19-7 and 19th in the nation, they played 10 home games. State played 20 in Reynolds. "I'm not criticizing State," Bradley said. "I just wish we didn't have to play on the other team's court so often. It's tougher to win away from home, and even tougher when you are going into the other team's gym."

Officiating could make a difference, too. In the first year of the ACC, 1954, the Blue Devils wound up 22-6. They won the school's only Dixie Classic, beating Navy in the finals, 98-83. They upset State twice, 87-85 in Durham and

90-89 on Don Tobin's lone basket of the game. That gave Bradley three straight wins over Case, just the second time that anybody ever had done that.

But in the ACC semifinals, State won 79-75, as the Wolfpack made 28 of 50 free throws and Duke hit 15 of 25. The Blue Devils had seven more field goals and shot 44.2 percent to State's 33.8. "I liked the officiating tonight," said Case, whose team was playing in Reynolds.

Bradley got off to a rocky start with his Duke players when he arrived, unknown, from Hartwick. At the initial practice, the only drill was to run to the free-throw line and shoot. Groat didn't know what to think.

But the coach turned his star loose immediately. In the opening game against Hanes Hosiery, he scored 31 points, breaking the school record of 30 held by Koffenberger. It was one of nine times that the 6-0 guard broke the record that season.

He scored at least 20 points in 28 of 33 games. He averaged 25.2 points and nobody else on the 20-13 team was in double figures. He almost doubled the school record for points, getting 831 to lead the nation. Koffenberger's 416 disappeared by late January.

As a senior, Groat was even better, raising his average to 26 points. He also averaged 7.6 assists. Both numbers were second in the nation and resulted in considerable speculation during the season.

Hall of Fame sports columnist Ritter Collett of the *Dayton Daily News* wondered how anybody could lead the country in scoring and assists, as Groat was doing at the time. *The Raleigh Times* even wrote that the statistics at Duke were being padded.

Fortunately for Duke, Groat and the statistician, the Blue Devils played back-to-back games at the most famous arenas in the nation, Madison Square Garden and the Palestra in Philadelphia. Not only did Duke defeat NYU and Temple to start a 15-game winning streak, but Groat had 10 assists in the Garden and a building-record nine in the Palestra. The Duke book had him credited with one fewer assist in each game.

That ended the controversy. Collett wrote a column saying he was wrong, that Groat was a remarkable player who either scored himself or passed for a basket. At the end of the year, he had 780 points and had assisted on 558 more, or 57.7 percent of the team's total of 2,320.

Groat broke the Southern Conference scoring record of 47 points when he got 48 in his home finale against UNC. In the tournament, the 12th-ranked Blue Devils upset West Virginia, 90-88, in the semifinals. Groat scored 31 points but fouled out with 1:18 left. His substitute, baseball star Dick "Footsie" Johnson, broke an 88-88 tie with a left-handed shot at the buzzer while sitting on the floor. Fortunately for the Devils, Johnson, who later played with the Chicago Cubs, was a southpaw.

Groat fouled out again in his last game with 4:08 left after scoring 27 points in a loss to State. "Dick Groat is the Ben Hogan, the Phil Rizzuto of the Southern Conference," wrote Charlotte columnist Sandy Grady.

Even his opponents loved him. Jake Wade, the sports information director at Carolina, said, "He's the greatest player I've ever seen."

After Groat, Duke had a lot of very good players under Bradley, but never could quite reach the top.

Bradley accepted the Texas job on March 23, 1959. Six weeks later, Vic Bubas, just 32, was hired away from his job as an N.C. State assistant. In a mere decade of coaching, he would take Duke to unprecedented heights and begin the extraordinary basketball success that exists today.

He won an ACC championship in his first season. He coached Duke into the school's first Final Four in 1963, and did it again in '64 and '66. And it all started in a hurry. The day after he accepted the Duke job, Bubas talked Art Heyman into reneging on his commitment to North Carolina and to sign with the Blue Devils.

FEBRUARY 29, 1952

Before a crowd of 7,000, All-American Dick Groat played his final home game as Duke thrashed arch-rival North Carolina, 94-64. Groat scored a career-high 48 points, which stood as the school scoring record for better than 37 years, until Danny Ferry had 58 in a game at Miami.

Groat's previous high was 46 points, scored against George Washington two weeks before. He scored 22 of the points—nine field goals and four free throws—in the final quarter. (College games were played in four 10-minute periods). The total also broke the Big Four (Duke, UNC, N.C. State and Wake Forest) record of 47, which was held by the Wolfpack's Sam Ranzino.

On his final goal, Groat drove toward the goal when he was fouled by UNC defender Cotton Thorne. With his body parallel to the court, "I switched the ball to my left hand, threw it up at the backboard, and somehow it went in," he said in a 2004 interview.

With 15 seconds left, Coach Hal Bradley pulled him and he was given a long standing ovation. Groat made eight consecutive baskets at one point in that last quarter after the Tar Heels had reduced the deficit to 58-50. He made nine of 12 shots overall for the period.

His teammates swarmed around him, even though the game wasn't over, and Groat broke into tears. Afterward, Groat addressed the crowd on the public address system, where, in a choking voice, he said, "As captain of the team I would like to thank you fans for your support during the season. We are sorry that we lost five games but we hope that we can win the conference championship for you."

The Blue Devils lifted Groat onto their shoulders and carried him into the dressing room, where he continued to cry. "I never thought I'd do that," he said of the record performance.

Groat's parents and two sisters arrived from Pennsylvania shortly before the game and witnessed Dick's greatest performance. Two months later, he became the first Duke player to have his jersey retired.

Groat was not the only hero for Duke, which finished that season 24-6 after losing in the Southern Conference Tournament finals to host N.C. State.

Junior forward Bernie Janicki, who stood only 6-3, grabbed 31 rebounds, a Duke record that likely will stand forever.

Groat had 17 points by halftime, and Duke led 50-32. In the final quarter, he personally outscored the entire Tar Heel team, 22-12. He made 19 of 37 shots and missed just one of 11 foul shots.

Showing the respect that the enormously popular Groat had with everybody who watched him play, the Carolina players came into the Duke locker room after the game to shake his hand.

CHAPTER 5

VIC BUBAS

Duke basketball had a decent tradition by 1960, but certainly not on a national scale. The school had won six Southern Conference championships, but the best that it had done nationally was to finish the 1958 season ranked 10th in the nation.

The Blue Devils had not won a championship in the ACC in the six seasons of its existence, and played in just one NCAA Tournament game, losing to Villanova, 74-73, in 1955. Duke only was playing in the postseason because league champion N.C. State was on probation.

All of that began to change—and change rapidly—after May 5, 1959. On that afternoon, Victor Albert Bubas stepped out of the office of Duke dining hall manager Ted Minah into the Union

VIC BUBAS (LEFT) SOUGHT OUT STUDENT SUPPORT AS SOON AS HE WAS HIRED.

lobby, where athletic director Eddie Cameron was prepared to announce the school's new coach.

Bubas, 32, had been hired after a six-week search upon the resignation of Hal Bradley. Once a red headed guard and a member of Everett Case's Hoosier Hotshots at N.C. State, he had stuck around after graduation and served as an assistant coach for the Wolfpack.

Cameron had 135 candidates for the job. When he selected Bubas, he told the media, "Gentlemen, this is Vic Bubas, our new basketball coach. We hope he is our coach forever."

Bubas, a native of Gary, Indiana, was one of the all-time bargains. He confirmed years later that his starting salary at Duke was $8,500.

He did not coach forever. In fact, his coaching career at Duke lasted merely for the decade of the '60s, but had it not been for John Wooden at UCLA, Bubas would have been the national coach of that period.

His overall record was 213-67, which included 17-11 in his first season (when Duke won its first ACC tournament), and 15-13 in his finale. From 1961 through 1966, the Blue Devils were dominant. They won 141 and lost 28, the best record in the nation. They appeared in the school's first three Final Fours. They finished in the top 10 every one of those years, and were No. 2 in the final poll in 1963 and 1966.

Playing at home in the indoor stadium, the Bubas teams were nearly unbeatable. Overall, they finished 87-13. Eight of those losses were in the first and last years of his realm. In the eight years in between, Duke was 76-5.

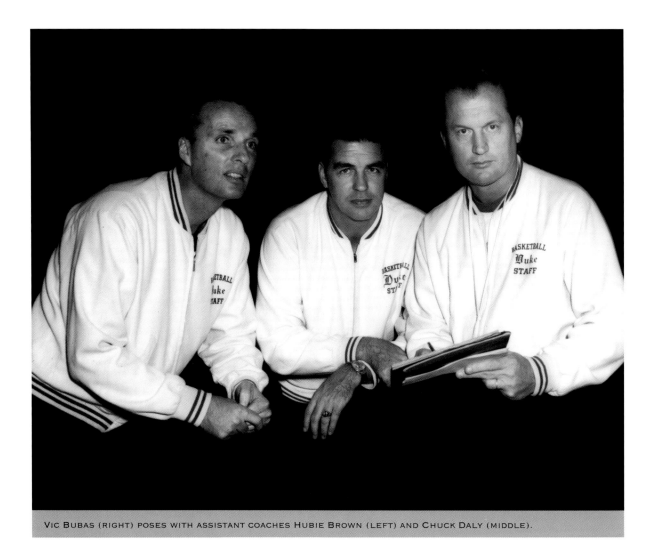

While Bubas's only real coaching experience had been with the State freshman team, he was hardly unknown in the region. But he wasn't exactly a big name, either.

Yet Duke sports information director Ted Mann was immediately convinced. He wrote to Joe Sheehan of the *New York Times*, "It is my firm conviction that he will be one of the great coaches in the game. He just simply has all of the requirements, including the knowledge of working with members of the press."

Doing things first class was a Bubas trait. It started with assistant coaches. Every Duke assistant coach went on to become a successful head coach, starting with Bucky Waters, another for-

mer State player, and ex-Duke player Fred Shabel, who had been on Bradley's staff.

At one time, the Duke staff consisted of Bubas, Chuck Daly and Hubie Brown. The latter two became most famous as professional coaches. Daly won two NBA championships with Detroit's Bad Boys, and the 71-year-old Brown has turned around the franchise of the Memphis Grizzlies, who set a team record for victories in 2004.

Bubas was a superior recruiter, and he started it immediately. The day after taking the job with Duke, he was in the New York home of Art Heyman, a scholastic superstar who had committed to North Carolina. In short order, Bubas had convinced Heyman to come to Durham, not Chapel Hill.

Heyman would be the first of a succession of Bubas's All-Americans. They came almost one every year. Heyman, who graduated in '63, was followed by Jeff Mullins, '64, Jack Marin, '66, Bob Verga, '67, and Mike Lewis, '68.

But it was the one open year in that pattern, 1965, that prevented Duke from being even more powerful than it turned out to be.

In June 1961, a player graduating from high school in Missouri stood up at the ceremony and announced that he was going to Duke. One week before classes were to begin in late summer at Duke, Bubas learned that Bill Bradley was going to Princeton instead.

It is almost mind-boggling to imagine how good the Blue Devils would have been had Bradley become a teammate of Heyman and Mullins. In what would have been his first year of eligibility

in 1963, sophomore Bradley would have played with junior Mullins and senior Heyman.

Even without Bradley, Duke was undefeated in the ACC in 17 games, went to the Final Four, and finished 27-3. The next season, when Bradley would have been a junior and Mullins was a senior, the Blue Devils were 26-5 overall, 17-1 in the ACC, and lost to UCLA for Wooden's first NCAA championship. They were second and third in the final polls those years.

In '65, Duke finished 20-5 and was upset in the ACC championship game. Bradley, meanwhile, was good enough to take a non-scholarship Princeton team to its only Final Four that season. In the third-place game against Wichita State, he scored an NCAA-record 58 points. There's simply no telling how good the Blue Devils would have been with him, because that '65 team av-

DUKE CELEBRATES ITS FIRST ACC CHAMPIONSHIP IN 1960, VIC BUBAS'S FIRST YEAR AS HEAD COACH.

eraged 92.4 points, which is still the school record. During Bradley's three varsity seasons at Princeton, Duke finished 73-13, including 46-5 in ACC games.

And there was more to the what-if story. If Bradley had told Duke in the early summer that he wasn't coming, it would have given the Blue Devils an available scholarship to go after a 6-8 Virginian, Fred Hetzel.

Hetzel had been recruited by Duke, but there was no scholarship available. He wound up signing with Duke alum Lefty Driesell at Davidson, where he became a two-time All-American. As a sophomore, Hetzel led the Wildcats to a 72-69 victory over Duke, one of just two regular-season defeats.

Those situations notwithstanding, Duke began its unprecedented period of success in the 1960 ACC Tournament, which the Blue Devils entered with a 12-10 record, including 7-7 in the ACC. Included among those league losses were two to North Carolina by 26 and 25 points, and two more to Wake Forest by 17 and 19. The Blue Devils also had been trounced by 22 points in the Dixie Classic by UNC.

Duke lost its regular-season finale to Carolina, 75-50, and finished with five defeats in its last seven games. The Devils obviously looked like anything but champions.

Led by juniors Doug Kistler, Carroll Youngkin and Howard Hurt, the Blue Devils defeated South Carolina to set up a fourth meeting with Carolina. Before the game, Bubas told his squad, "We have everything to gain and nothing to lose. We have been manhandled three times, so there is no reason for you to be tight this time. To the contrary, I want you to be loosey-goosey. Just go out there and play basketball."

Led by Youngkin's 30 points and 17 more from Hurt, Duke upset the Tar Heels, 71-69. Bubas always considered that one of his greatest victories.

That sent Duke into the finals against Wake Forest, where controversy awaited. Dave Budd, the Deacs' star, had gotten into a fight in the semifinals and ACC commissioner Jim Weaver had ruled him ineligible for the title game.

But the ACC's executive committee overruled Weaver and permitted Budd to play. Whether that distraction bothered Wake Forest nobody ever will know, but Duke was in command most of the way and pulled off the shocker, 63-59, as Kistler scored 22 points and Hurt added 14. Budd was limited to 10 points and without question the Blue Devils had earned the championship.

Entering the NCAAs for just the second time, the Blue Devils pounded Princeton, 84-60. In the East regional at Charlotte, Duke upset St. Joseph's 58-56 to reach the finals against power-

ART HEYMAN GOES FOR A REBOUND AGAINST N.C. STATE.

JEFF MULLINS DRAWS PLENTY OF ATTENTION FROM NORTH CAROLINA'S DEFENSE.

In his career at Duke, Bubas took his teams to the title game all but two years, and registered an ACC tournament record of 22-6. The Blue Devils were the toughest kids on the block.

Heyman joined Kistler, Youngkin and Hurt on the varsity in '61 and the Blue Devils played like league favorites. They lost just once in their first 16 games, to Carolina and Doug Moe in the Dixie Classic finals.

When the teams met in Durham, Heyman scored 36 points while Moe shot two of 14 and fouled out. Duke won but the game would prove to be extremely costly to the Blue Devils.

Heyman, who clinched the victory by making two foul shots with 15 seconds left, fouled Carolina guard Larry Brown six seconds later. The play occurred in front of the UNC bench. It was Heyman's fifth foul, but referee Charlie Eckman tossed him out of the game for the rough play against Brown.

Once again, Weaver stepped in. He banned Heyman, Brown and Donnie Walsh for the remainder of the ACC games. Duke was never the same after that.

Eckman reversed himself after watching the film of the incident. "I realize that Heyman did not start the fight. The first two punches were thrown by Larry Brown. Heyman was merely defending himself."

The Blue Devils worked Heyman back into the lineup for non-league games (plus a game at Wake Forest where he was allowed to play). But the chemistry was gone. Duke dropped five of its last 11 games, three without Heyman. Wake Forest, led by Len Chappell and guard Billy Packer,

ful NYU. It was the Blue Devils' sixth game in 10 days, and on the way back from the Princeton game they had been snowed in at Washington and had to bus the remainder of what became a 13-hour trip.

NYU won, 74-59, and Duke's first chance at a Final Four was gone. "When you get down to realism, it would have been incredible if we had gone to San Francisco," Bubas said.

But he was elated with what his team had done in the postseason. "The way our conference has it set up, and as long as it remains that way, we're going to play it as the most important. I remember what a coach told me when talking about championships, 'It's fine to be a national champion, but first you've got to be the toughest kid on your block.'"

The big fight at the end of the game didn't impact the outcome, but it did signal that the Duke-North Carolina rivalry had reached a unique standard. Although the schools always had been rivals, they rarely had been good at the same time.

This was the first time that the neighboring schools met when both were ranked in the top five. Duke, 15-1, was No. 4; UNC was 14-2 and No. 5. Each team was 7-0 in the ACC. And the Blue Devils' only loss had come in the Dixie Classic finals, 76-71, as Doug Moe shut down sophomore star Art Heyman.

Heyman won the individual duel easily. He made 11-of-13 field goals and added 14 free throws for 36 points. Moe shot 2 for 14 from the field and fouled out with 7:06 to play. Duke won 81-77.

But the real story was the brawl just prior to the end of the contest, after Heyman made two clinching free throws with 15 seconds to play that gave Duke an 80-75 advantage.

Heyman fouled UNC's Larry Brown. It was a hard foul and Brown took offense. They squared off, and Heyman threw a punch. He was immediately ejected by referee Charlie Eckman, although it also was his fifth foul.

The Carolina bench erupted, and leading the way was Moe, who took wild swings at anybody he could find, including Duke students who had gone on the floor.

UNC Coach Frank McGuire got into a verbal exchange with Duke trainer Jim Cunningham, who had shouted at Tar Heel player Deiter Krause.

McGuire expressed concern about the future. "I hope I am wrong, but I'm afraid this is only the beginning. I'm just afraid that the situation might get worse."

Duke athletic director Eddie Cameron said, "It's a shame to have such a grand ball game ruined by such an incident. But there's one common factor in these basketball fights we've had in the Atlantic Coast Conference during the last few years."

He refused to elaborate on the "common factor," but media members pointed out that Carolina teams had been involved in most of the free-for-alls.

The foul that started it came in front of the UNC bench. Heyman grabbed Brown as the Tar Heel guard dribbled under the basket. Both players tumbled to the floor. The two squared off and began swinging fists.

Led by Moe, players came off the Carolina bench and swarmed over Heyman. Duke fans then joined the melee, which was quickly broken up by police in a couple of minutes. Earlier in the game, Heyman and Moe nearly had come to blows.

Heyman was the lone player ejected. Brown made two foul shots, then Duke made one to end it.

Duke lost three of its next four games, and fell to the Tar Heels in the rematch in Chapel Hill, 69-66, in overtime. There were no incidents, but the rivalry had heated up and remains the best in all of college basketball more than 40 years later.

trounced the Blue Devils 96-81 in the ACC finals. Duke finished 22-6, ranked 10th nationally. Even that matched the school's highest final ranking, but it could have been much better.

With four senior starters gone, Heyman was joined by Mullins and other sophomores for the '62 season. The two worked well together and Duke roared to a 14-2 start.

But Heyman suffered a severely sprained ankle, and though he played sparingly against UNC and missed two other games, he never was the same. In the five games that he sat out in his first two seasons, Duke lost four. With the All-American playing, the Devils were 41-7.

Heyman still wasn't himself for the ACC Tournament. Although he insisted he was healthy, he shot five for 16 in a 71-58 win over Maryland, then missed 20 of 27 attempts in the semifinal loss to Clemson, 77-72. It remains the only time the Tigers ever reached the finals, where they were beaten by Wake Forest.

Duke finished 20-5 and Heyman averaged 25.3 points. In his other two years, his scoring average was 25.2 and 24.9. Unhappy after the loss, he predicted that '63 would be far better.

Heyman was a man of his word, aided substantially by Mullins. Duke went undefeated in the conference. There was just one close game, 56-55 at State, and most of the others were blowouts.

After consecutive losses at Davidson and Miami, Duke won 20 straight games. The team shot 51.7 percent, a school record although Heyman made just 45 percent of his attempts. Nevertheless, he finished his career with the highest scoring average of better than 25 points, was first in career field goals and free throws and second in rebounds.

Wake Forest coach Bones McKinney called Duke "one of the great teams the ACC has fostered. They're as talented a bunch as the ACC has ever seen and maybe the most talented."

In the NCAAs, Heyman played poorly, but Mullins was sensational as Duke defeated NYU and St. Joseph's to reach its first Final Four, to be played in Louisville. There, No. 2 Duke would meet Loyola Chicago, while No. 1 Cincinnati took on Oregon State.

The Blue Devils picked a bad time for their worst game of the year. They shot under 30 percent and fell behind the quick Ramblers by 17 points. Heyman, who scored 29 points, led a desperation rally that cut the margin to 74-71 with 4:22 left, but Duke was out of gas. Loyola scored the next 14 points and won 94-75.

The Blue Devils crushed Oregon State, 85-63, in the third-

JACK MARIN WAS A CONSISTENT OUTSIDE SCORING THREAT.

BOB VERGA AND BOB RIEDY HELPED DEFEAT UCLA IN BACK-TO-BACK GAMES IN 1965.

place game, and in an extraordinary vote, Heyman was named the Final Four MVP. That had never happened before. Two years later, it would happen again. Bradley got the nod for his 58-point outburst.

Even with Heyman gone and Bradley at Princeton, Duke was still rolling during the 1963-64 season. The Blue Devils went 26-5 and were ranked third in the nation. Mullins averaged 24 points, was runner-up for national player of the year, and Duke went back to the Final Four.

Just before Christmas, Duke was crushed at

No. 1 Michigan, 83-67, where the Wolverines featured All-American Cazzie Russell and center Bill Buntin. After losing to No. 2 Kentucky, 81-79, in the final of the Sugar Bowl tournament, the Devils won 10 straight.

Wake Forest then upset Duke, 72-71, ending a streak of 28 games against ACC foes. That was the last defeat until the NCAA finals. The ACC tournament was won in record fashion by margins of 31, 16 and 21 points.

In the NCAAs at Raleigh, Mullins played all 40 minutes against Villanova and made 19 of 28 shots while scoring 43 points with 12 rebounds. Duke won 87-73. Nobody else had more than three field goals.

The regional final was against Connecticut, coached by former Duke assistant Fred Shabel. The Blue Devils romped, 101-54, as Mullins scored another 30.

The 1964 Final Four was played in Kansas City. The trip got off to a bad start. Terrible weather closed the K.C. airport and the charter had to land in Municipal Airport, rarely used for commercial traffic. The plane slid off the end of the runway and was stuck deep in mud.

The team arrived at the Muehlbach Hotel, adjacent to the Kansas City arena. On the dais, there was a sign, "Welcome Tar Heels." And the *Kansas City Star* constantly referred to Duke as the Tar Heels. Nobody was pleased.

Bubas discovered that the locker room was being painted, so he had the team dress in the hotel for practice and take the tunnel to the arena. Seven-foot beds which had been ordered for the 6-10 towers, Jay Buckley and Hack Tison, weren't available. And standing in Duke's way was Michigan.

In the first Michigan game, Buckley had been outrebounded 18-2 by Buntin. A Charlotte writer called Jay the "weak link" of the team. His teammates called him by his new nickname, "Link."

Buckley played the game of his life against the Wolverines. He scored 25 points, making 11 of 16

shots, and added 14 rebounds. Mullins added 21, and Duke won what Bubas later called one of his "most satisfying" games, 91-80.

That sent the Blue Devils into their first national championship game against undefeated UCLA. It was only the second time (UNC '57) that an ACC team had reached the finals.

This was to be the start of the incredible run by the Bruins, coached by the Wizard of Westwood, who won 10 NCAA crowns in 12 years. Duke's team was taller; Wooden's was faster.

The Blue Devils led 30-27 when UCLA went on a 16-0 run that sealed the victory. The Bruins were led by an unheralded guard, Kenny Washington, from Beaufort, S.C., who scored 26 points and had 12 rebounds. He was averaging 3.9 points. All-American Gail Goodrich scored 27 against a Duke team that had 29 turnovers against the UCLA press. The Bruins won, 98-83.

"When you play for the national championship, you have to play a great game," Bubas said. "And UCLA played a great game." The Blue Devils had six days to get ready for Michigan. They had just a few hours to prepare for the Bruins, as the Final Four was played on Friday-Saturday.

The '65 Blue Devils didn't have a typical Bubas superstar, although Jack Marin became an All-American the following year, and sophomore Bob Verga would become such a player before he graduated.

Duke still had excellent talent, and the Blue Devils were the school's highest-scoring team ever. Among the 20 wins was a record 136-72 stomping of Virginia, when all 14 players scored as they shattered all school and ACC records, making 55 of 93 shots.

With four new starters, the Blue Devils still got off to an 18-2 start, with both losses at home, to Michigan and UNC. But the lack of experience showed in defeats at Maryland and Carolina to close the regular season in which Verga averaged 21.4 points and Marin 19.1.

In the ACC semifinals, top-seeded Duke blitzed Wake Forest, 101-81, to gain a meeting with homestanding N.C. State, also 20-4. The Wolfpack was on an emotional high, having been coached since the early part of the season by Press Maravich, who replaced the gravely ill Everett Case.

Although Duke led at halftime, 43-40, the Wolfpack rallied in the second half behind reserve forward Larry Worsley, who made nine of 13 shots, mostly from the corner to win, 91-85. He finished with 30 points in front of Case, who died not long afterward.

Bubas actually felt Duke had done as well as possible. Of the three leading scorers, Verga had been on the freshman team the previous year while Marin and Vacendak had been reserves.

But the '66 Blue Devils were loaded. Verga, Marin and Vacendak were joined by sophomore center Mike Lewis, who Bucky Waters had recruited out of Missoula, Montana, and 6-6 Bob Riedy.

The team lost an early two-pointer at South Carolina, then trounced two-time defending NCAA champ UCLA in consecutive games at Durham and Charlotte by 16 and 19 points.

The Blue Devils were 15-1 when they were upset on the road by West Virginia, now coached by Waters, 94-90. The only other regular-season loss was a stunner at last-place Wake Forest, 99-98. Duke got revenge in a big way a week later in the ACC Tournament, 103-73. That set up a third meeting with North Carolina in the semifinals. The Blue Devils had beaten UNC easily twice during the campaign.

Dean Smith, the young Carolina coach, had decided if he played Duke again, he would unveil his stall game. They called it the Four Corners. The Tar Heels, who never substituted, placed a player in each corner and one at the top of the key.

There was no shot clock. Duke didn't press. And the Blue Devils led 7-5 at halftime as many in the Reynolds Coliseum crowd booed. Ironically, it was to be the last time the ACC Tournament was to be played in Raleigh.

For awhile, it appeared Smith's strategy might work. The Tar Heels took a 17-12 lead midway through the period. But Duke battled back to tie it at 20 on a basket by Vacendak with 2:09 to play. Carolina missed a free throw, the Devils rebounded and held for the final shot.

Lewis broke free for a layup with four seconds left and was fouled hard. He missed the first but made the second for a 21-20 victory. "When I walked to that foul line, I was so nervous my knees were almost knocking. In fact, they might have knocked, and I wouldn't have known it," he said.

BOB VERGA WAS A PHENOMENAL LONG-RANGE SHOOTER.

JACK MARIN AND MIKE LEWIS BATTLE AGAINST WAKE FOREST.

litis. He wound up playing against the Wildcats with a fever above 100 degrees.

Kentucky also had ailments. Guard Larry Conley was very ill. But, like Verga, he played. Conley had one first-half basket, as did Verga, which came on a breakaway layup. Duke led 42-41 as Kentucky couldn't stop Marin, Lewis and Vacendak, who would combine for 67 points.

Verga played 28 minutes and scored a career-low four points. He made two of only seven shots. His counterpoint at guard, Louie Dampier, led Kentucky's 83-79 victory with 23. Conley scored 10 points and made the biggest basket of the game.

"He had a 102-degree fever last night but we fixed that with some old-fashioned goose oil and a vaporizer," said Kentucky coach Adolph Rupp.

Despite a severely sprained ankle early by Lewis, Duke defeated Utah in the third-place game. In the finals, Texas Western's all-black starting team gained immortality by upsetting Kentucky's all-white squad. It's doubtful if there would have been the social uproar had it been Duke against Texas Western, because Rupp had the reputation of being a bigot.

"This was the best team I ever had," said Bubas. It certainly wouldn't be replicated by any of his last three squads.

In '67, Duke got off to a 3-4 start that included two crushing losses at UCLA, which would start its string of seven straight titles, and an 83-82 defeat against Ohio State despite 41 points from Verga.

The title game against State was won by Duke, 71-66, as Vacendak led the scoring with 16 points. He would be named the ACC Player of the Year, although he didn't make first-team all-conference.

In the NCAAs, No. 2 Duke struggled past St. Joseph's, 76-74, then defeated Syracuse, 91-81, to win the East Regional. That sent the Blue Devils to College Park, where they would face No. 1 Kentucky in the semifinals.

In what became one of the most memorable Final Fours in history, Duke had to deal with a serious illness. All-American Verga was first diagnosed with strep throat, later revised to tonsil-

The Blue Devils rallied to win 11 of 12 games before losing for the second time to Carolina, 82-69. That defeat left Duke second in the ACC at 9-3 behind the 12-2 Tar Heels, ranked third nationally.

In the tournament, Duke reached the finals and Verga finished with 76 points. But UNC won, 82-73, as Larry Miller made 13 of 14 shots.

The Blue Devils then became the first ACC team permitted to play in the NIT. It was a difficult situation. Two days after losing to the Tar Heels, Duke lost to eventual NIT champion Southern Illinois and Walt Frazier, 72-63, in Madison Square Garden.

That ended the season at 18-9 and the team was rated 19th in the nation, the lowest ever for a Bubas team.

Even though Verga had graduated, Duke rebounded in '68 to finish 10th in the nation with a 22-6 record. The Blue Devils were 11-3 in the league, one game behind fourth-ranked North Carolina, which would make it to the Final Four.

Lewis averaged nearly 22 points and more than 14 rebounds, and got double-figure help from Dave Golden, Joe Kennedy and Steve Vandenberg. None had played significant roles before.

In the home finale, Duke upset UNC, 87-86, in triple overtime. Lewis fouled out, but his sub, Fred Lind, paced the Blue Devils to the win with 16 points and nine rebounds. He had scored 29 points all season.

That all but ended the scoring for the season. In the ACC opener, Clemson slowed it down and Duke was fortunate to escape, 43-40. Compared with what was to occur against State in the semifinals, it was a shootout. State held the ball and won, 12-10.

Duke was off to the NIT again, where the Blue Devils defeated Oklahoma City, 97-81, before getting blown out by St. Peter's 100-71, as All-American Lewis fouled out after just 7:18 of playing time.

The final season of Vic Bubas's coaching career—1968-69—was different for variety of reasons, very few of them positive.

His team finished 15-13, his worst record ever. There were four losses at home, including one to East Tennessee. That came immediately after a loss at Virginia, the only game Bubas ever lost to the Cavaliers.

MARCH 8, 1968

Duke was used to playing against teams that froze the ball. Both Wake Forest and South Carolina had done it, and in the '66 ACC semifinals, Dean Smith unveiled the four-corners and top-seeded Duke had to rally for a 21-20 victory.

But nothing could set the stage for the ACC semifinal game against N.C. State at Charlotte. No. 6 Duke played a zone, and the Wolfpack held the ball. And held it.

It was 4-2 Duke at halftime. In the second half, because play continued without a timeout, the North Carolina radio network went to commercial during the non-action. When they returned to the air, play-by-play man Bill Currie said, "You haven't missed a thing. This is as exciting as artificial insemination."

During the 14-minute period without a shot, Everett Case called Eddie Biedenbach to the sidelines for some advice. He was followed by Duke guard Tony Barone, who unabashedly listened to the conversation.

The unhappy fans threw coins on the court. "It's always pennies, never quarters," complained referee Otis Almond.

The only action came in the final minute. Duke took a 9-8 lead on Dave Golden's free throw, but then fouled State's Bill Kretzer. He missed, but an offensive stickback by Dick Braucher made it 10-9. Vann Williford added a foul shot with 16 seconds left.

Golden was fouled with six seconds on the clock. He made the first but missed the second. Braucher was fouled at :03 and made the foul shot that ended the bizarre 12-10 contest. Duke made two field goals in the entire game; State had four. "I don't fault our strategy not to chase them," Bubas said. "Missed foul shots and offensive rebounds beat us."

The only highlights were the home game against No. 2 North Carolina, which the Blue Devils won in an 87-81 upset as Vandenberg scored a career-high 33 points, and gaining the finals of the ACC Tournament.

In the tournament, Duke defeated Virginia and No. 13 South Carolina to reach the finals against North Carolina. The Blue Devils even led 43-34 at halftime, before All-American Charlie Scott took over. In the second half, Scott made 12 of 13 shots, most of them deep jumpers that would have been three-pointers today. He scored 28 of his career-high 40 points and the No. 4 Tar Heels won, 85-74.

There never was an official announcement about the Bubas retirement until well after the season, when he accepted a job as a Duke vice president, and would be an assistant to the school president, Douglas Knight.

On February 13, *Durham Sun* columnist Elton Casey broke the news that Bubas was retiring. Casey had the accurate news about the next job for the coach. There was no attribution in the story.

The next day, Bubas met privately with then-baseball coach Tom Butters, who later would become Duke athletic director until 1997. "He told me he wanted to broaden his horizons," Butters said.

On February 15, Duke played West Virginia, coached by Bucky Waters, in Charleston. Incredibly,

not a single North Carolina newspaper covered the game. The only ACC-area paper to have a reporter there to interview Bubas was the *Roanoke, Virginia, Times.* The Blue Devils lost the game, 90-88.

In reflection, Bubas called the 1960 team his favorite because it overcame so many obstacles to win the school's first ACC championship. The '66 team was labeled his best and he said that the loss to State in the '65 ACC finals was "the only time we should have won it and didn't."

His top players, he said included Mullins (best medium-range shooter) and Verga (from long range). Marin was the best all a round, Lewis the finest center, Buckley the best defensive center. Kennedy was the most improved and Vacendak was the best competitor ("not even close.") Heyman was the player who would win the tough games.

And what would Bubas miss most about coaching? Practice.

"The people," he said. "The fantastic association of being with young people, sweating together, smiling together, crying together. You're in the arena and you look around, and there's no place to hide. You do it or you don't. I don't think anything else can approach it—except maybe war."

Bubas was just 42 years old when he quit coaching. He remained at Duke for seven more years. He left in 1976 to return to sports as the commissioner of the new Sun Belt Conference.

CHAPTER 6

TRANSITION YEARS

For a basketball program that has known so much success for the past 45 years, one decade stands out when Duke was less than the best—the 1970s. Even then, by the end of that period, the Blue Devils had righted the ship and played for a national championship.

But things didn't begin that way, and in the middle of the '70s, they were downright devastating.

Rumors were flying on the night that North Carolina defeated Duke in the ACC finals at the Charlotte Coliseum, the final game of the coaching career of Vic Bubas.

Assistant coaches Tom Carmody and Hubie Brown were huddled in a reporter's motel room, constantly on the telephone with Bucky Waters.

When Bubas stunned the Duke community in mid-February by saying that he was quitting at the end of the season, attention on a successor was directed at Waters, then the 33-year-old coach at West Virginia.

Waters had appeared to be the logical person to follow Bubas. He had come to Duke with Bubas in the spring of 1959, like Vic a former player at

N.C. State and a member of the coaching staff of the Wolfpack.

Waters coached the freshman team at Duke for four years before moving up to the No. 1 assistant for two more. He then became the nation's youngest head coach when he got the West Virginia job, where he had just completed his fourth season.

Waters was 19-9 each of his first three years in Morgantown before what would be his final team finished 12-13. One of those wins was over Duke, two days after the Bubas retirement story broke. He also had beaten the Blue Devils, 94-90, in 1966, his first year as a head coach. Duke was No. 1 in the nation at the time.

For the three weeks before the ACC tournament, rumors had swirled that Waters was coming back to Durham. But on the evening after Duke had lost that title game, there was word that a strong push was being made for Duke grad Lefty Driesell, who had built a powerhouse at Davidson.

Although there were reports that Bubas had campaigned for Waters, Vic later denied that and stated that the choice always was athletic director Eddie Cameron's to make.

BUCKY WATERS RETURNED TO DUKE FROM WEST VIRGINIA TO REPLACE VIC BUBAS.

there was media speculation over whether or not Duke should have hired Driesell, who took the Maryland job after the Blue Devils made their decision.

Driesell said his intentions were to make Maryland the "UCLA of the East," and in 1973, the Terps appeared to be well on the way. They were ranked in the top 10 regularly, and the only thing that stood between them and a chance at the national championship was N.C. State with David Thompson.

Had Driesell gotten the Duke job, he certainly would have remained for a very long time. It was only the cocaine-related death of Len Bias in 1986 that forced him out at Maryland. No matter how long Lefty would have coached, it's a cinch that Mike Krzyzewski never would have come to Durham. In that regard, the choice of Waters proved enormously beneficial in the long run.

Waters was a proven recruiter. He brought in blue-chip prospects Jim Fitzsimmons, Richie O'Connor, Jeff Dawson, Gary Melchionni and Alan Shaw that first year. The freshman team went undefeated, although leading scorer Fitzsimmons

Regardless, Carmody—who had taken the job at Rhode Island—and Brown spent several hours on the telephone trying to see what was going to happen.

Eventually Waters got the job. His Duke teams were good enough to play in the NIT the first two seasons when they went 17-9 and 20-10. But his third team fell off to 14-12, and in what proved to be his final campaign, slumped to 12-14 and 4-8 in the ACC. It was the school's first losing season in 34 years.

As Waters's program slipped badly, primarily because several blue-chip players transferred for a variety of reasons,

BRAD EVANS LOOKS TO FEED ALL-AMERICAN RANDY DENTON IN THE POST.

became the first player to transfer, going to Harvard at midyear.

On the court, Waters did a marvelous job, the best he would do in his four seasons at Duke. He didn't start a senior, but the team went 17-7 in the '70 regular season against a most difficult schedule. The only non-conference loss was to No. 1 Kentucky. There also were losses to nationally ranked South Carolina (twice), UNC and State. Duke defeated the latter pair in the final week.

The record would have been even better except point guard Dick DeVenzio broke his foot during the Christmas holiday, and the Devils lost four games in succession. DeVenzio returned to action but he didn't have the quickness he had possessed before the injury.

The Duke star was center Randy Denton, a junior, who averaged 21.5 points and 12.4 re-

LARRY SAUNDERS SCORES AGAINST CLEMSON.

RANDY DENTON SCORES IN AN EASY VICTORY OVER MICHIGAN IN '70.

bounds. He went over the 30-point mark five times, including 37 at Clemson.

During the losing streak, the Blue Devils were awful at the foul line, missing 51 of 90 free throws in the four games. But in its upset victory over UNC in the finale, Duke made the first 21 foul shots and 23 of 24 in the first half en route to a 14-point lead.

The Blue Devils won, 91-83, although they took just 45 shots and had 24 turnovers, while Carolina got 83 shots and had a mere 10 floor mistakes. "I thought Duke couldn't shoot foul shots," said Dean Smith.

A thrilled Waters said that his team had completed basic training, "and we are peaking. I believe we are destined to win the tournament." It was a quote that would come back to haunt the coach.

Duke not only didn't win the tournament, it didn't win a game. In the end, an inability to achieve in the postseason became Waters's Waterloo. The Blue Devils were guilty of looking past Wake Forest, a team they had defeated three times during the year.

Duke players were quoted about their expectations of beating South Carolina in the semifinals. The Gamecocks had gone undefeated in the ACC. That game never came about. Charlie Davis scored 23 of his 25 points in the second half, and the Deacs pulled off the shocker, 81-73.

So that sent Duke off to the NIT along with North Carolina, which also lost in the first round. Down 76-75 with five seconds left against Utah, guard Ray Kuhlmeier missed a short jumper and the Devils were eliminated. Again playing "what if?", Denton said, "I think if we had made that shot we would have won the NIT."

DICK DEVENZIO PLAYED ON VIC BUBAS'S FINAL TEAM.

The next season, Duke had an unusual situation, with four seniors and four sophomores. Except for one game that Melchionni missed with a sprained ankle, the eight players participated in every contest and seven of them got at least 10 starts. The eighth player, sophomore backup center Shaw, averaged 20 minutes.

Denton was the only player to start every game. He was All-ACC. Most of the time he was joined by sophomores O'Connor and Dawson and seniors DeVenzio and Larry Saunders. The others were senior Rick Katherman and sophs Melchionni and Shaw.

Duke started the year rated ninth in the nation and behind only South Carolina in the ACC. After seven games, they were 3-4 and the ranking was gone. The team finished last in the Big Four Tournament.

But the Devils finally got it together and won their last eight games in the regular season. They got revenge against Maryland and N.C. State, and shot 62 percent in defeating North Carolina at home. Duke finished fourth in the nation in free-throw shooting and was the best rebounding team in the ACC. It also was second in field-goal percentage, and that winning streak got it to 19th in the nation in the final poll.

But tournament time again proved a jinx. Duke promptly lost to sixth-seeded State, 68-61, after leading by seven at the half. Those great foul shooters made five of 10; the Wolfpack hit 16 of 24.

So, once again, Duke headed to the NIT, again with Carolina. This time the Devils won twice, whipping Dayton and Tennessee, before going against the Tar Heels in the semifinals. UNC won, 73-67, which was bad enough. In the consolation game, the Devils showed little interest against St.

Bonaventure and blew a 20-point halftime lead to lose in overtime.

There was obvious dissension on the squad. According to Denton, who averaged better than 20 points, "We had a conflict with some of the players. There were too many personal conflicts, like seniors against sophomores. We fell apart in the NIT."

DeVenzio had a different slant. "I loved Vic Bubas and his theory of basketball. Coach Waters has his own ideas on how the game should be played. He was sincere and he had reasons, but it completely changed my style of play.'"

Despite all the problems, Duke did win 20 games. It would be quite a while before it won that many again.

In the next six seasons, the Devils would lose six more games than they won. Their ACC record was 19-53. They finished last in the league for the first time in 1973. In the three seasons that followed, Duke was last again one time and tied for last in the other two.

The best record during that stretch was 14-12 in '72, and that year was filled with controversy. Dawson, a double-figure scorer as a sophomore, transferred in September to Illinois.

After the opening game with Richmond, 6-10 sophomore Dave Elmer, who led the freshmen in scoring the previous year, announced he was leaving because of Duke's run-and-shoot style of play. He wound up at Miami of Ohio, where he became a star.

Then, in midyear, came the biggest surprise of all. O'Connor, the leading scorer with a 15.4 average, quit the team. His reason was the same as Elmer's, but by now Duke had returned to patterned play because of lack of depth. Even more frustrating, O'Connor remained in school for the rest of the semester, when he transferred to Fairfield.

And in May, sophomore Ron Righter said he was leaving over the lack of playing time. That made it seven players who had left since Waters got the job.

The only highlight for the season came when the indoor stadium was dedicated to the retiring athletic director,

STU YARBROUGH REBOUNDS AS DUKE UPSETS MARYLAND IN '72.

JANUARY 22, 1972

Cameron Indoor Stadium was officially named for the veteran athletic director and former basketball coach, Eddie Cameron. He had come to Duke in 1926 and planned a leave of absence on February 1. His official retirement date was August 31.

Cameron coached the basketball team for 14 years, posting a 226-99 record while winning three Southern Conference titles. He had first designed the building that still bears his name on the back of a matchbox.

Chancellor John Blackburn announced the naming of the building at halftime of the game against North Carolina. He read a statement

from school president Terry Sanford, who said, "It is only fitting to rename the building in Cameron's honor for his outstanding and distinguished service to the university over the last 46 years."

The once-beaten, third-ranked Tar Heels were heavy favorites over a Bucky Waters-coached team that was 7-6.

But Duke won 76-74 on Robby West's basket with three seconds left.

West had been involved in an officiating decision moments earlier. The fifth foul called on UNC's Bobby Jones sent Blue Devil star Gary Melchionni to the foul line. The officials conferred and decided that West had to shoot.

West had shot just 10 free throws all season and was averaging 2.8 points. But with 31 seconds left, he made the first shot for a 74-72 lead. He missed the second, and UNC's Bill Chamberlain tied the score with 13 seconds to play. "I don't know what happened on the one and one," West said. "I thought Melchionni was going to shoot it."

Duke took a timeout with eight seconds left, and Melchionni passed the ball to West, who was near midcourt. He heaved—and the shot went in.

The Duke student body—perhaps the initial Cameron Crazies, mobbed West on the floor, thinking the game was over. But the officials ruled that there were three seconds left. Carolina's George Karl threw a fullcourt pass to leading scorer Dennis Wuycik (23 points), who was in the left-hand corner.

Wuycik immediately shot, but the ball hit the rim and bounced away. Duke had inaugurated Cameron Indoor Stadium with a victory. West was again in the middle of a student celebration. Only this time, the game was really over.

West's parents had planned to attend the game, but his mother got the flu. Although the game was on TV, it wasn't carried in New Jersey, where they lived. "The last shot wasn't planned for me," said the senior guard. "It could have gone to Melchionni or Richie O'Connor."

West, making his first start of the year, explained, "When my shots leave my hand, I can just about tell what it will do. I felt it was a good shot. It felt smooth when it rolled off my fingertips."

CHRIS REDDING AND DUKE DEFEATED SANTA CLARA IN 1972-73.

Cameron, on January 22, and Duke upset UNC on a last-second shot by Robbie West.

As bad as '72 was, the next season was even worse. It all started when Duke was placed on NCAA probation for one year because, unknown to any member of the coaching staff, a Duke alumnus took prep superstar David Thompson to the 1971 ACC Tournament and bought him a sportcoat.

N.C. State also landed on probation, but it got Thompson. In that season, the Wolfpack went undefeated at 27-0 and won the ACC Tournament. State fans happily accepted their penalty.

This was the first year that freshmen were eligible, and Duke had 12 rookies—freshmen and sophomores—on the roster. The only experienced players were seniors Melchionni and Shaw and junior Chris Redding. And the schedule made it more difficult. The Devils played 14 of the first 17 games on the road.

GARY MELCHIONNI, WHOSE SON LEE IS ON THE CURRENT DUKE TEAM, WAS AN ALL-ACC SELECTION.

the season was a first as Duke ended the nation's longest skein of winning seasons.

The question then became whether Waters, who had been the target of the media, would be around for the final year of his contract. Duke never had fired a coach, and the new athletic director, Carl James, insisted that Bucky would return.

Uneasy with the situation, Waters asked for a vote of confidence from the Duke administration. He didn't get it. On September 14, he announced that he was quitting to become administrative assistant to Dr. William Anlyan, vice president of Health Affairs at the university. Waters worked more than 30 years as an executive with Duke Hospital, primarily in the area of fund raising.

It was just a month before the '73-74 season was to begin. Duke, which had been picked last in the ACC and was facing a schedule that would be ranked the nation's most difficult, had to find a coach in a hurry.

The initial news was the biggest shock of all. James was prepared to hire Adolph Rupp as an interim coach for one season while searching the nation for what the AD called a "super coach."

Rupp, then the winningest coach in NCAA history, had been forced to retire at Kentucky when he reached the age of 70. But before there was time to determine if the Baron of the Bluegrass was physically up to the job Duke was offering, Rupp called back and withdrew his name. The manager of his farm had died and Rupp couldn't leave Lexington.

Duke simply was unable to meet the challenge and finished under .500 at 12-14 for the first time since Cameron had his only losing season in 1939. The only consistent players were Melchionni and Redding. Shaw even lost his starting job to sophomore Bob Fleischer.

The lone highlight came when Duke upset a Maryland powerhouse that featured All-American Tom McMillen, Len Elmore and Durhamite John Lucas, 85-81. Melchionni, who never before had scored more than 21 points, had an unbelievable game and finished with 39.

The Devils lost their last five games, including to Virginia in the opening round of the ACC Tournament. The five-game losing streak to finish

NEILL MCGEACHY REPLACED BUCKY WATERS AS COACH RIGHT BEFORE THE START OF THE 1973-74 SEASON.

In the game at Durham, the Tar Heels were ranked No. 3, but Duke stayed close behind Kevin Billerman's 22 points. With 2:37 left, he gave his team a 71-70 lead, but also collected his fifth foul on a charge into Mitch Kupchak. His free throw tied the game.

Duke held until Paul Fox, Billerman's sub, double-dribbled. Then, with six seconds left, Walter Davis missed for UNC and the Devils rebounded, taking a timeout with four seconds to play. Poor Fox. He made the inbounds pass, aimed at Fleischer, but Bobby Jones intercepted at the foul line and made the winning layup.

That loss was mild compared to what happened in Chapel Hill in the regular season finale. With Billerman getting 14 assists, Fleischer claiming 18 rebounds and Willie Hodge coming off the bench to score 20 points, Duke held an 86-78 lead with 30 seconds left.

At 0:17, Jones made two foul shots. McGeachy called a timeout and reminded his team to be safe with all passes. Davis promptly stole the inbounds pass and fed John Kuester for the layup that made it 86-82 with 13 seconds left.

Another turnover, a missed shot by Davis, but a stickback by Jones and now it was a two-point game with six seconds to play. The Tar Heels fouled Pete Kramer, who missed, and with three seconds left, UNC took a timeout.

The pass went to Davis at midcourt. He took two dribbles, then heaved the ball at the basket. It slammed into the glass, and back into the goal and the game was going into overtime. "No, I didn't try to bank the ball," he admitted.

Carolina won in the extra period. It was a microcosm of the Duke season. After a 19-point loss to Maryland in the ACC Tournament, a committee was formed to search for a new coach. The unfortunate McGeachy, extremely popular with his players, was one and done.

Now there was no time left for James to conduct any kind of search. On October 18, he announced that 31-year-old Neill McGeachy, Waters's top assistant, would be the coach for the upcoming season. There were no guarantees that he would get to stay any longer than that.

There simply was no way McGeachy could succeed. Duke would not have won no matter who the coach was. The roster was depleted, and recruiting had not gone well because of all the talk about Waters' future. And the Blue Devils would lose 10 games to teams in the top 10.

The result was a 10-16 season and last place in the ACC for the first time. Two losses to North Carolina were a perfect example of a year gone wrong.

CHAPTER

7

RETURN TO GLORY

In exactly three weeks, Duke had its new coach—Bill Foster of Utah, whose team had just lost in the NIT finals. Foster had rebuilt programs at Rutgers and Utah, and he was only 43. He was a Pennsylvanian, so it wasn't that difficult to lure him back East.

Foster was a salesman. He said his team would be the Running Dukes, and although they finished last or tied for last for three straight years, he was slowly rebuilding the enthusiasm for Duke basketball.

He sold Duke to anybody who would listen—the students, the townspeople, the media. He recruited great players—but not nearly enough of them.

First came Jim Spanarkel, a pigeon-toed guard from New Jersey. The next year, it was 6-11 Mike Gminski from Connecticut. Foster began recruiting him when he learned that Gminski was going to graduate a year early, when he was 16.

Finally, Duke signed Gene "Tinkerbell" Banks, a forward from Philadelphia who was the co-national player of the year along with Albert King, who went to Maryland.

Each of them became a great player, and they combined to take Duke from last place in the ACC to the national championship game against Kentucky in 1978. But there were never enough other recruits. Gminski was the only player in the '76 crop.

BILL FOSTER RETURNED THE EXCITEMENT TO DUKE BASKETBALL.

71

BOB HARRIS

The voice of the Blue Devils is passionate about all things Duke. Bob Harris will have done play by play for the school for nearly 29 years as the 100th anniversary season begins. "No," he insists, he wasn't there for the first game. But many people who listen to the Duke radio network can't recall the time that he wasn't the voice they heard.

For the record, Harris became the Duke play-by-play man on February 7, 1976, in a contest at Maryland. Duke lost, by the way, 102-91.

Harris, 62, and a native of Albemarle, North Carolina, had been working for less than six months as a salesman at WDNC in Durham. He had become the color man for Add Penfield, another longtime Duke announcer. But Penfield became ill and missed the team plane to Maryland.

Harris was still in Durham, preparing to drive to College Park the next morning with engineer Donnie Tuck. But sports information director Tom Mickle called and told him to get on the road immediately, that he would be replacing Penfield, and that an eight-inch snowstorm was on the way.

Harris actually had worked three Duke games already, in the Big Four tournament at Greensboro and at Wake Forest.

Since that eventful phone call, Harris has been at the microphone for 945 games ("my record is 704-241," he said). He has missed 11 games in the 28-plus seasons, only one of those—at Georgia Tech—because he was ill.

The other games all were because he was broadcasting Duke football except for a contest at Northwestern, when he already was in Evanston when he learned his father had died.

Popular with Duke fans, many of whom turn down the sound on television to listen to him, Harris said he has learned in recent years "what it's like to be a Yankee fan. Duke has won so much that a lot of people simply don't like us."

Because the Duke network (like other ACC affiliates) carries all of the league tournament games, Harris said his total of games broadcast is actually 1,102, including 90 NCAA games. It's always apparent when you hear him that it's a labor of love.

Foster's first team finished the '74 season 13-13. It didn't win an ACC road game, which extended Duke's streak of losses to three years. There was little quickness, but the Devils ran anyway. They scored 109 points against Wake Forest; the trouble was that the Deacons had 122. It was the first time Duke had scored 100 points and lost.

The Blue Devils scored over 100 four times. The problem was that the opposition did the same.

There were injuries to Billerman and sophomore Tate Armstrong. George Moses, 26, became Duke's first junior college transfer, and flunked out within one semester. The team finished 13-13, but 2-10 in the ACC.

The seniors, Fleischer, Billerman and Kramer, ended frustrating careers. "I was going to a basketball powerhouse," said Fleischer, "and then the bottom dropped out. But what really bothers me is that we're nobody's team. We'll come back to visit in a couple of years, and we won't have belonged to anybody. Coach Waters is gone. Coach McGeachy is gone, and we're not really Coach Foster's players. Everyone who claimed us is gone."

Foster recruited Spanarkel, who averaged better than 13 points and shot 54.8 percent. But he wasn't nearly enough. The ACC's rookie of the year couldn't turn things around by himself.

Duke went 13-14 in '76, but the Blue Devils at least were the most exciting last-place team ever. They broke the school record for field goal percentage at 52.3. They averaged 88.7 points, sixth in the nation, and beat opponents on the backboards by an average of 3.4 rebounds.

None of that was good enough. Armstrong, a 6-3 junior from Texas, scored 34, 37, 38 and 40 points in successive games—and Duke lost them all. He averaged 31.3 in ACC road games, yet for the fourth straight year the Blue Devils lost them all. There were three defeats in overtime, seven by three points or fewer.

Spanarkel played well, then sprained his ankle and missed the last three games. All were losses.

Armstrong made 11 consecutive shots from 20 feet or beyond—all would have been three-pointers today—against Maryland and Driesell said in amazement, "I've never seen anybody shoot like that." Despite the individual heroics, the Devils were beaten, 102-91.

The ACC Tournament described Duke's season perfectly. It was played in Landover, Maryland, the first time ever outside of North Carolina. The Blue Devils met the homestanding Terps, who were the co-favorites.

Armstrong made his first eight shots. "Hell, ain't he ever going to miss?" said Driesell. Tate would score 33 points.

With 13 seconds left, Duke led 74-72 and Mark Crow, the team's best free-throw shooter, was on the line for a one and one. He missed, but Moses, his eligibility restored, claimed the rebound. He got the ball to Paul Fox, the unfortunate goat of the UNC game the year before and Spanarkel's replacement. Fox was fouled. He missed, and Moses once more claimed the rebound.

Moses passed to Crow, who was fouled with six seconds left. Again, Crow missed. This time, Moses fouled Steve Sheppard on the rebound. Two free throws sent the game into overtime. Maryland won, 80-78, on a rebound basket by Lawrence Boston with three seconds left.

Afterward, Armstrong pulled off an appropriate t-shirt in the locker room. Superman. But this time Superman didn't win. "We deserved to win this one," he said. "But you've got to be able to handle the pressure part of the time, and we didn't do that too well."

Foster was succinct. "I'm getting tired of this," he said.

What he couldn't know was that things would fall apart again after a great start. Duke couldn't shake the black cloud that hung over the program.

TATE ARMSTRONG WAS AN ALL-ACC SELECTION AND A 1976 OLYMPIAN.

Gminski was the only recruit the next year, but he would become Duke's greatest center. He had just turned 17 when he matriculated, but he played well beyond his years. He joined with Armstrong and Spanarkel to give the Blue Devils scoring balance—for a while.

Duke lost to Wake Forest by a point in its '76-77 season opener, then won 10 straight including at Tennessee, which had Bernard King and Ernie Grunfeld. The streak was broken in overtime at Clemson and then the Devils lost at UNC, but they still were 10-3 when they arrived at Virginia. They were, however, carrying the burden of a five-year, 28-game ACC road losing streak.

In the first five minutes, Armstrong fell heavily on his right wrist. But he never left the floor, and Duke ended its losing ways 82-74 in overtime. Armstrong had 33 points, 31 after he was injured. He played all 45 minutes.

The next day, it was determined that his wrist was broken and he was out for the season. He was

ALL-AMERICAN MIKE GMINSKI STARRED FOR BILL FOSTER'S DUKE TEAMS.

tainly didn't want to recall the immediate past. "I wouldn't want that out," he said. "Could you see the headline? 'Foster glad it's over.'"

But there were signs things would improve. Banks had signed. So had Kenny Dennard, a 6-7 forward from South Stokes, North Carolina. And—extremely rare for Duke—there were two transfers, guard John Harrell, who left North Carolina Central for a chance at Division I, and Bob Bender, who started his career at Indiana.

Bender was a freshman when IU won the national championship with the last undefeated team in college basketball. But he didn't have a good relationship with Bobby Knight. Foster got a call from Knight. Did he want to talk with Bender? "It was worked out from his end," Foster said.

leading the ACC in scoring with a 22.7 average while shooting better than 55 percent.

It was too much for Duke to overcome. Down to seven scholarship players, the Blue Devils lost 10 of their last 13, including five of the last six, to finish 14-13. Spanarkel almost never left the court. He played 329 of 330 minutes in the next eight ACC games, two of them overtimes. Gminski averaged better than 15 points and 10.5 rebounds and tied State's Hawkeye Whitney for ACC Rookie of the Year.

Foster had been at Duke three years and his record was 40-40. In the ACC, however, he was just 7-29 and never out of the cellar.

Spanarkel said he was confident of the future. Foster was happy to look ahead. He cer-

ORIGINALLY ENROLLED AT INDIANA, BOB BENDER WAS A RARE DUKE TRANSFER.

Banks arrived with enormous hype. Coincidentally, Duke had renovated Cameron with a new floor, new bleachers and refurbished offices for the coaches. For the first time since Bubas resigned, interest had returned to the basketball program. It had been eight long years. Some 5,000 people came to watch the opening practice on October 15, 1977.

Even though Duke was scheduled to start freshmen Banks and Dennard at forward along with sophomore Gminski, who had just turned 18, the Blue Devils were picked second in the ACC behind North Carolina in the preseason poll.

Spanarkel and Gminski were chosen All-ACC, and Banks was picked on the second team and rookie of the year before he ever had played a game.

The Blue Devils lost to UNC in the Big Four Tournament and on the road at Southern Cal in overtime. They were 7-2 when they played undefeated Virginia Tech in Roanoke.

Gminski was unstoppable with 33 points. Spanarkel and Banks each had 19 and Duke won, 86-79. It set the tone for the rest of the season. In their next game, the Blue Devils won at No. 12 Maryland, 88-78, as Spanarkel scored 33 points. "The Terps were Spanarkeled," wrote Ken Denlinger in *The Washington Post*.

Later, Foster would call those two road wins, so rare in the past, "the key to the season."

Bender became eligible, and shared time with Harrell at the point as erstwhile starter Steve Gray went to the bench. In a smashing win at Clemson, where Gminski, Banks and Dennard combined for 66 points and 23 rebounds, they also claimed a new nickname, the Duke Power Company.

Playing at home against No. 2 North Carolina, the Blue Devils won 92-84 and Duke made 65.5 percent of its shots. Gminski had 29 points and 10 rebounds and was named *Sports Illustrated*

BILL FOSTER AND JIM SPANARKEL SHARE A MOMENT AFTER WINNING THE 1978 ACC CHAMPIONSHIP.

Player of the Week for three games in which he made 31 of 43 shots.

That elevated Duke into the top 20 for the first time in seven years, but when Gminski hurt his toe at Virginia, the Devils lost by a point. He missed the next two games, one a 19-point loss at Wake Forest.

After he returned to singe Virginia in a 100-75 romp, Duke regained form and carried a 20-5 record into the finale at Chapel Hill. The Devils couldn't stop Phil Ford, who had 34 points in his final home game, and the Heels won, 87-83.

But Duke had played well. Banks, Spanarkel and Gminski each scored 20 or more points. Banks made all eight shots in the second half. The Blue Devils did indeed finish second to Carolina and were eager for the ACC Tournament.

In 1978, the NCAA field had been expanded to 32 teams. The ACC, where for the first time everybody had an overall winning record, was certain to have its second-place team selected. The title game was to be on ABC, also a first. The format was changed—games on Wednesday and Thursday, an open date on Friday.

In the opener, Duke beat Clemson 83-72 as Dennard scored 22 points, more than double his

KENNY DENNARD PUNCTUATED DUKE'S TRIP TO THE
FINAL FOUR WITH A REVERSE DUNK VS. VILLANOVA.

Foster had a team in the ACC finals. So I apologize for the weather."

Wake Forest led at the half by five, but Foster switched to a zone in the second half, and ordered Gminski to stay near the basket. Gminski and Banks took over as Duke won the rebound battle, 27-11. G-Man and Tinkerbell scored 34 of Duke's 48 second-half points and the Blue Devils won, 85-77, for their first ACC title in 12 years.

Banks was on the cover of *Sports Illustrated*. "Before we had trouble getting on the cover of the school paper," Foster said. But there were concerns about the infamous *SI* jinx, and they were justified.

The 23-6 Devils went against 24-6 Rhode Island in the NCAA first round in Charlotte. There was a chance of a letdown from the ACC, and it happened.

Gminski, Spanarkel and Banks scored 57 points. The rest of the team had six, with one basket. Rhode Island, behind Sly Williams's 27 points, actually led 62-59 when G-man scored with 41 seconds left.

With 17 seconds left, Gminski rebounded a Rhode Island miss and was fouled by Williams, his fifth. Earlier at Virginia, he had missed a one and one and Duke lost by one, "I said then if I ever got another chance, I'd stick them," he said.

Gminski's first foul shot hit the front and back of the rim before going through the net. He did swish the second and it was 63-62. As the buzzer sounded, he swatted a rebound out of bounds and the Devils had survived.

Duke advanced to Providence, where it would play Penn. Villanova and Indiana were in the other bracket of the NCAA East Regional.

The Blue Devils continued to struggle against the Quakers, whose star guard, Bobby Willis, had turned down a scholarship offer from Duke. Midway in the second half, Penn led 64-56 and Willis was penetrating the zone defense with ease.

average. Upon reflection, Duke's Bill Foster (the Clemson coach also was Bill Foster) quipped, "We usually lose and I go home. In the past, I've just packed a handkerchief and that's about it. But this time I packed for the whole week, and so did the team." He was clairvoyant.

While Duke was winning, Carolina was upset by Wake Forest. The Blue Devils knew they now had to win the tournament to get an NCAA bid, because the Tar Heels, as regular-season champs, would get one for sure.

Duke pulled away in the second half to beat Maryland, 81-69, while Wake Forest also advanced. During the open-day media conference, it began to snow heavily. Foster deadpanned, "They said it would snow in Greensboro before

Penn coach Bob Weinhauer went to a spread, designed to make it easier to drive against the zone. It worked, too, until the guards reached Gminski. Three times he batted away layups. He got two of the rebounds himself and Banks got the third. Duke scored each time and the game had turned around.

In a seven-minute span, the Blue Devils went on an 18-2 run for a 74-66 lead and they held on to win, 84-80. "The last one was an escape," Gminski said. "Why don't we say we're still escaping and not getting caught?"

Villanova had upset Indiana, and stood between Duke and the Final Four. But the Devils got an emotional lift from Weinhauer and some of his Penn players. "I see Villanova winning by six," said the coach, an ACC critic. "Gminski, Spanarkel, Dennard and Bender are slow. Banks is a decent moving forward. Harrell is the only guy on the team with any quickness."

Willis, who must have had brainlock, commented, "I don't think Gminski's especially intimidating. He's kind of slow reacting. Every time we got two on one, we'd beat him." Willis apparently had forgotten G-Man's seven blocks.

Penn forward Tony Price chipped in, "They're awfully slow afoot; that's going to hurt them against Villanova."

Inspired by the negative comments, Duke never let Villanova in the game. It was 21-6 after seven minutes, and the lead grew to 21 before halftime. The Blue Devils made 39 of 60 shots (65 percent) and romped, 90-72. "Our guys were really ticked off about all that stuff that's been written. I think we showed a few people today," said assistant coach Lou Goetz.

Duke was 26-6 when it headed to St. Louis, where it would meet No. 6 Notre Dame. No. 1 Kentucky and Arkansas were in the other semifinal. Foster brought with him the youngest team ever to reach the Final Four. "This is the greatest thing that's happened to me in coaching," he said.

The Irish, with Bill Laimbeer, Dave Batton and Kelly Tripucka, were huge up front. Even their guards were big, and they had rolled to three easy wins in the Mideast, including 20 points over No. 3 DePaul in the championship game. Asked if he had ever seen a team as large, Foster replied, "Yes, when I was coaching football."

What about an edge in quickness, Foster was asked? "When we were playing Penn, we were a slow team. Two days later, we were quick. That was an amazing job of coaching I did."

Tall as they were, the Irish had no answer for Gminski. The 6-11 sophomore made 13 of 17 shots for 29 points. Duke led by 14 points at the half and finally muted a late rally to win, 90-86.

The best foul-shooting team in the nation, Duke made 32 of 37, including 12 straight by Spanarkel. He, Gminski and Banks combined for 71 points as the Blue Devils made it to the championship game for the second time in school history. Their opponent would be No. 1 Kentucky.

The Wildcats were grim. Retiring coach Joe B. Hall said if his team didn't win, the season would be a failure. The Duke players were too young to know better. Dennard showed up for the open-day media conference wearing an Arkansas hog hat.

Duke got all the good press after Hall called his team's 29-2 record "a season without celebration." But what the Blue Devils couldn't do was put the clamps on a goose—Kentucky forward James "Goose" Givens. One of four seniors in the lineup, he constantly flashed into the middle of the zone for 41 points, on 18-of-27 shooting.

One of his shots, from the deep corner, hit the side of the backboard and went in. "When you make one like that, you just know it's your night," he conceded. Kentucky won, 94-88.

Somebody other than Hall was serious about Kentucky winning. There were two death threats made on Banks's life, one to a St. Louis TV station and the other at the arena. Foster and athletic director Tom Butters had been told, but the

MIKE GMINSKI IS DUKE'S ALL-TIME LEADER IN BLOCKED SHOTS.

to release a story calling Gminski, Spanarkel and Banks each the best player at his position in college basketball.

Duke blew big leads and lost to Ohio State in overtime and St. John's by three points. Just when they seemed to have gotten it together, the 17-3 Blue Devils lost at home to Pitt and Sam Clancy, 71-69.

In the last 10 games, the Devils went 5-5. They were beaten by 21 points at Clemson, before beating UNC 47-40 in the home finale as Dean Smith stalled away the first half and saw his Tar Heels trail, 7-0.

Duke beat Wake Forest and State to reach the ACC finals against North Carolina, but before the game, Bender suffered an attack of appendicitis. He was in the hospital when UNC won, 71-63.

decision was made not to notify Banks until after the game.

The youthful Duke team wasn't all that upset. Stepping out of the shower, Banks said, "We'll be No. 1 next year."

He was correct about that—at the beginning. Duke was No. 1, but '79 was to be a season of frustration.

Gminski, Spanarkel and Banks all saw their scoring averages drop. For Spanarkel, the best free-throw shooter in Duke history, there was a slump to 73.4 percent from 86.3. Gminski dropped to 72.9 from 84.1. The same players who led the nation at the foul line with 79.1 percent shot below 70.

The team that began the year No. 1 fell to 11th by the finish. The scoring average dropped precipitously from 85.6 to 71.9.

Actually, the slump didn't begin until late December in the Holiday Festival at Madison Square Garden, as *Sports Illustrated* was prepared

GENE BANKS SCORES AGAINST NORTH CAROLINA IN THE ACC TOURNAMENT.

Duke was ranked sixth in the nation, but was coming off a 21-point loss at Clemson. North Carolina was rated fourth. But UNC coach Dean Smith decided that he wasn't going to play against the Blue Devils in the first half.

So UNC held the ball against the Duke zone. And held it.

Duke scored in the opening minute on a rebound goal by Vince Taylor. Then the Tar Heels held it for 12 minutes.

Finally, Duke forced a turnover when it double-teamed Rich "Chick" Yonakor in the corner. Yonakor later turned it over again when his bounce pass bounced on the endline. But it was his missed shot that would become the basis for a now-infamous cheer.

Carolina was trailing 3-0, late in the half, when Smith finally permitted his team to shoot. Yonakor, under pressure, tried a 10-foot jump shot from the side that went nine feet, hitting nothing. Instantaneously, the Duke student body—now officially the Cameron Crazies—began to scream, "Air ball, air ball."

It was the first air-ball cheer, and obviously the start of something that spread across the nation.

The first half ended with Duke leading 7-0 and pitching a no-hitter. The only other Carolina shot came from Dave Colescott from halfcourt just before intermission. It didn't reach the basket. The Tar Heels, 21-4 coming into the game, had played an entire half without having a shot even hit the rim.

At halftime, a member of the bored press corps said cynically, "If they score in the second half, do you think they'll go for two?"

Smith elected to play in the last half, and each team scored 40 points, giving Duke a 47-40 victory. The Blue Devils led by as many as 15 points, and the eventual margin was as close as UNC came.

In the final minute, Gminski accidentally decked Carolina's Al Wood with an elbow, which got the Duke All-American ejected. Smith was furious and yelled at the 6-11 center. Later, both denied that the coach had accused the player of anything.

The win tied Duke for the regular-season title with Carolina, but the Tar Heels won the draw the next day and received a first-round bye for the ACC Tournament.

Both the Devils and Tar Heels were sent to Raleigh for the NCAAs. It proved to be Black Sunday, as they both lost.

What happened to Duke was almost beyond belief. With Bender sidelined, the Devils also lost Dennard, who sprained an ankle playing in a pickup game with some football players.

On game day, Gminski became sick. He played but became nauseous several times. Harrell, who replaced Bender, got a finger in an eye and missed 10 minutes of the second half.

With all that, Duke still led by a point when Vince Taylor fouled out. Harrell, a six-footer, replaced him, and with three seconds left, 6-3 Reggie Carter posted up Harrell and made the basket that won the game, 80-78.

Bender and Dennard would have been available for the regionals, which were played in Greensboro. Instead, Penn—which defeated UNC—beat St. John's before a half-full coliseum. It was a low point in ACC history.

If anything, 1980 was even more bizarre. Duke began the year rated No. 3, even though Spanarkel had graduated and the bench was composed almost entirely of freshmen. But the Devils won their first 12 games and became No. 1.

They stumbled for the first time at Clemson, 87-82 in overtime. It was the fourth overtime of the season and Duke had won the first three. The Blue Devils would beat the Tigers by the same score in an extra period in their next meeting.

Then it really became astonishing. It was good-Duke, bad-Duke. There were four games with UNC. Each team won twice. All were blowouts. There were two losses to Virginia and 7-4 freshman Ralph Sampson, and a 19-point defeat at Maryland, which was revenged in Cameron.

Dennard missed nine games with an injury. Gminski, consistent throughout his career, suffered his first slump. Duke lost five of its last seven before the ACC Tournament.

While all this was happening, there were constant stories that Foster was leaving Duke for

South Carolina, which made no sense, except it proved to be true.

The team that had been No. 1 limped into the ACC Tournament tied for fifth with Virginia, and even lost the tie-breaker to the Cavaliers. That meant the Blue Devils would have to beat the 3, 2, and 1 seeds to win, which was the only way to make the NCAAs and extend the season. They did that, just as Foster confirmed the rumors were true.

In what would be the lame-duck coach game, Duke beat N.C. State, 68-62. Norm Sloan was leaving the Wolfpack for Florida, perhaps for some of the same reasons that were sending Foster to South Carolina. Neither could handle the constant pressure of competing with Dean Smith.

Gminski and Banks made 26 straight free throws and combined for 46 points. That sent the Blue Devils into the semifinals against a North Carolina team that had embarrassed them 96-71, less than a week before.

Duke did everything right in another stunning turn of events. Banks limited All-American Mike O'Koren to four points. Gminski made 11 of his shots, and matched his career high with 19 rebounds. The Devils led all the way and made it a 40-point turnaround with a 75-61 victory. "What a difference a week makes," UNC's Smith said.

That sent Duke into the title game against Maryland. Then it snowed, and snowed some more. Greensboro was crippled by the blizzard. Only 10,392 fans made it to the game. But Duke was happy. The Blue Devils had never lost a game during a major snowstorm.

Maryland led during the first half as Albert King went wild. He would finish with 27 points, 81 for the tournament. But in the second half, Duke rallied by sinking 15 of 19 shots. The

Devils 56.6 percent for the game; Maryland was almost as good at 53.6.

Late in the game, Taylor missed a jumper, but Gminski tapped in the basket that gave Duke a 73-72 lead. With five seconds left, King shot under severe pressure. The ball bounced on the rim three times, then fell away. Duke had pulled off its third upset.

Later, TV replays showed what had happened. As the ball was bouncing, Dennard threw a body block on Buck Williams under the basket. Both players rolled out of bounds and no foul was called. The Blue Devils were on their way to the NCAAs.

Sports Illustrated's Curry Kirkpatrick got it right. "The Blue Devils are a schizoid's delight, having lost their coach—Bill Foster, who will take over at South Carolina—and found their soul at about the same time."

The next day, with a record four ACC teams headed to the NCAAs, Foster announced officially that he was leaving. "He's still our coach," said Banks. "We want to win the national championship for him, and for ourselves."

The Blue Devils, seeded fourth in the Mideast, got a first-round bye, then defeated deliberate Penn, 52-42, at Purdue. Gminski led the way with 21 points. "They're better than we are," said Penn coach Weinhauer, taking a different stance from two years before. "If we played them 10 times, they'd probably win all 10."

So Duke advanced to the regional semifinals, against Kentucky—at Kentucky. The Blue Devils had beaten the Wildcats in overtime in the season-opening Hall of Fame game. Then they were ranked No. 3 and Kentucky had been No. 2. Since then, UK had won 29 of 33 games. But, Duke pulled off the upset, 55-54.

Duke was now one win away from a totally unexpected Final Four, but there were no more miracles left. Joe Barry Carroll, a seven-foot center, outscored Gminski 26-17. Taylor had just one field goal. In the last half of the 68-60 Purdue victory, the Boilermakers shot 26 free throws and Duke shot five.

"I'm sick," Foster said. "I wanted to win the game so damn bad. That's how I feel."

Several years later, Foster told Ron Morris of the *Durham Morning Herald,* "I guess it was just my time to leave, I don't know. Those were my most memorable days in coaching. But I never did enjoy it. I don't know what it was. It didn't really sink in and that's my own fault. I don't blame anybody for that. I certainly can't blame Duke. I just never relaxed."

Foster had a special place in his memories for his Final Four team, and its three stars— Spanarkel, Gminski and Banks, who would become the school's first 2,000-point scorers. In 1986, when another Duke team went to the Final Four, Foster said, "You know, I still hear from those guys. I really loved those players."

MIKE GMINSKI LED DUKE TO AN UPSET OVER
KENTUCKY IN AN NCAA GAME PLAYED IN LEXINGTON.

MARCH 13, 1980

Ranked first in the nation for several weeks after starting the season with 12 straight victories, Duke fell upon hard times and wound up with a 7-7 ACC record and in fifth place.

The Blue Devils also had lost their coach. Bill Foster had accepted a job at South Carolina after the season.

By the time the ACC Tournament rolled around, Duke was no longer ranked and forced to play three Top-20 teams in succession. The Blue Devils upset No. 19 N.C. State, trounced No. 10 North Carolina by 14 points, and then shocked No. 7 Maryland, 73-72, to win the championship.

In the NCAAs, Duke defeated Penn, 52-42, to advance to the Southeast Regional at Lexington, Kentucky, where the Blue Devils would take on fourth-rated Kentucky, the home team.

The teams had met in the season opener, in the Hall of Fame game at Springfield, Massachusetts, and Duke had won. But, playing at Rupp Arena, the homestanding Wildcats were solid favorites.

Duke opened the game by scoring the first seven points, and the Wildcats never did lead and were tied only once, in the final seconds, at 54. By halftime, it was 37-23 and the big upset looked to be in the bag.

After intermission, however, Duke started to fall apart under the constant pressure with 23,330 fans screaming for their boys in blue. The Blue Devils made just 11 of 23 free throws. Even All-American Gminski, a career 80-percent shooter, missed two of three.

In the closing minutes, Duke missed the front end of two one and ones and also had a three-second violation. Kentucky tied the score with 36 seconds left as Freddie Cowan scored. Cowan, who had 26 points, made 15 consecutive points for the Wildcats.

With 22 seconds left, Duke forward Gene Banks drove for the basket and was fouled by Derrick Hord. He made one free throw and the Blue Devils led, 55-54.

Kentucky worked the ball around, finally passing it to All-American Kyle Macy in the corner. He was guarded by Vince Taylor, a native of Lexington who had left the area to play for Duke.

Macy shot. The ball bounced high off the front rim and was slapped into the backcourt by Duke as time expired.

"We figured Macy would get the ball," Taylor said. "When he went up, he spun a little. I just held my hands straight up. There was contact. I guess that was incidental. It came after the shot. He came into me."

Kentucky coach Joe B. Hall, who had beaten Duke in the '78 NCAA finals, didn't complain. "I asked Kyle if there was a foul and he said no. We didn't really have a play. We ran our man-to-man offense even though they were in a zone. We either wanted to get the ball to either Macy or Cowan."

Two days later, Duke lost to Purdue in the regional finals and Foster headed off to South Carolina. Shortly thereafter, Duke hired Mike Krzyzewski.

CHAPTER

8

SPELL IT K

The biggest questions when Mike Krzyzewski was named the Duke coach on May 4, 1980 were (a) who's he? and (b) how do you spell his name? If you played Scrabble, you learned in a hurry. Think of all those extra points.

As an athletic director, Duke's Tom Butters always thought big. His first choice, years later in football after Steve Spurrier resigned, was Bill Walsh of the 49ers. Spurned, he elevated assistant coach Barry Wilson.

Knowing that Bill Foster was leaving for—at best—a lateral move to South Carolina, Butters started at the top. He asked Bobby Knight if he were interested. The Indiana coach said no, of course, but did recommend Krzyzewski, who played for him at Army and later was on his IU staff.

The reason that Butters called Knight was because "I wanted the best defensive coach in the country. Knight

MIKE KRZYZEWSKI WAS INTRODUCED AS
DUKE'S HEAD COACH IN 1980.

suggested Krzyzewski," who had just completed his fifth season at his alma mater.

There were four serious contenders for the job. Of that quartet, Krzyzewski was easily the least known. The others were Bob Weltlich of Mississippi (also a former Knight assistant); Paul Webb of Old Dominion; and Foster's top assistant, Bob Wenzel.

Krzyzewski was 32. He had served in the Army for five years after his graduation from West Point. In the final three ('72-74), he got a start on his eventual career as coach at U.S. Military Academy Prep at Fort Belvoir, Va. Upon discharge, he joined Knight's Indiana staff as a graduate assistant.

After that '75 season (IU was unbeaten in the regular season and No. 1 in the nation until star Scott May was injured), Krzyzewski got the job as head coach at his alma mater. He was 28, the youngest head coach in the nation.

In his second year, he took Army to a rare 20-win season. The following season, the Cadets were 19-9 and played in the NIT. The last time that had happened, Knight was the coach and Krzyzewski was his point guard.

But in 1980, his fifth and final year, Army slumped to 9-17. It was then that the Duke job opened, as did the position at Iowa State. That job paid big money and matching Cadillacs, but Krzyzewski took a chance. Duke still had not made a decision. He said no to the Cyclones, who hired Johnny Orr.

He interviewed three times with Duke. The first two were off campus. The third time was in Durham. "I just couldn't get Krzyzewski out of my mind," Butters said. "Knight convinced me he was one of the brightest young coaches in America, and the more I talked with Mike, the more I was convinced that Knight was right."

After the final interview, the Krzyzewskis headed for the airport. But Butters had made up his mind. He told his assistant, Steve Vacendak, "I like that guy. Go get him back here." So Vacendak brought Mike back from the airport, while his wife Mickie flew home.

Krzyzewski was offered the job and accepted on the spot. Then he called home. "Mickie, I got the job," he said. "Good," was the reply. "What is your salary?"

"I don't know," said Duke's new basketball coach. "We didn't discuss it."

The Duke interviewing team of Butters, chancellor Ken Pye and vice president Chuck Huestis, had not painted a rosy picture. They had not tried to romance the youthful coach. "They said we would have one decent year, then we'd go through rebuilding," Krzyzewski said years later. "They painted a rougher picture than what I thought it would be."

The Duke people were correct. Although the Blue Devils had played for the national championship in 1978 and won the ACC in '80 and ad-

FEBRUARY 28, 1981

The first game that Mike Krzyzewski ever coached against North Carolina in Cameron also was the regular-season finale for senior forward Gene Banks.

Prior to the game with the heavily favored Heels, Banks threw four red roses into the crowd. Then he played a critical role in an upset victory.

With two seconds left in regulation, the 11th-ranked, 22-6 Tar Heels took the lead, 58-56, on two foul shots by Sam Perkins, who led his team with 24 points.

Duke had only one timeout remaining, and Carolina had only four personal fouls, so it had two it could give without penalty. Dean Smith instructed his team to do just that.

But Duke senior Kenny Dennard threw a perfect pass to Chip Engelland at midcourt, and he called that final timeout before he could be fouled. One second remained.

The play set up by Coach K was to have Banks set a screen for Engelland, while Vince Taylor was creating a pick for Tom Emma. "That would have given our two best perimeter shooters a chance," Krzyzewski said. "We sort of used Gene for a decoy."

But Dennard passed inbounds to Banks, guarded by Perkins at the top of the key. "I was saying, 'Please don't block that son of a buck,'" Krzyzewski said. And Perkins did barely touch the ball, but Banks's shot fell through the basket and the game went into overtime.

"With one second left, we were lucky to get that good a shot," Engelland said. "It was the best we could have possibly gotten. That shot was so incredible. But that's the kind of situations that Gene loves. Perkins was on him, so it had to be a perfect shot. But Gene, I think he'd rather have a tough shot like that than an easy one."

In the overtime, Banks scored six of his game-high 25 points, including the game winning basket with 12 seconds to play. That one was easy—and lucky.

Taylor missed a shot from inside the foul line, and it bounced off the hands of UNC's Al Wood directly to Banks, who simply laid it in the basket for the victory with 12 seconds left. Mike Pepper missed a jumper for the Heels just before the buzzer.

"I was like a magnet," Banks said of the way the ball just seemed to come to him.

"That's the breaks," said UNC's Wood. "It just bees that way sometime." Ungrammatical, but accurate.

Not only had Banks scored two key baskets on shots that UNC defenders touched, but he also had a third in the overtime after the ball slipped through the hands of the Heels' Matt Doherty. "Gene has a knack for it," Taylor said.

vanced to the regional finals, recruiting had not gone well in Foster's last seasons.

With seniors Gene Banks and Kenny Dennard and junior Vince Taylor, Duke was good enough to win 17 games in 1980-81 and play in the NIT. "I was not aware of how good the conference was until I got in it," Krzyzewski said. "Everything was harder than what I thought—recruiting, playing, everything. I knew about the top guys, but I wasn't aware of the talent from three through eight. And the coaching was so good."

Krzyzewski decided that while coaches from other areas think they know about the ACC, "there's no way you know until you've been a part of it."

Obviously, the key had to be recruiting. Taylor was the only blue-chipper who had been recruited since that '78 season. "When we took over, it was

VINCE TAYLOR WAS ONE OF COACH K'S EARLY STARS.

late," Krzyzewski said. "We busted our butts, and came up with Doug McNeely, who was a complementary player. We should have just given up on that year and recruited juniors."

The NCAA had just established an early signing date for basketball recruits in November, and that put Duke even farther behind. "We didn't forecast that," Krzyzewski said. "We were undergoing a recruiting revolution and the people who were out there recruiting juniors were way ahead of us."

Still, the Duke staff tried to make up the lost ground. They came close on some great players, most notably Chris Mullin, who went to St. John's. But in the recruiting game, second isn't close, it's last. Duke continued to strike out.

In his second year, the Blue Devils fell to 10-17 and were last in the ACC. But the staff, including Chuck Swenson and Bobby Dwyer, had enormous success on the recruiting trail, and in time it would be the beginning of what has become the nation's top basketball program.

Coach K—that was now his moniker because so many, especially in the media, couldn't spell or pronounce his name correctly—understood that Duke could recruit nationally. He was supported budgetarily by Butters.

While the Blue Devils struggled with Taylor as the lone ACC-caliber player, the staff got a commitment from Johnny Dawkins of Washington, D.C., who would become the school's all-time leading scorer.

Mark Alarie, 6-8 from Phoenix, became a 2,000-point scorer along with Dawkins, and two-time All-ACC. Center Jay Bilas came from California, Weldon Williams from Chicago and forward David Henderson from nearby Drewry, North Carolina.

The sixth recruit, Bill Jackman, came from Nebraska and transferred home after one season. He never became a fulltime starter in college.

"The way we recruit is good for Duke," Krzyzewski said. "We don't want numbers. I don't foresee us having 15 scholarships. We'll have between 11 and 13. I prefer 12."

Even though the NCAA lowered the number of scholarships for men's basketball to 13, Coach K never has had the full complement with recruited players. In 2004 had 10, and one of them transferred early in the season. Lack of numbers hasn't been a problem.

"I've found in this league you have to have eight who can play. The talent pool is smaller. I'd liken it to a river that's very wide, but very shallow. There are not that many (prospects), and they're spread all over. You have to make decisions early on, and you have to sink or swim with those decisions."

(Over the years, recruiting has continued to evolve, and now Duke is perhaps the No. 1 school at evaluating sophomores and getting commitments from juniors. It is simply another example of understanding the workplace).

Coach K always has believed in close relationships with his players. Before senior night, every Duke senior is invited to a dinner with the Krzyzewski family. "I personally want to feel comfortable. I like our kids. This is a family here. I want our players to come by the house."

The family also relates to his position with the school and its administrators. "At Duke, the game is put on by the university, not me."

Over the years since his hiring, Krzyzewski has become ever a more important member of the Duke family. His involvements also include the community. He's the current chairman of the Duke Children's Miracle Network Telethon and has played vital roles in the Duke Children's Classic and the Jimmy V Foundation.

He is the chairman of the Emily Krzyzewski Family Center, named for his mother. The Basketball Legacy Fund was formed to endow all of the scholarships for the program, plus the salaries of the coaches. The Krzyzewskis have endowed

MIKE KRZYZEWSKI IS INVOLVED IN SEVERAL COMMUNITY PROJECTS, INCLUDING A FAMILY LIFE CENTER NAMED IN HONOR OF HIS MOTHER, EMILY.

one of those scholarships, and they also created the Krzyzewski Family Scholarship Endowment for Duke students from the Carolinas.

The Coach Michael W. Krzyzewski Human Performance Laboratory was opened in 1996. The K-Lab is dedicated to research on athletic performance to prevent injury.

Coach K signed a lifetime contract with Duke on November 14, 2001. But in 1984, there were people who wondered why Butters had given a contract extension to a man whose team had lost three straight games, and would lose to N.C. State that night.

But that first great recruiting class was in the process of turning around Duke's basketball fortunes.

When Dawkins and friends were freshmen in '83, the Blue Devils continued to take their lumps. They again finished last in the ACC and suffered a record 109-66 beating at the hand of Virginia and Ralph Sampson in the opening round of the tournament.

At a 3 a.m. meal in a fast-food diner in Atlanta, Duke sports publicist Johnny Moore said, "Here's to never remembering this game." He was interrupted by Krzyzewski. "Here's to never forgetting it," he said. The Blue Devils had lost nine straight to the Cavaliers. Coach K was 0-7 versus University of Virginia. After that early-morning declaration, Duke won the next 16 games in the Virginia series.

That team, despite its youth, played man-to-man defense throughout the season, even though critics insisted that Duke might be better off in a zone.

The low point came when Duke lost at home, 84-77, to a Wagner team that had just been beaten by 50 points by UNLV. Boos echoed through half-filled Cameron, and a Durham writer acknowledged that Krzyzewski was on the hot seat. A year later, the Blue Devils were on their way to the NCAAs and Krzyzewski was the ACC Coach of the Year.

It was in 1984 that the Blue Devils began their move toward the top, where they have all but resided for the next 28 seasons. Duke entered the ACC season at 14-1, but with just one league game played—a win at Virginia.

The Blue Devils promptly lost the next three ACC games and, on January 26, Butters summoned Coach K into his office. Krzyzewski didn't know what to expect. The athletic director awarded him a contract extension.

"It shows real commitment from the athletics and school administration," Krzyzewski said. "But the administration always has been supportive. I'm really pleased with it. I love Duke. My background fits into the principles they want to teach their students. I try to do that. It also gives us more credibility in recruiting. This year our players have been asked what my status was. People used that against us."

Years later, Butters would say, "That was the smartest thing I ever did next to hiring Mike in the first place. I wanted him to know he was our coach, no matter what." The Blue Devils promptly lost to N.C. State to fall to 1-4 in the ACC.

But Duke, with four sophomores and freshman Tommy Amaker starting, rallied to finish 7-7 in the league. There were two defeats, the last in double overtime at Chapel Hill, to No. 1 ranked UNC. In the ACC Tournament, the Devils defeated Georgia Tech in overtime in their opener, then upset the favored Tar Heels of Michael Jordan, Sam Perkins and Kenny Smith, 77-75, in overtime.

"It's the greatest win any of these players have realized," Coach K said.

"I still can't believe it," said forward Danny Meagher. "I looked up and saw all the fans go crazy. I just kept hearing how that the Heels are so good. I've heard so much talk, but we're good, too."

Even though Duke lost in the ACC finals to Maryland, and to Washington, 80-78, in the opening round of the NCAAs played at Pullman,

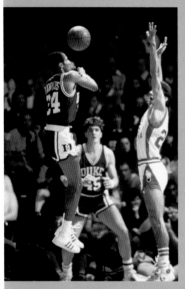

After one transition year and then two seasons in last place in the ACC, Mike Krzyzewski had his first good team, featuring four sophomore starters plus freshman Tommy Amaker. The Blue Devils were nationally ranked for the first time under Coach K by mid-February, and were rated 16th when they faced No. 1 Carolina in the ACC semifinals in Greensboro.

Duke had lost twice to the Tar Heels, who swept all their ACC games. But the second defeat, at Chapel Hill a week earlier, had come in double overtime. There was no fear of playing them again. "We're too young to know better," said guard Johnny Dawkins.

"I don't know if we match up with them well," said Coach K. "But I think we're a confident team when we're playing." Duke was 23-8; UNC was 27-1 and featured National Player of the Year Michael Jordan in what turned out to be his final season as a junior.

"We act like a much more mature team when we play Carolina," Krzyzewski observed. "But when we're playing other teams. . . . I don't know if we show maturity through the whole 40 minutes."

The taller, deeper Tar Heels led in rebounding, 39-28, but behind sophomore center Jay Bilas's 10 points and 11 boards, Duke was able to score 11 points via offensive rebounds. "I think that has to do with the mental part of getting so fired up. You jump a little higher," Dean Smith said.

Duke outhustled UNC in the first half, once owning a 10-point lead. But with nine minutes to play, Carolina took a two-point edge when Jordan had an emphatic dunk.

Krzyzewski immediately took a timeout. "He told us to hang in there," said David Henderson. "Don't try and do anything out of the ordinary and we'll be all right." The Blue Devils promptly scored the next five points. "Duke never died on us," said Sam Perkins.

Duke held on the rest of the way, winning 77-75 as Mark Alarie scored 21 points, Dawkins had 17 points and seven assists, and Henderson had 14 points and six assists. Four free throws by Henderson in the final 42 seconds kept the Blue Devils in front for the upset.

"We came down here to win the ACC Tournament," said Bilas. "As good as we feel now, we would feel that much better if we could come out tomorrow with a win and win the tournament."

Years later, Bilas, now an ESPN broadcaster, said, "The reaction after the game was so wild, and we hadn't really won anything. We were acting as if we had won the championship." He was correct. The next day, Maryland dominated Duke as Coach Lefty Driesell, a Blue Devil alumnus, won his only championship.

Washington, the team had finished 24-10 and ranked 14th in the final polls. It was the first of many national rankings for Krzyzewski's teams.

The '85 team started the year ranked No. 6 and won its first 12 games before losing consecutive overtime contests with Maryland and Wake Forest. Then came a trip to Chapel Hill, where the sixth-ranked Tar Heels had won every year since 1967 against Duke. The Blue Devils broke that 19-year jinx with ease, 93-77.

Dawkins played all 40 minutes, matched his career high with 34 points, eight rebounds, four assists, four steals and a single turnover. Bilas had one of his best games with 17 points and 11 rebounds as shorter Duke won the battle of the boards, 42-30.

JOHNNY DAWKINS REGULARLY PLAYED ALL 40 MINUTES AS A COLLEGIAN.

"Look around the league," Krzyzewski said. "There's a lot of great athletes and we don't have many of them. I'm not bad-mouthing my team. If we were a bad team, I'd tell you. What we are is a good team, but we're not a great team." That would not come before another year.

The ACC was especially strong. Duke would finish fourth, but with a 21-6 mark, they had the best regular-season record.

The most difficult defeat came at home against North Carolina. The Blue Devils were shooting 54.2 percent for the season and were held to a woeful 33.8 as the Tar Heels won, 78-68, behind 23 points and 12 rebounds from Brad Daugherty.

Duke forced 20 turnovers and got off 32 more shots. But the Devils couldn't find the range. Nobody shot 50 percent, including Dawkins, who scored 25 points. Alarie, who was shooting better than 60 percent on the year, missed his first 11 and finished five for 19. "We're the type of team that will benefit from a loss like this,"

MARK ALARIE SCORES AGAINST VIRGINIA.

he said. "We now know we're not an imposing team."

The ACC Tournament was in Atlanta. Duke opened with one of its finest performances, beating Maryland 87-73 as Dawkins scored 27 points and Alarie, on track again with 10-of-13 shooting, getting 21. But late in the game, Alarie fell heavily and suffered a hip pointer. He was considered doubtful for the semifinal game against Georgia Tech.

Alarie never had missed a start in three years at Duke. And he started against top-seed Georgia Tech, which had finished in a three-way tie during the season with Carolina and N.C. State, just ahead of the Devils and Maryland in the closest ACC race ever.

DAVID HENDERSON WAS PART OF COACH K'S FIRST GREAT RECRUITING CLASS.

But it was obvious the 6-8 junior forward couldn't go. He left the floor after a minute and didn't return. Mark Price, Bruce Dalrymple and John Salley led Tech to a 75-64 victory, and the Jackets went on to win the league championship.

Duke got an NCAA bid and was seeded third in the Midwest. Alarie played in the opener vs. Pepperdine and scored 16 points with nine rebounds, even though he could only go at half-speed. Led by David Henderson's 22 points, the Blue Devils won their first NCAA game for Krzyzewski, 75-62.

In the second game, the injury bug hit Duke once again. Henderson suffered a severe sprained ankle in the first half and left for good while the Blue Devils were breezing.

With Alarie and Bilas (whose knee required post-season surgery) also slowed, Duke suddenly was in trouble in the front court. Bilas did score 15 points and claim 13 rebounds, but Boston College edged the Blue Devils, 74-73.

Dawkins was a consensus All-American, the first of many for Krzyzewski. Alarie was all-district, and all five starters returned for the 1986 season. That would be the year that propelled Duke to the top of college basketball's charts, where, except for '95 and '96, it has remained.

Duke began the 1986 season ranked sixth in the nation. Georgia Tech was No. 1, UNC No. 2. The Tar Heels moved into the top spot on Nov. 26, after the first games had been played, and remained there until the next-to-last poll on March 4. They wound up eighth, two slots below Tech. N.C. State was 20th until the last poll. The ACC was as strong as it had ever been.

Television took note, with special attention paid to Duke. In February, four consecutive home games were televised either by NBC or CBS. The ratings were among the best ever. The networks were delighted.

All told, in a period of eight weeks, there were 10 Duke games on national television. It never

had happened before. The exposure was over-whelming, and others noticed.

What television was showing, week after week after week, was Duke's best team, a team that set an NCAA record with 37 victories that remains today.

The Blue Devils did everything except win a national championship. In the finals against Louisville, they led at halftime but were defeated, 72-69, as freshman center Pervis "Never Nervous" Ellison grabbed an airball and made the winning basket.

But just about everything else Duke did that season was right.

Krzyzewski's best recruiting class was in its final year. Duke started four seniors—Dawkins, Alarie, Henderson and Bilas—and junior Tommy Amaker. Another senior, Weldon Williams, was a reserve. The Blue Devils had the most experienced team in the nation, one that was coming off back-to-back NCAA appearances.

The freshmen who arrived in the fall of '82 were to become the highest-scoring class in history. Dawkins finished with 2,556 points, still a Duke record and second in the ACC behind Dickie

JAY BILAS, NOW A TELEVISION PERSONALITY, HELPED DUKE DEFEAT DEPAUL IN THE SWEET SIXTEEN.

TOMMY AMAKER WAS NATIONAL DEFENSIVE PLAYER OF THE YEAR.

Hemric of Wake Forest, who played his first two seasons in the Southern Conference.

Alarie finished with 2,136, which remains 20th all-time in the ACC. It was the first time any team ever had a pair of 2,000-point scorers in the same class. Henderson, a 6-5 forward, tallied 1,570, and Bilas, the hard-working center, scored 1,062.

Including the 126 points from Williams, the Duke seniors had a career total of 7,450 points. Amaker, the junior, finished his career with 1,168 points. It was a potent offensive machine.

But in many respects, the sum was greater than the parts. There wasn't much size, and Duke simply didn't look all that dominating. All it did was win.

At the Final Four in Dallas, N.C. State coach Jim Valvano accurately described the Blue Devils. "They will go down as the greatest not-great team ever."

But Duke took on all comers, and came out ahead most of the time. Its only two defeats in the regular season, back to back, came at North Carolina and Georgia Tech. Both home teams were favored. Until the loss to Louisville in the 40th game, the Blue Devils had won every single game in which they were favored and several when they weren't.

It started with the preseason NIT, the first time that event (called the Big Apple NIT) had been held. That turned out to be a preview of the Final Four.

The semifinalists at Madison Square Garden were Duke, Louisville and Kansas, all eventual Final Four participants, and homestanding St. John's, which would win the Big East and become the No. 1 seed in the NCAA West.

Duke's four seniors were backed up by freshmen Danny Ferry and Quin Snyder. They were expected to be good, but they wound up playing great from the beginning. In the ACC, the Devils were selected third, well behind Carolina and Georgia Tech.

But sports information director Tom Mickle wrote in a questionnaire for a preseason magazine, "Despite back-to-back 24-10 and 23-8 records, this team is out to prove they are winners. They want to get to the Final Four and they want to win the ACC title. I think they can do it."

They did it without Bilas, who missed the first six games because of knee problems. He was replaced by 6-10 rookie Ferry, the top prep player in the nation as a senior. "It may have been the best thing that happened to us," Coach K said later. "Ferry got to play a lot in big games."

Dawkins, Alarie, Henderson and Amaker started every one of the 40 games as Duke stayed away from any serious injury. Once Bilas returned, he came off the bench for the next 15 games. But when Ferry's play leveled off, Bilas was returned to the starting job. And Ferry responded to the lineup change by playing much better as a reserve. His playing time actually did not decrease.

Including four NIT games, Duke would open the season with eight games in 17 days, the first six without Bilas. "It's like playing an NBA schedule," Alarie said.

The eighth game was in Cameron against Virginia in the ACC opener. The team was tired.

FEBRUARY 15-16, 1986

Duke had risen to second in the Associated Press poll as it headed into its toughest stretch of the season. The Blue Devils played at Stetson on Tuesday night, then had a game scheduled at No. 17 N.C. State on Saturday, followed by a 1 p.m. game on Sunday in Cameron against 14th-ranked Notre Dame.

National television was a consideration. But Duke would have to play two games within 16 hours.

State, coached by Jim Valvano, was desperate for a big win that would impress the NCAA tournament committee. The Wolfpack led much of the game, and with the score tied at 70 in the closing seconds, worked the ball for a layup try by Chris Washburn. But he shot too hard and Duke rebounded.

The clock was running down, and Johnny Dawkins had the ball deep in the corner. He went up for a shot which missed, but a foul was called on State's Nate McMillan, although he protested vigorously.

Dawkins, who may have won his National Player of the Year award in this weekend, made both shots for the 72-70 victory.

The next afternoon, the exhausted Blue Devils stayed even almost the entire game against Notre Dame, and with six seconds left, held a 75-74 lead. But the Irish had the ball at midcourt.

Duke anticipated the inbounds pass would go to Irish star David Rivers. "No way did we think Rivers would pass off, either," said Dawkins, who was defending the Notre Dame point guard.

Rivers went up the side, rather than try the middle and a play coach Digger Phelps had designed. As the clock ticked down, Rivers went up for a shot and Dawkins blocked it cleanly, after which the Cameron Crazies swarmed onto the floor.

Speaking of Dawkins, Coach K said, "He's the premier player in our conference. Whatever role we put him in, he came through."

With Tommy Amaker limited to 18 minutes because of foul trouble, Dawkins played the point for more than half the game. He scored 18 points in 37 minutes after getting 24 points in Raleigh just hours before.

"Dawkins has been consistently excellent for four years here," Krzyzewski said. "I'm a better coach because of Johnny Dawkins."

One week and two more victories later, Duke was elevated to No. 1 for the first time in Coach K's tenure.

It missed 10 of 16 first-half free throws. But Henderson continued his hot streak with 20 points, including a basket with 1:20 left that gave Duke a four-point edge. The Devils won, 72-64, as Amaker missed the school record by one with 13 assists.

After the holidays, 11-0 Duke played at College Park against Maryland. The Devils won 81-75, and it wasn't that close as the Terps scored the final 10 points. "I think this is the best team in the country," said Tom Newell, personnel director for the Indiana Pacers. "Winning the NIT gave them a playoff fever that you usually don't get until March."

Duke took a 16-0 record to Chapel Hill to play 17-0 and No. 1 Carolina, which was dedicating the Dean E. Smith Student Activities Center, to become instantly known as the Dean Dome.

UNC won 95-92. The Tar Heels ran back-door after back-door against the aggressive Duke man to man, and Steve Hale scored 28 points, almost all on layups. Carolina led by 16 in the second half, but the Devils rallied and made it close at the finish.

The next game was at Georgia Tech, also unbeaten in the ACC. It was a matchup of All-Americans, Dawkins against Mark Price. Tech got 25 points from Price and 21 from running mate Bruce Dalrymple and won, 87-80.

It looked like the preseason picks were accurate. But Alarie disagreed. "We could have won both games. We've got a good team. We just need to improve."

They did just that. Duke won its next 21 games, taking care of business all the way.

Maryland's Len Bias scored 41 points, but Duke won, 80-68. "We felt we could beat them by doing what we usually do," Coach K said. "We're not going to mess ourselves up with any trick defenses."

In the rematch with Georgia Tech, Duke shot poorly in the first half but managed to lead by a point. In the last half, the Devils played like a

KRZYZEWSKIVILLE

How formal have things become at Krzyzewskiville, college basketball's first—Duke students would insist only legitimate—tent city?

At the start of the previous school year, an eight-page "Statute of the Duke Student Government: Undergraduate Admissions Policy for the 2003-2004 Men's Basketball Season" was published.

It included nearly 5,200 words of instruction, and caution, to the Duke students, about the habit of tenting outside Cameron Indoor Stadium merely for the right to eventually claim the best seats for two home games, against Maryland (February 22) and North Carolina (March 6).

When the six-story Schwartz-Butters building was dedicated on April 15, 2000, a sign proclaiming Krzyzewskiville was officially placed near the walkway to Card Gym. But Duke's tent city got its start in 1986.

According to legend, K-Ville (as it is more familiarly known on campus) had its humble beginnings when a group of students, having played a game of quarters throughout the night, decided to rent a tent from U-Haul and pitch it on the quad on a Thursday night in anticipation of a game against rival North Carolina on Saturday.

There are no student tickets at Duke. It's first come, first enter, although for many years the whole process is monitored officially by jacketed students. It wasn't a case of just getting into the contest against the hated Heels, but to achieve first-row status in the bleachers behind press row, opposite the team benches.

The better to be seen by television, of course.

In '86, Mike Krzyzewski's program had made a breakthrough. It was ranked No. 1 and went all the way to the NCAA finals, where the Blue Devils lost to Louisville. They had won a collegiate-record 37 games.

The initial tenting was spontaneous, and soon was followed by other students doing the same thing. But the spontaneity didn't last long as the legend of the tent city grew rapidly. Originally, there would be cardboard signs recording the population of K-Ville, where up to 10 students (now 12) were in each tent.

The first tent in 2004 was in place on December 26—some 70 days prior to the UNC game and two weeks before the Christmas holiday break would end. By the time the Maryland game rolled around, more than 100 tents were in place.

Duke has tried to regulate K-Ville, out of health fears for students who sleep outside in the middle of the winter, snow, rain and cold be damned. The unofficial record was some 170 tents.

The rules have changed repeatedly over the years, as Krzyzewskiville has become more and more official. No matter when the first tent went up, in 2004, nothing became official until February 1.

At that time, each tent had to be occupied by at least eight members from 11 p.m. until 7 a.m. and from 2 a.m. until 10 a.m. on Friday night and Saturday morning. At all other times, at least one person must occupy the tent. Students work in shifts, normally of two-hour duration during the daylight hours.

In the interest of safety—not comfort—after February 1 the line monitors can call a grace period any time the temperature falls below freezing. Prior to that, the residents of Tent 1 have the right to send everybody to the comfort of their dorm rooms or apartments.

However, for walkup overnighters, or in the 48 hours before either of the tent games, there are no grace periods. No matter how dreary the weather, the students have to be in their tent home.

What started out as simply an idea hatched by a night of

frivolity has become serious business. Very serious business.

The line monitors run the show. The head monitor, elected by the student body, is in charge of K-Ville. He mediates disputes and makes the rules. And when those rules are broken, the tent inhabitants may be banished entirely, or bumped to the end of the line.

But the school has worked hard to make conditions much more liveable. There are ethernet ports in the base of all quad lights. The whole place has internet access. Students can watch DVDs on laptops and there are extension cords everywhere, reaching to nearby outdoor wall outlets. Every tent has its TVs and nintendos. Hungry? Just call local pizza delivery. They'll be only too happy to service K-Ville.

Krzyzewskiville is co-ed, roughly on a 60-40 male basis according to a *Sports Illustrated* on Campus cover story in January, 2004. The females do not get any extra benefits.

Maryland only recently became an official game, benefiting a rivalry that that mushroomed in importance in recent years, when the Terps went to back-to-back Final Fours and won a national championship in 2002, a season in which UNC slumped to an unimaginable 8-20.

Now that Roy Williams has returned to Chapel Hill, the Duke students believe that the UNC rivalry will regain its white-heat status, but they're still willing to contend with the "other" Williams, Maryland coach Gary, who considers Duke public enemy No. 1.

While the K-Ville inhabitants gain initial entry for the two "official" games, they don't have any extra privileges for other home games in legendary, ancient and (relatively) tiny Cameron. Like all other students,

the tent residents have to line up to enter the building.

The line monitors send them in groups, and the head monitor calls a halt if he determines that the student section is full. Actually, it is mostly overflowing, and it's rare that anybody is turned away.

Krzyzewski has worked hard over the years to both court and shape the tenting students. He constantly reminds them they are a part of the team. On the night before the Carolina game, he will send pizzas to K-Ville, and the students will be invited into the old arena to listen to encouraging words from their leader.

They may be shown highlights of previous Duke-Carolina games. And they will be told what to look for in the next day's game, or as the case in 2004, a 9 p.m. Saturday night regular-season finale.

Once the UNC game has ended, Krzyzewskiville is abandoned. The place is a mess. There is mud and empty cans and pizza boxes, their contents long since devoured. It looks for all the world like an abandoned town, which, in a sense, it is.

It usually takes four days to clean up the place, and nearly a year before the grass can grow back. Just in time for the next Krzyzewskiville.

Krzyzewskiville is unique. It is Duke and nobody else has one. Duke basketball stands apart, and on its own, and one of the reasons is the tent city. Outsiders simply can't comprehend why bright young people with those absurdly high SATs would spend countless hours over many days, braving the wet and the cold when it wasn't necessary, to be assured of being admitted to a basketball game they were entitled to attend. For free. Although they would have to stand the entire time.

K-Ville is different. For that matter, so is Duke basketball.

machine and handed the Jackets their worst loss in two years, 75-59. "We were flawless offensively and defensively in the second half," Krzyzewski said.

Before a 93-84 win against Oklahoma in another made-for-TV game, Dawkins became the third player to have his jersey retired. (Groat and Gminski were the first two). "This is an awesome thing," he said.

The home finale was against Carolina, of course. It was the last game in Cameron for the five seniors. The Tar Heels shot 64.2 percent during the game and dominated the rebounding, 38-22. But Duke won, 82-74. It was the first outright regular-season title in 20 years.

"The seniors handled it better than I did," Coach K said. "That just shows their maturity. The key to the whole game was our senior class being able to handle the atmosphere. I mean the things on the periphery."

He wouldn't talk about the upcoming tournament. "Four years we've been working, and we're going to enjoy this." The Blue Devils were 29-2, and they had beaten nine teams that were ranked in the top 20 at the time of the game.

Duke struggled in the ACC opener against Wake Forest. With 5-3 Muggsy Bogues controlling the tempo, the Devils led by one point at halftime. It didn't get much better in the second half, but the nation's No. 1 team managed to win, 68-60.

The semifinal against Virginia was equally tough. The Cavaliers hit almost 60 percent from the field and led 38-33 at halftime. It wasn't until a three-point play by Henderson gave Duke the lead at 67-66 that the Blue Devils were able to take control.

Henderson did it again, basket and free throw, and Duke was up by four. The Blue Devils closed it out, 75-70. "I thought we threw our best punch at them and they absorbed it," said UVA coach Terry Holland.

So the Blue Devils were in the finals against Georgia Tech, which beat Maryland in the other semifinal. It would be Dawkins against Price, two of the all-time ACC great guards. They had each won the same number of games in their career.

It was close all the way. Duke led at halftime and by nine points later, but Tech rallied to lead 63-62 on a basket by Duane Ferrell with 1:57 left. After the teams traded baskets, Alarie gave Duke a 66-65 edge with 44 seconds to play.

Tech wanted to go to Price, but Dawkins covered him like a blanket. He spun the other way and ran into Amaker in a double-team. So Craig Neal ended up with a jumper from the corner. It hit the rim and bounded away. Dawkins got the ball and Price fouled him.

"Ice," said Amaker. Dawkins did just that. He made them both and Price's uncontested basket at the buzzer left Duke the winner, 68-67.

Dawkins scored 60 points in the three games and was named MVP as Coach K got his first ACC championship. "This is something we'll reflect on the rest of our lives," Dawkins said. "There haven't been too many negatives, that's for sure."

The opening NCAA game also was in Greensboro, against No. 16 seed Mississippi Valley State. At halftime, the Blue Devils trailed 40-37. Would it be the biggest upset in NCAA history?

Dawkins made sure that didn't happen. In less than five minutes, he scored 16 points and Duke won, 85-78. The Blue Devils had 23 turnovers and forced just 10. "We weren't prepared for their quickness," Coach K said. "I don't know if we had recovered from the ACC Tournament."

After the game, a couple of the Mississippi Valley State players were collecting Duke auto-

MARK ALARIE SCORES AGAINST NAVY TO LEAD DUKE TO ITS FIRST FINAL FOUR UNDER COACH K.

graphs. "They're my favorite team," said one of the Delta Devils.

It was a wakeup call for Duke. The Blue Devils never gave Old Dominion a chance. Amaker had seven steals by halftime. Dawkins scored 25 points, and the rout was on, 89-61.

In the NCAA East Regional, the next foe was DePaul, another low seed which had beaten Virginia and Oklahoma. Duke won, 74-67, although it led by 14 points with two minutes to play. Dawkins scored 25 and had a season-high 10 rebounds, most of them offensive. "There were holes in their zone," he said. "I just looked for the open areas and went to the boards."

In the region finals at the Meadowlands, Duke was paired against Navy. The military school had

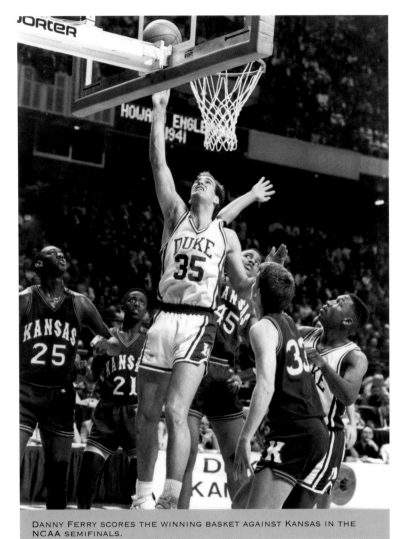

DANNY FERRY SCORES THE WINNING BASKET AGAINST KANSAS IN THE NCAA SEMIFINALS.

The Cameron Crazies on hand—maybe a couple hundred of them—started chanting near the end, "Abandon ship, abandon ship."

Alarie summed it up as Duke prepared to head for Dallas and the Final Four. "I can't believe we're 36-2, that we've played this many times without playing a really bad game. We've won every game we were supposed to win."

Three favorites were on hand. No. 1 Duke would take on No. 2 Kansas in the headliner. The Blue Devils had whipped the Jayhawks in the Big Apple NIT. No. 7 Louisville, which had been beaten twice by Kansas, went against the darkhorse, LSU.

The Blue Devils, other than Dawkins, continued to shoot poorly. But if Alarie was cold from the field, he also was stifling on defense. He played against 6-11 Danny Manning, who had scored 24 points the first time against Duke.

Manning got in early foul trouble. When he returned in the second half, he had just one field goal. Eventually, he fouled out with a mere four points. "That was defense at its best," Krzyzewski said. "How many times did Manning have the ball in scoring position?"

Still, cold-shooting Duke trailed 65-61 with 4:18 left before rallying to tie at 65 on a dunk by Alarie. After the teams traded baskets, Duke took a timeout with 58 seconds left. The idea was to take the first good shot. Alarie took it, an 18-foot jumper that missed. Dawkins got his hand on the loose ball, keeping it alive, and freshman Ferry scooped it up and made the layup that put the Devils ahead 69-67.

never been a factor in basketball before, or until it recruited David Robinson and saw him grow to 7-1.

The Blue Devils got an edge they didn't need when CBS analyst Bill Raftery said Bilas would get in foul trouble early against Navy—and Robinson. "That really ticked me off," he said. "I was so upset I couldn't sleep."

Duke breezed, 71-50. Dawkins made nine of 10 shots in the second half and had 28 points and the Most Outstanding Player award. Bilas, who had no fouls in the first half, had 10 rebounds, high for the season. "I told you so," he said to Dawkins.

Ferry then made a defensive stop, drawing a charge from Ron Kellogg with 11 seconds left. He missed the free throw, but Kellogg threw up a wild 25-footer that had no chance. Amaker got the ball and was fouled with one second to play. He made them both and Duke won, 71-67.

That sent the Blue Devils into the championship game against Louisville, which handled LSU.

At the Sunday media conference in which each team brought its starting lineup, it became a Blue Devil love-in. Each team featured seniors. All of the Duke players were graduating; none of the Cardinals were.

Most of the writers were delighted with how articulate the Blue Devils were. *The New York Times'* Pulitzer-Prize winning columnist, Dave Anderson, wrote that "Duke does it the right way." That was the tone of most of the stories, which praised Duke, its players and its coach, Krzyzewski. Only a handful of reporters supported the Cardinals.

But Louisville won the game.

Dawkins and Amaker dominated the first half. A press forced 14 turnovers, but Duke led only 37-34. The Blue Devils failed on five fastbreak chances when they had three-on-two or two-on-one. It would come back to haunt them.

Louisville coach Denny Crum made a decision that would lead his team to the title. "We weren't going to let Dawkins beat us," he said. So the Cardinals went to a diamond-and-one zone, with the one chasing Dawkins everywhere. Guarded by five different players, Johnny got just two shots the rest of the game. He wound up with 153 points in the six games.

That left other players open. But the forwards, Alarie and Henderson, couldn't hit. Duke led for the last time, 65-64, on two free throws by Dawkins. Louisville regained the lead on a jumper by Billy Thompson.

Henderson missed, but Dawkins soared for the rebound. He had a 10-footer, a shot he had made throughout the tournament. "I thought I made it," he said. But it bounced away, Louisville got the ball, and then came the play of the game.

With 48 seconds left, Crum took a timeout with 11 seconds on the shot clock. He wanted either Jeff Hall or Milt Wagner to drive, but Dawkins and Amaker had the lane blocked. Hall had the ball, guarded by Dawkins, and he had to shoot. He threw up a weak airball.

It turned out to be a beautiful pass. Ellison caught the ball and made a layup, and the Cards were up by three. Moments later, the freshman center locked up the MVP with two free throws.

Duke rallied to cut it to 70-69 on Ferry's basket with four seconds left. But the obligatory foul sent Wagner to the line with two seconds to play, and he made them both to clinch the championship.

"We played well and extremely hard," Krzyzewski said. "But we did not shoot well. We took the same shots we always take, and we would take the same shots again."

Years later, after he had coached his team to NCAA titles in '91 and '92, coach K reflected back on that '86 title game. "If I had known then what I know now," he said, "I could have helped my team. But we were very weary, except for Dawkins and Amaker, who never got tired. We had no legs, and we were short on our shots."

Although he has won national championships since, the '86 team always will be his favorite. "They really started the program, especially the seniors. We grew up together. They were the building block for what we have become."

CHAPTER

9

STARTING A DYNASTY

Mike Krzyzewski had taken his team from last place in the ACC to first in the national polls in a mere four years. But now, in 1987, he faced his most severe rebuilding effort.

Gone were four four-year starters—that never again will happen to an NCAA contender—and 75 percent of the offense that carried the Blue Devils to a national-record 37 victories.

The lone returning starter—the only senior who played significant minutes—was guard Tommy Amaker, known more for his defense and leadership skills than for his scoring.

But Amaker's 6.4 average in '86 made him the highest-scoring player on this team. And his point norm was barely more than his assist average of 6.0. He started his last year as the No. 1 assist man in school history. He's still third on the list, behind Bobby Hurley and Chris Duhon. He started all 138 games of his career, one fewer than Hurley's record.

The seven players who had been on the NCAA runner-up squad collectively averaged 23.7 points, or less than Johnny Dawkins. The ACC media thought so little of Duke's chances that the Blue Devils finished sixth in the preseason poll. (The team has never been voted that low since).

The question was whether Coach K had produced one great team—or actually had built a successful program. This team answered those questions. It finished 24-9, including 9-5 (third place) in the conference. The Blue Devils wound up 17th in the national polls.

It wasn't spectacular, but it proved to be the perfect bridge campaign that transitioned Duke into a five-year run of Final Four appearances, climaxed by back-to-back national championships in 1991 and 1992.

In '87, Krzyzewski demonstrated that he was one of the best coaches in the nation. By the end of the run, he was widely considered the finest.

The team succeeded despite some deficiencies. Freshman Phil Henderson, a 6-4 guard, scored 15 points in just nine minutes in an upset of Alabama at Duke's home away from home, the Meadowlands in New Jersey in December. After one more game, he was lost for the rest of the year because of academic deficiencies.

The lineup was peculiar from a purist's perspective. John Smith, a 6-7 frontcourt player who

DANNY FERRY (LEFT) AND BILLY KING WERE STARTERS ON THE 1987 TEAM.

in a row ('99-01). Only 10 other schools have won the award.

Despite the modest predictions, Coach K was confident. "We'll have a new look," he said. "I don't know how well we'll start, but by the time the ACC begins, we should be all right. We should improve. I'm just glad we don't start the conference season early this time."

Actually, the Blue Devils got off to a fast start after they lost their second game, to Illinois in Hawaii. They won 10 straight, including the Alabama game in which Henderson came off the bench to hit a bunch of three-pointers.

This was the first season for the three-pointer, and Krzyzewski didn't like it. "I think it's too short," he said of the 19'9" distance. But just because of his distaste that didn't mean Duke wouldn't shoot from outside. The Blue Devils benefited because both Ferry and Smith could make the three and also draw their defenders away from the basket.

Before the season began, Coach K said, "I like our team. There's not a kid who isn't a good player. We're not going to sit on our hands. I really believe this will be a fun year."

Part of the fun came early when Duke demolished Northwestern, 106-55. Not only was it the most points scored all season, but it came against a team coached by Bill Foster, the man whose resignation in 1980 had led to Krzyzewski's hiring. It was the worst loss in school history for the Wildcats. "Long night," Foster said. "I came all the way for that, huh?"

Duke won at Maryland as Ferry, whose father was general manager of the Washington Bullets,

scarcely had played as a freshman, became the starting center.

Danny Ferry, a 6-10 sophomore who had been a key reserve on the previous powerhouse, lined up at forward. He went on to become the first, and still only, Duke player to lead the team in scoring, rebounding and assists.

Defensive specialist Billy King was the other forward, while either junior Kevin Strickland or sophomore Quin Snyder lined up with Amaker in the backcourt. After the loss of Henderson, the only other member of the normal rotation was freshman Robert Brickey.

It wasn't an imposing group, and it was one that often had offensive problems. Yet, Duke played well enough together that nobody suggested the program was in any trouble.

Amaker went on to win the first Corinthian Award, the trophy that goes to the nation's top defensive player. It is an award that virtually has become personal property of the Blue Devils.

King would win it the next year. Grant Hill won in 1993, current assistant coach Steve Wojciechowski in 1995, and Shane Battier established his reputation by winning three times scored 20 points and grabbed 19 rebounds while playing before friends and family.

Duke took an 11-1 record into a home game with third-rated North Carolina, the ACC's preseason (and postseason) favorite. The much smaller Blue Devils actually led, 72-71, with 2:41 left before the Tar Heels rallied to score 12 consecutive points to win, 85-77. When it counted, UNC scored on six straight possessions.

Against the smallish Duke frontcourt, the Tar Heels had their way behind 6-10 seniors Joe Wolf and Dave Popson and freshmen J.R. Reid and Scott Williams. Carolina dominated the backboards and outscored the Blue Devils from the foul line, 26-14.

"I don't know how good this team can be," Krzyzewski said. "We have to see how they handle a loss, how they handle conference games. They have a long way to go before they can consider themselves a good team."

That answer came at Clemson, where the Tigers had won their first 17 games and where 11,000 fans overflowed Littlejohn Coliseum. Duke trailed by 11 points when Ferry picked up his fourth foul with 10:40 left to play in regulation. He never got another one, and made the game-winning shot in overtime as the Blue Devils persevered, 105-103. After his basket, Ferry blocked a last-second three-point try by Michael Tait to preserve the victory.

"It was a great basketball game," Coach K said, "one of the best I've been associated with as long as I've been coaching."

Despite the high score of that game, Duke was winning on defense. That began with Amaker. "Our defense starts with ball pressure," Ferry said. "Tommy's the thing that makes our defense go." As if to prove a point, Amaker held Wake Forest star Muggsy Bogues scoreless in the next game, a 69-49 victory.

When the teams next played, a Ferry tap-in with two seconds left provided the winner in a 62-60 contest that left Duke with a 16-4 record,

5-3 in the ACC. "I was just the right guy in the right place at the right time," Ferry said.

Duke ran its record to 20-4 before losing, in overtime, at Notre Dame. But it lost more than a game. Billy King broke his wrist and was lost for the rest of the regular season.

The Blue Devils struggled the remainder of the season. They lost for the second time each to Georgia Tech and North Carolina, then were upset in the opening game of the ACC Tournament by No. 6 seed N.C. State, 71-64 in overtime. The Wolfpack went on to capture the title by beating UNC in yet another upset.

King was back, but Duke's offense was missing in action. The Blue Devils got an NCAA bid, the third seed in the Midwest. They played in the Hoosier Dome in Indianapolis, where they defeated Texas A&M (58-51 with Strickland scoring 20 points) and Xavier (65-60, as Strickland had 12 points, nine rebounds and nine assists).

Moving on to the Sweet 16 in Cincinnati, Duke went against top seed Indiana, No. 3 in the land and the eventual national champions. The Blue Devils scarcely were in good shape as Ferry had a hip pointer and Snyder had the flu before the first coaching meeting between Krzyzewski and his mentor, Bobby Knight.

Despite 23 points from Amaker in his final game and 20 more from a somewhat hobbled Ferry, the Hoosiers advanced with an 88-82 victory.

But the 1986-87 season had been a success, much better than forecast. Amaker and Ferry were second-team All-ACC, but the story of this team was its balance.

"They (players) did everything I could have expected of them. We knew it would be different from last year, but this team had a great season."

In the preseason for '87-88, Duke was selected second in the ACC and 15th in the nation. When the regular season concluded, Duke finished third in the ACC but fifth in the nation. First-place UNC was seventh nationally, second-place N.C.

State (with two wins over Duke) was 14th.

But it was in the post-season that the Blue Devils shined, setting the stage for an amazing success story.

Duke not only won the ACC Tournament, defeating Carolina in the title game for its third victory over the Tar Heels, but the Blue Devils advanced out of the NCAA East to the Final Four, their second in three seasons. It was evidence that 1987 truly had been a transition season. Mike Krzyzewski's program had arrived.

Even after No. 2 seed Duke upset No. 1 Temple to advance to the Final Four, nobody could have guessed that this was just the beginning.

Coach K also led his squad to four more Final Fours in succession, and the five in a row set a modern-day record that quite likely never again will be matched.

The only longer streak in NCAA history is the 10 straight Final Fours by UCLA from '67-76, including seven consecutive championships behind centers Lew Alcindor and Bill Walton. The only other team to go to five straight Final Fours was Cincinnati ('59-63).

But Duke's quintet of Final Four appearances came after the NCAA expanded its field to 64 teams in 1985, balancing the brackets and requiring six games to win. All of Cincinnati's seasons and all but one of UCLA's came when only champions played, and it required just two games for the top seeds to get to the national semifinals.

The highlights for Duke would come in 1991 and 1992, when it won the NCAA, thus becom-

CURRENT MICHIGAN COACH TOMMY AMAKER'S FINAL GAME CAME AGAINST INDIANA IN THE SWEET SIXTEEN.

ing the first repeat winner since UCLA's skein ended in 1973. To give another example of just how dominating the Blue Devils were, the only other schools to go to as many as three straight Final Fours since '85 were Kentucky ('96-98) and Michigan State ('99-01).

Since the NCAAs began in 1939, the only other ACC school to make three straight Final Fours was North Carolina ('67-69). Counting its appearance in 1986 and again in 1994, Duke made it to the Final Four an astounding seven times in nine years.

While some experts believe that is every bit as amazing as UCLA's victory march, at the least it is the second-greatest achievement in basketball history. Considering the number of Division I schools (now 326), the fact that one team could get as far as the Final Four so often is beyond comprehension.

Unlike '87, the '88 team had plenty of experience. The only real loss was Amaker, the four-year starter at point guard. He was replaced by junior Quin Snyder.

The regulars were Ferry, a junior; Strickland, also a junior; senior Billy King and junior John Smith, who was replaced at the start of the ACC campaign by sophomore Robert Brickey.

Phil Henderson, back in academic good graces, sophomore Alaa Abdelnaby and freshman Greg Koubek gave Coach K a nine-player rotation.

After five blowouts against modest competition, Duke played in the Fiesta Bowl Classic in Tucson in a field that included No. 1 Arizona and

No. 7 Florida. The fourth entry was Michigan State.

The Blue Devils, who had averaged 101.8 points in those first five games, disposed of Florida, coached by Norm Sloan, 93-70, to advance to the final against homestanding Arizona.

Thanks to 31 points by Sean Elliott and good work at the free throw line, the Wildcats won, 91-85. Duke shot 54 percent to Arizona's 44, but were hampered by 30 personal fouls and a technical on Coach K. Arizona attempted 42 foul shots and made 32. Duke was 17-22. Ferry and Strickland each had 25 points, although the latter was one of two Blue Devils to foul out.

Even with the tough loss, Duke had proven its point. It could compete with the best. It had

DANNY FERRY, DEFENDED BY FORMER BASEBALL STAR KENNY LOFTON, HAD A BIG GAME AT ARIZONA IN 1987.

made over half its shots in each game and shown that it could score.

The team returned home and won four more games to make its record 10-1, including a victory at Virginia where Ferry was unstoppable. It was the 10th straight time Duke had beaten the Cavaliers (the streak eventually would reach 16).

Then came the most unexpected defeat in three seasons. Playing in Cameron, Duke led Maryland 69-64 with 2:42 left, and never scored again. The Terps pulled off the upset, 72-69, on five straight points by Keith Gatlin and a dunk by Derrick Lewis with 22 seconds to play.

Ferry had 23 points for Duke, but needed 25 shots for his eight baskets. He had been sick for two days, and it wasn't certain he would play until game time. The Blue Devils fell behind 16-4 at the start, expended a lot of energy in rallying, and fell apart at the end.

"Maryland did everything they had to do in the last three minutes," King said. "They got the loose balls, they got the big rebounds and they made the shots."

The next game for the Blue Devils was at No. 2 North Carolina. They had won there just once in 21 years, and never in the Dean Dome. But Duke pulled off the upset, 70-69.

The Blue Devils couldn't stop freshman J.R. Reid, who scored 27 points, many of them as the Heels rallied from an 11-point deficit to tie the score at 69. But good defense by Duke kept Reid from touching the ball in the final minute.

Duke took the lead when Ferry made the front end of a one and one with 52 seconds left. Neither team scored after that, but the Tar Heels had their chances.

Carolina missed a shot by Jeff Lebo and a tap-in by Pete Chilcutt. Duke rebounded, but the Blue Devils missed a free throw by Henderson ,and the same player had a turnover with 16 seconds left.

Duke had Reid blanketed, so Chilcutt had to shoot, and missed from 20 feet. With five sec-

have been well beyond the NBA stripe.

One of the Crazies went on the floor, placed a dollar bill on a spot, and indicated to Magid to shoot from there. The player came over, took his jumper, and when he made it, put the money in his pocket.

Other Terps were part of the Crazies' legend. Longtime coach Lefty Driesell, a Duke grad, was mostly bald. One year, Maryland arrived at Cameron with Driesell's foot in a cast. Perhaps he had broken it kicking a chair, as he often did.

A dozen or so students showed up in line, all wearing casts. They also had on skull caps, with empty and full inscribed. For Lefty, the needle was placed on the "E". Asked for his autograph, Driesell went along with the joke and signed the skull cap with a large X.

Nobody can be quite certain when the Cameron Crazies, the most famous student body cheering section in the nation, got their name. The building was dedicated in Eddie Cameron's name in 1972, but even before then, the fans could get rowdy.

What is certain is that the Crazies have been the most publicized student group for many years, for which a great deal of the credit must go to the constant reminders of television analyst Dick Vitale.

What also is certain is that, as Duke basketball has become dynastic, the Crazies aren't quite as crazy as they once were.

In the early '70s, for example, Maryland had a forward with bright red hair, Jim O'Brien, a dead ringer for Bozo the Clown. In a game at Cameron, several of the Duke students showed up in clown uniforms with floppy shoes and red wigs.

While the Maryland players were doing a layup drill, one of the imitators actually jumped into the line behind O'Brien, who apparently got a kick out of the attention.

Just a few years later, Maryland sharpshooter Brian Magid had a habit of coming out early to practice. This was before the three-point line, but just about every shot Magid took would

What makes the Crazies so unique has been their instantaneous responses to what occurs on the floor. During a 1979 game against North Carolina, coach Dean Smith elected

to have his team stall for the entire first half, which ended with Duke ahead 7-0.

Late in the period, the Tar Heels took their first shot of the game. It was a 10-footer from the wing by forward Rich "Chick" Yonakor, and the ball went nine feet. Immediately, the Crazies began the yell, "Air ball, air ball." If it wasn't an original cheer, nobody has thus far disputed it.

Six years later, Washington All-American Detlef Schrempf was greeted as he attempted a free throw with "fehlwurf"—German for airball.

The height of the craziness came in the early and mid-'80s, as Mike Krzyzewski was in the process of what has now become his own dynasty.

Vitale might show up hours before a game to interact with the students, and he would be willingly hoisted, hand over hand, from the front row to the back of the bleachers.

Jim Valvano, another fun-loving coach, enjoyed the attention from the crowd. Once, the Crazies

yelled at Jimmy V to sit down. He did—on the floor. The students promptly yelled, "Roll over, roll over." And Valvano did as commanded, with a smile on his face.

After he was let go at State, Valvano showed up at Cameron as a TV analyst along with Brent Musburger, once the play-by-play voice of the Final Four. Seeing the pair doing a preview from courtside, the Crazies interjected, "You both got fired."

There were times in which the students went over the line when abusing a player on the other team. The worst came in 1984 when the Crazies threw condoms and other items on the floor at Maryland's Herman Veal, who the previous season had been accused of making sexual advances and placed on probation.

Veal played well, Maryland won, and *Washington Post* columnist Ken Denlinger blasted the student body as "several thousand Duke students majoring in smartass." University president Terry Sanford admonished the Crazies in a letter in the *Duke Chronicle*, asking them to clean up their act. "We can cheer and taunt with style; that should be the Duke tradition." He signed the letter Uncle Terry.

At the next game, against archrival Carolina, when the Crazies protested an official's call, they chanted, "We beg to differ."

There was a banner that read, "We're sorry, Uncle Terry. The devil made us do it." The students wore aluminum halos. They yelled, "Go to heck, Carolina, go to heck." Another sign read, "A hearty welcome to Dean Smith." When the Tar Heels shot free throws, instead of arms waving behind the basket there was a sign that read, "Please miss."

Television—and not just Vitale—added to the Crazies' resume. In 1986, Al McGuire called the scene at Duke a zoo. He showed up for the game wearing a pith hat and carrying a whip. He flicked the whip at the students while play-by-play man Dick Enberg threw peanuts to the crowd.

There is an obvious reason why the Crazies have become such a part of the scene at a Duke home game that Krzyzewski

refers to them as the team's "Sixth Man." The students are courtside, in bleachers that were narrowed—three new rows were added—during a mid-90s renovation.

Nobody sits down. Not before, during or after a game. The Crazies, many painted blue and white, stand and yell and point.

Press row is immediately in front of them. It doesn't matter. They reach over the heads of the reporters to slap hands with the Blue Devils or to point at an offending official.

Some other schools, seeing the attention that the Crazies merited from the national media, have moved students near the floor, where they can be every bit as obnoxious as the originals.

Student line monitors handle the crowd, which does not require tickets. There are approximately 1,200 numbered seats for the students. Donald Wine, head monitor for the '03-04 season, said the average attendance had been around 1,500, which means that for most games, the bleachers are filled to every nook and cranny.

When they aren't, or when the Crazies aren't in good form, Krzyzewski may comment about it in his postgame media conference. Over the years, he has shaped the student crowd to his liking, which is to primarily cheer for Duke, and never abuse visiting players.

About as strong as it gets toward the opposition now is for the Crazies to mock N.C. State star Julius Hodge with a "Jul-e-us" chant, repeated often as the all-conference player suffered through a seven-point, seven-turnover game in Cameron in 2004.

The students still are noisy and disruptive when opponents shoot free throws, while being quiet as church mice any time a Duke player is at the line. The graduate students sit in the end zone, where a couple of years ago, one fan stood as the opposing player was ready to shoot, rapidly stripped and boogied while clad only in a brief bathing suit. Thus was the legend of Speedo Guy born. Yes, the foul shot missed.

CAMERON CRAZIES
(continued)

Whenever an opponent fouls out, the Crazies point their arms in the direction of the bench and chant. When the player finally takes a seat, they yell, "See yah!" That has gone on so long that visiting players know what's coming. Sometimes they remain standing by their bench. Others will fake sitting down. Eventually, the Crazies tire of the wait and yell, "You're not worth it."

Coach K may remind the Crazies in advance not to taunt an opposing player who may have gotten in trouble. Before the St. John's game last season, Duke students had been e-mailed by some students of the opponent to yell "Fire Jarvis" at beleaguered coach Mike Jarvis. They did so. Briefly.

Krzyzewski jumped to his feet and screamed at them to stop. Which they did. Immediately. Jarvis, a close friend of Coach K, nevertheless was fired a couple of weeks later.

The Crazies are extraordinarily receptive to their Hall of Fame coach's requests. And they politely applaud when he comes out, just before the game and after halftime, even though it means the passageway to the concession stand is blocked temporarily until Krzyzewski has passed by.

The amazing thing about the Crazies is how the traditions get passed down, year after year. Freshmen are indoctrinated immediately, and there are seniors every season who claim they never have missed a home game.

Duke usually wins at Cameron, often by a wide margin. But that doesn't halt the perennial enthusiasm. And, judging by the Duke boards on the Internet, once a Crazy, always a Crazy.

ALAA ABDELNABY SCORES AGAINST VIRGINIA IN THE ACC TOURNAMENT.

onds left, the Blue Devils knocked the ball out of bounds. The Devils double-teamed Reid, so it was left to Lebo to shoot from the corner. Brickey rushed out, got a hand on the ball, and victory was assured.

Despite the closeness of the score, Duke trailed only at 2-0. It was just the second home loss for North Carolina in the Dean Dome, which opened in 1986.

That started a five-game winning streak for the Devils, who moved to fourth in the polls. But they again were upset at home by N.C. State, 77-74, as the Wolfpack overcame a 14-point deficit in the second half.

That was a Saturday night game. The next day, Duke was home to Notre Dame and All-

American David Rivers. It was the fourth contest in seven days. Thanks to defense by King, who would win the Corinthian Award, the Blue Devils won, 70-61. Rivers, averaging 24 points, was limited to nine by King.

Four more victories later, including a revenge game against Maryland at College Park, Duke arrived at Kansas for a late-season non-conference outing. The Blue Devils, now ranked sixth, won in overtime, 74-70. Ferry's defense on Danny Manning at the end of regulation saved the win for Duke. "I was forced into a shot I really didn't want to take," said Manning, an All-American from Greensboro.

Six weeks later, the Jayhawks would end Duke's season in the Final Four.

Suddenly, the Blue Devils went into a tailspin. They lost three straight ACC road games.

DANNY FERRY SHOOTS AGAINST KANSAS IN THE NCAA TOURNAMENT.

The first two were against nationally ranked N.C. State and Georgia Tech, but the third was to seventh-place Clemson, 79-77. Upcoming was the finale at home against No. 6 Carolina, which had wrapped up the regular season.

The score was tied at 36 at halftime. The second half turned into one of the most remarkable shooting exhibitions ever. Carolina shot 60 percent, and was outscored by 15 points as Duke won 96-81. The Blue Devils made 11 of their first 12 shots, hitting 73 percent for the period. They scored 26 points in the first six minutes to open a 17-point lead, and even after a UNC rally, the margin was never less than five.

In the ACC Tournament, defense saved the Blue Devils in the opener against Virginia. They won, 60-48. The semifinal was against State, which had beaten Duke twice. This time, the Blue Devils pulled it out, 73-71, on a jumper by Ferry with 1:15 left. The defense provided the winning stop, forcing a last-second turnover by Charles Shackelford.

North Carolina again was the opponent in the title game. Unlike the previous meeting, this one was all about defense. Duke shot a mere 36.8 percent, but held the Tar Heels to 33.3.

With Duke ahead 61-59, Ferry rebounded a missed free throw by King and scored for a four-point lead. After Carolina scored, Snyder made two free throws with four seconds to play to clinch Duke's third win against the Tar Heels.

"We've accomplished something," Strickland said. 'Last year we had a great season, but we didn't have anything to show for it. We wanted to turn that around."

The ACC title sent Duke to Chapel Hill and the Dean Dome for the NCAAs. The Tar Heels, who all along had assumed they would be playing at home, wound up in Salt Lake City. "They won the tournament and they beat us three times," conceded Dean Smith.

Not having to travel helped weary Duke. The Blue Devils were able to cruise past Boston

University, 85-69, and SMU, 94-79. That sent them to the East Regional at the Meadowlands, where they had won in '86.

Awaiting was underdog Rhode Island. It proved to be a tough test. Duke won 73-72. No. 2 seed Duke now faced Temple, 32-1, in the East championship game. The Owls were rated first in

DECEMBER 10, 1988

Senior Danny Ferry came into the game at Miami after the shortest performance of the season in the previous contest with Stetson. Duke's leading scorer fouled out in 12 minutes.

Against the Hurricanes, at Miami's new pro arena where the half-full crowd of 6,654 was still a school attendance record, the 6-10 Ferry collected two fouls in less than nine minutes and headed to the bench.

But Duke trailed 32-28 against hot-shooting Miami, so Ferry was reinserted in the lineup by Mike Krzyzewski. He took over the game.

By the end of the half, Ferry had made 15 of 17 shots for 34 points, and the Blue Devils were in charge. He kept shooting—three-pointers, layups, and everything in between. It seemed they all went in. Actually, he missed three of 26 shots.

In the 117-102 Duke victory, Ferry scored a school and ACC-record 58 points. Dick Groat held the Blue Devil record of 48 for more than 36 years. The ACC record of 57 was held by N.C. State superstar David Thompson against Buffalo State in 1974.

Ferry, who once scored 13 points in succession in two and a half minutes, also set new Duke standards for field goals with his 23. The record of 19 had been held by Groat and Jeff Mullins.

"I was confident and the guys were yelling at me to shoot," Ferry said. "He's capable of a game like this," said his dad, Bob, general manager of the Washington Bullets who witnessed the performance.

Ferry's best friend, Quin Snyder, put it in perspective. "As you can see, he didn't beat me and the rest of the team. We got 59; Dan only got 58. He was in the groove. You could see it. We kept telling him to shoot. He was unbelievable."

In football-crazy Florida, however, Ferry wasn't the big news. Also on hand for the game was Florida's new grid coach, Steve Spurrier, fresh from Duke. He was surrounded by the media after the game.

Duke shot 75 percent for the first half and 67.2 percent overall in what was one of the highest-scoring games in school history. "One of the most phenomenal I've ever seen," said Miami coach Bill Foster. "And he wasn't getting any gimmies. Hell, we hammered him and he still made them. He amazed me."

the nation and freshman Mark Macon had been unstoppable all year. Until he went against Billy King.

Macon shot six for 29. He had six airballs and the Owls shot 28 percent. Duke won, 63-53, with its offense coming from Strickland (21 points) and Ferry (20). "The defense was great," Coach K said. "To play it without fouling was the key. We wanted to make Macon and (Mike) Vreeswyk put the ball on the floor and take away the three-point shots."

Duke advanced to the Final Four in Kansas City, where it once again would meet Kansas. The Blue Devils not only had beaten KU in the regular season, but also in the '86 NCAA semifinals.

It didn't happen again against the underdog Jayhawks, who had 11 losses during the season. Kansas scored the first 14 points, and led 18-2 and 24-6. Duke staged a second-half rally to cut the margin to 55-52 with 4:17 left, but could get no closer.

It was still three points with 2:11 to play, but Danny Manning had a tap-in off a missed shot, and Duke eventually lost 66-59. "Danny and the Miracles" won the NCAA, upsetting an Oklahoma team that had beaten them twice.

"We had a marvelous year," Krzyzewski said. "The start killed us. We were always fighting back, and that takes a lot out of you." Duke finished at 28-7 and Ferry, an All-American, was the ACC Player of the Year.

Duke started the 1989 season ranked No. 1 in the nation, an acknowledgment of the Final Four appearance and a veteran team led by seniors Ferry, Snyder and Smith and juniors Henderson, Brickey and Abdelnaby. There also was one prominent freshman, 6-10 Christian Laettner.

The Blue Devils looked the part in their opener against Kentucky in the Tipoff Classic at Springfield, Massachusetts, home of the Basketball Hall of Fame. Behind Ferry's 23 points, Duke romped 80-55. It was one of the worst defeats in history for the proud Wildcats.

QUIN SNYDER PASSES AGAINST NORTH CAROLINA.

The Blue Devils won their first 13 games and continued to be the No. 1 team. That included Ferry's ACC and school record 58 points at Miami, and league wins over Wake Forest, Virginia and Maryland.

It also included an ACC record for Abdelnaby, who made his final two shots against Kentucky, went eight for eight against The Citadel and nine for nine against East Carolina, and hit his first shot against Northwestern. His streak of 20 consecutive field goals broke the league record of 15, but fell short of the NCAA mark of 25 set by American's Ray Voelkel in 1978.

Sophomore guard Joe Cook flunked out after the first semester, leaving the team with two traditional backliners, Snyder and Henderson. The first move was to put the 6-5 Brickey on the perimeter, although he lacked playmaking skills. After that,

the season turned topsy-turvy and Coach K went in search of different lineups in an effort to create more consistency.

Duke's fall from grace—and in the national polls—began in stunning fashion, a 91-71 defeat to North Carolina in Cameron. And that was just the beginning. The Blue Devils also lost at Wake Forest and N.C. State, blitzed Clemson by 30, but were beaten on the road by Georgia Tech.

In a win at Maryland, Ferry suffered a badly strained back. He played against UNC, but was ineffective with 14 points, 11 below his average.

Duke actually led 50-45 with 14 minutes left, but the Tar Heels went on a surge, led by reserve center Scott Williams, who scored 22 points and grabbed 11 rebounds. Carolina hurt Duke badly on the boards, 43-27, and pulled away as guard King Rice filled in for Jeff Lebo, who was out with a sprained ankle.

The Blue Devils were No. 1 no longer. Losing to UNC was one thing, but a 75-71 defeat at seventh-place Wake Forest was another. Quin Snyder analyzed the defeat this way: "It isn't just

DANNY FERRY GRABS A REBOUND AGAINST N.C. STATE IN 1989.

the last two games. It's been there all along, just like a bomb that finally exploded. We haven't put together 40 minutes all year."

Things didn't improve. Ferry missed the N.C. State game with his bad back. He had played in 123 consecutive games in his career and started the previous 88. Duke actually shot 64.6 percent, but lost 88-73, as the Wolfpack forced 21 turnovers and had only nine floor mistakes.

The victory over Clemson meant little, because the Tigers had six players suspended by Coach Cliff Ellis for skipping study hall. The Tigers suited up the remaining six players and a manager.

By the time the slump was over, Duke had fallen to 14th in the polls and seemingly out of the national picture. But Krzyzewski kept changing the lineup, and finally came up with one that seemed to work. Laettner had gotten his first start at State, but played just 13 minutes and didn't take a shot.

Laettner, who would go on to one of the most distinguished careers in NCAA history, replaced Abdelnaby at center. Henderson and Snyder started every game as did Ferry, other than the loss at State.

A defeat at Georgia Tech left the former No. 1 team at 4-4 in the ACC. Coach K made another lineup change, bringing the explosive Brickey off the bench even though "he's one of our top three players, along with Ferry and Snyder." Duke promptly won seven straight, including routs of Notre Dame and Kansas.

The 102-88 triumph at South Bend represented the most points scored against the Irish in the 18 years Digger Phelps had been the coach. Ferry had 27, beginning a stretch in which he scored at least 24 in nine straight games except for a blowout at Harvard.

Before the Kansas game, Ferry's jersey was retired and he responded with 26 points and 10 rebounds as Duke crushed the Jayhawks, 102-77, who were being coached in his first year by Roy Williams. The Blue Devils easily gained re-

venge on Georgia Tech (91-66) and N.C. State (86-65).

Again playing another name team outside the ACC, the Blue Devils—in front of former president Richard Nixon—were defeated, 77-75, at the Meadowlands by No. 2 Arizona. Duke had a chance to tie at the finish but Laettner missed the front end of a one and one.

He was consoled by Nixon, a Duke law school grad. "I know you feel badly, young man," Nixon said. "But everything will be fine. I know. I've won a few and lost a few myself." It was to be the last critical shot that freshman Laettner would miss in his college career.

Duke was upset at Clemson to end a chance for the regular-season title, but the Blue Devils responded with their own upset, 88-86, at UNC. It cost the Tar Heels a tie for first place with State. Instead, Carolina and Duke each finished at 9-5.

The ACC Tournament was played in Atlanta. After a season in which five teams had a chance at first place, there were six blowouts in as many games as Duke and Carolina advanced to the finals.

UNC won, its first title in six years, 77-74. Duke shot just 38 percent and Ferry was only 6-20 with 14 points. Laettner led Duke with 15. The physical game wasn't decided until Ferry's three-quarter-court heave bounced off the rim at the buzzer. Dean Smith commented, "It was so close an old man could have had a heart attack."

Duke was seeded second in the East as six ACC teams got NCAA bids. UNC was sent to the Southeast as the No. 2, a move that irritated Dean Smith. However, there was no way that the committee was going to pair fifth-ranked Carolina in the same region with No. 2 Georgetown. Duke had finished ninth in the final polls.

The Blue Devils won easily over South Carolina State by 21 points before struggling past West Virginia in Greensboro, 70-63. The seven points represented the largest lead of the game.

ROBERT BRICKEY SHOT 54.8 PERCENT FROM THE FIELD AS A COLLEGIAN.

PHIL HENDERSON DUNKS OVER ALONZO MOURNING TO LEAD DUKE TO A FINAL FOUR.

Ferry didn't make a basket in the second half, but was nine for nine rom the foul line.

In the regional at the Meadowlands, Duke trounced Minnesota, 87-70, with Brickey scoring 21 points. On the previous night, UNC lost to eventual champion Michigan and Smith commented, "I would rather have played Minnesota."

Awaiting was Georgetown, which had squeaked past N.C. State. The Hoyas were led by freshman center Alonzo Mourning, but it was Laettner who got the best of the duel.

Early in the game, Mourning blocked Laettner's first shot. But Christian picked up the ball and scored. He would finish with a career-high 24 points and nine boards on the same floor where he missed the foul shot against Arizona. Henderson ignited the crowd with a vicious slam over the 6-10 Mourning as Duke established a 14-point lead in the last half.

But from a 75-61 deficit, the Hoyas scored 12 straight points. "You knew they were going to make a run," Krzyzewski said, "because they play such good defense." Snyder fouled out, but Ferry made two foul shots and after a miss by the Hoyas, Duke closed out the victory with eight straight at the free throw stripe to end it, 85-77.

That created the third Final Four for seniors Ferry, Snyder and Smith. Duke did not cut down the nets, a decision by the players. "I didn't know," said Coach K. "I had my scissors ready."

The Final Four was at the Kingdome in Seattle, Snyder's hometown. Duke would play Seton Hall, which had won the West as No. 1 Arizona stumbled in the Sweet 16. The others were Illinois and Michigan from the Big Ten.

Duke got off to a blazing start—or rather Ferry did. The Blue Devils led 26-8 and Ferry had 14 points. But in the first three minutes, Brickey had been injured. He returned briefly, but didn't score in 11 minutes and didn't play in the second half.

Laettner fouled out with just under 10 minutes left, and Duke had nobody to help Ferry, who

QUIN SNYDER PLAYED IN THE 1989 FINAL FOUR IN HIS HOMETOWN OF SEATTLE, WASHINGTON.

ed the ball by Coach K at the start of fall practice and gave it back four years later.

He was joined in the starting lineup by seniors Henderson, Abdelnaby and Brickey and sophomore Laettner. The lineup changed only when Brickey missed eight games over three weeks in January, when he was replaced by Greg Koubek.

Besides Koubek, a junior, the bench consisted of sophomore Brian Davis and freshmen Billy McCaffrey and Thomas Hill.

Despite playing on such a veteran starting unit, Hurley averaged over 33 minutes, highest on the team. The baby-faced kid from Jersey ended up breaking the school record for assists with 288 as the Blue Devils not only made the Final Four for the third year in a row, but played in the title game.

This team averaged better than 89 points, most since 1964. Henderson was the leading scorer at 18.5, but Laettner made third-team All-America

scored 34 points in his college finale. The Pirates, led by Australian rent-a-star Andrew Gaze (he was in the U.S. for six months), won going away, 95-78.

Duke was outscored in the second half, 62-40. "I couldn't have pictured too many teams here losing an 18-point lead," Ferry said. "That just doesn't happen." But without Brickey for almost the entire game and with Laettner in foul trouble, the Devils had insufficient help for Ferry.

Ferry was voted the National Player of the Year. "I feel bad for Danny," said Seton Hall coach P.J. Carlesimo. "He deserves to play in a championship game." That didn't happen for Ferry, but for his teammate Laettner, it was just the beginning.

When the 1990 season began, Duke had a new point guard. Freshman Bobby Hurley, son of a famous high school coach in New Jersey, was hand-

DANNY FERRY SCORED 34 POINTS IN HIS FINAL GAME VS. SETON HALL IN THE FINAL FOUR.

and led the team in rebounding while scoring at a 16.3 clip. They were the team's co-MVPs. No Duke player made All-ACC, however.

Duke got off to a fast start with three wins in which it scored over 100 points each time. Then came a couple of narrow defeats, which were more impressive than the victories.

In the ACC/Big East Challenge at Greensboro, the Blue Devils were beaten by No. 1 Syracuse, 78-76, as David Johnson made two free throws with three seconds left and McCaffrey's last-second three-pointer bounced away. Duke trailed by 15 points early, but rallied to tie early in the second half.

After that difficult loss, the Blue Devils played at Michigan, the defending NCAA champs, three days later. The Wolverines, with four senior starters, also jumped out to a big early advantage. Twice, Duke trailed by 18 points, but again showed the ability to rally.

Koubek's rebound of a Hurley miss at the buzzer sent the game into overtime, 94-94. In the extra period, the Wolverines made critical free throws for the 113-108 victory. Duke scored the most points ever by a visiting team in Crisler Arena, including 26 by Laettner and 22 by Henderson. "This wasn't a game that we lost," Krzyzewski said. "This was a game that was won. It was a game that had an incredible number of big plays.

"It was a good week for us. Those were exhausting, exciting basketball games. That's the way we planned it. I think it's been very good for our team."

Laettner agreed. "I think we learned that we can play with big, good teams. Now what we have to learn is that we can beat those kind of teams."

The Blue Devils won their next nine games, including three in Hawaii's Rainbow Classic, where Hurley joined Laettner and Henderson on the all-tournament team. The streak included ACC wins against Virginia, Georgia Tech and Maryland.

Now 12-2, Duke played at UNC, and got thumped 79-60. Brickey was sidelined with a knee injury, and Laettner (18 points, 13 boards) got little help. The Tar Heels had been slumping and had lost six times, but it was No. 8 Duke that looked lost.

After the debacle, Duke responded with six more victories, four of them in conference play, to make its league record 7-1. Four home games in succession against N.C. State, Georgia Tech, Clemson and Notre Dame helped.

Brickey returned for the game against the Irish, but he never regained the scoring form he had displayed before getting hurt.

The game against Tech matched Hurley against the Jackets' freshman point guard, Kenny Anderson, who 14 years later is still in the NBA. They had a passing duel. Hurley had 13 assists, while Anderson had 12 and scored 19 points.

Dennis Scott scored 36 for Tech, including five threes. But the biggest surprise was Blue Devil Brian Davis, who came into the game averaging 3.8 points. Used as a defensive stopper, Davis scored a career-high 16 points as Duke won a squeaker, 88-86. He also scored the final five points on a three-point play after a Hurley pass and two foul shots.

Krzyzewski praised the bench play from Davis and Thomas Hill. "I think only a coach can really understand that feeling when you see youngsters respond under those situations." Tech coach Bobby Cremins said, "I don't know if we can play any better."

Duke raised its record to 18-3 and was ranked fourth nationally by beating Notre Dame, 88-76. Digger Phelps praised the Blue Devils. "I like Duke's team," said the veteran coach. "I think they play, as usual, aggressive defense. I think they're very unselfish and make things happen on offense. Duke's one of the top teams in the country. I think the way Mike goes after it and the way they'll play in the NCAAs, I'm sure they'll advance the way they usually advance."

After such glowing remarks, the Blue Devils fell on their face, losing at Virginia, 72-69. Duke had beaten the Cavaliers 16 consecutive times since being trounced by 43 points in the '83 ACC Tournament. "I never thought some mystic power was going to have us win the game because of the way the series has been," Laettner said. "We were a real stupid team. We'd make a good play and they'd miss another free throw, then we'd come down and be stupid again."

Two days later, the Devils were at College Park and with less than four minutes to play, trailed by 10. But they forced seven turnovers in that span and took a 95-93 lead when Hurley made two free throws with two seconds left.

It turned out to be a long two seconds. Jerrod Mustaf threw a baseball pass to Vince Broadnax, who tried a 25-footer. But Brickey blocked the shot. Teyon McCoy picked up the ball and made a desperation shot and the officials said it beat the buzzer.

"I thought by the time they got the ball and I knocked it away, time would have run out,"Brickey said. So did the rest of the team, who were emptying the bench in the assumption they had won. But the refs cleared the court and they played five minutes more. Duke wound up winning, 114-111. "There is no explanation," Coach K said. "It's like your home is destroyed by a tornado and you go on living."

Duke lost at N.C. State, where it hadn't won since '86, although Abdelnaby had a career-high 32 points. In the next game, the Devils won at home against No. 8 Arizona, 78-76.

What once had been a two-game ACC lead was wiped out when Clemson won its 24th straight home game, 97-93, although Laettner broke a three-game shooting slump with 25 points and 12 rebounds.

Duke headed home for the finale against Carolina, needing a victory to tie for the regular-season title. Instead the underdog Tar Heels pulled off an 87-75 upset. The Blue Devils had lost their third straight league game heading into the ACC Tournament.

"We need to change our team around before the tournament," Laettner said. "We're not playing as a team. Our defense is just really horrible."

It didn't get any better in the first half of the tournament opener, which ended in a 48-48 tie with Maryland. But Coach K pulled a shocker after Hurley and Henderson each got a fourth foul. He switched to a zone. Behind freshman McCaffrey, who played the point for 10 minutes, Duke pulled away and won, 104-84.

But the slump wasn't over, just postponed. Duke was beaten 83-72 in the semifinals by Georgia Tech, and afterward in the locker room, Henderson exploded. "We've got a bunch of babies and too many quitters," he yelled. "There's too much faking going on with this team. It's ridiculous. I can't understand why you can't give everything you've got for 40 minutes."

It turned out to be the speech of the year. The next time Duke lost was in the NCAA finals.

Seeded third in the East Region, the Blue Devils practiced at home while the ACC finals were being held. Krzyzewski, who had heard of Henderson's outburst, asked Phil if he would like to repeat what he said. And the senior guard did just that, adding a few expletives. "I admire a little bit the way Phil expressed himself," Coach K said. "That didn't bother me. I like that. I've never closed my locker room."

Duke opened against Richmond, a team that had pulled off several NCAA upsets before. The Spiders never had a chance. The Devils romped, 81-46. "Obviously Duke was too big, too talented, too deep, and we just didn't belong on the floor with them," said Richmond coach Dick Tarrant. "Their second team could probably have beaten us." The bench outscored the Spiders, 41-6.

In the second round in Atlanta, Duke nudged St. John's 76-72 behind the play of Brickey, whose 22 points were a season high. With the score tied at 72 in the final minute, he rebounded a blocked shot by Abdelnaby and dropped it in the basket with 32 seconds left. After a St. John's miss, Brickey made two free throws with nine seconds left and the Devils advanced to the Sweet 16 for the fifth straight time.

Duke was headed to its favorite NCAA arena, the Meadowlands in New Jersey, where the Blue Devils previously had advanced to the Final Four three times after a 6-0 record. The opponent would be UCLA, another legendary basketball foe.

Duke won, 90-81, thanks to Henderson's heroics. The Bruins had erased a nine-point deficit to take a one-point lead. Early in the half, Abdelnaby and Laettner each collected his fourth foul within 10 seconds. But Henderson took it upon himself to score 13 consecutive points. His third three-pointer in that spree gave the Devils the lead for good at 70-68 and they expanded that to a 90-81 win with good foul shooting.

Jokingly, Coach K remarked, "It went just like we planned. We wanted to get everyone in foul trouble and then pray Phil would save us. That's exactly what he did."

That sent the Blue Devils into the regional finals against No. 3 Connecticut, the top seed in the East. The Huskies edged Clemson by a point on a buzzer-beater by Tate George.

The teams battled on an even basis for 40 minutes, going into overtime at 72-72 when Duke just missed on a lob from Hurley to Abdelnaby with 0.3 seconds left.

In the extra period, Duke led 77-76 when Abdelnaby was called for a rare goaltending on a missed free throw by UConn's Nadev Henefeld. He grabbed the ball off the rim and the whistle meant it counted for the tying point. Henefeld made the second one for the lead.

After misses by both teams, Duke had the ball out of bounds in front of its bench with 2.6 seconds left. Krzyzewski set up a play for Henderson, with options to Abdelnaby or Hurley.

PHIL HENDERSON DRIVES AGAINST CONNECTICUT IN THE 1990 EAST REGIONAL FINAL.

But when Coach K saw that UConn wasn't defending against Laettner, who was making the inbounds pass, he yelled at Brian Davis, "Special." Nobody on the team other than Davis or Laettner knew what was happening.

Davis accepted the pass and threw it immediately back to the uncovered Laettner. From 15 feet on the left wing, Laettner took a jumper that swished for the victory. It was to be the first of three NCAA game-winning scores for the 6-11 forward, who would become the all-time scoring leader in the postseason.

"Our guys cried in victory and their guys cried in the loss," Krzyzewski said. "That's how great a game it was."

Duke arrived in Denver for its fourth Final Four in five years as the underdog against Arkansas. Favored UNLV would play Georgia Tech in the other game. Coach Nolan Richardson promised

CHRISTIAN LAETTNER CELEBRATES THE GAME-WINNING SHOT AGAINST CONNECTICUT TO SEND DUKE TO THE FINAL FOUR.

sickness." He returned to play 36 minutes and handed out six assists.

Two previous Final Fours worked to Duke's advantage. "The seniors have been in those games for four years," Coach K said. "They realize it's a 40-minute game and to hang in there."

There was no way to hang in there against UNLV. The poised, veterans Rebels simply took apart the youngest team Duke had in a decade, winning in record fashion, 103-73.

It was the largest margin of victory in a title game, the most points scored and the most field goals, 41. Duke had 23 turnovers, 16 of them as a result of steals. "I don't know how much it was us," Coach K said. "They were just totally in control. I think it was the best that a team has ever played against me as a coach."

Playing in Denver, where the football Broncos never had won a Super Bowl, the Blue Devils were now 0-8 in Final Four appearances. Nobody knew it at the time, but all that was about to change. Revenge would be sweet.

"40 minutes of hell" for the Blue Devils. Instead, in the last four minutes, he found out what hell really looked like.

The Blue Devils trailed 69-62 with 10 minutes left. They outscored the Hogs 35-14 the rest of the way to advance to the championship game against UNLV, which rallied in the second half to defeat Tech.

There were obstacles from the beginning. There was an extraordinary scene as Hurley, who had battled the flu all week, left the court after just 4:40 of action with Duke ahead 16-5 and ran to the locker room, sick at his stomach. "I didn't want to embarrass myself out there on the court," he said. "I had to come back here and take care of myself." He threw up before the regional finals, "but that was just nerves. This time it was real

BOBBY HURLEY GOT HIS FIRST FINAL FOUR EXPERIENCE IN 1990.

CHAPTER 10

BACK TO BACK

Winning a first national championship was a long time coming, and when it did, in 1991, it was unexpected. Duke had been to eight Final Fours without a title, but only in 1986 it had been the favorite. But because the Blue Devils had been four times in five years, including the previous three, Krzyzewski's record was under the microscope.

The three-in-succession Final Fours all had been surprises. "Those three years, we shouldn't have gotten there," Coach K said. "In 1988, we weren't an awesome team. In 1989, we couldn't influence games. In '90, I don't know how we made it."

In 1991, Duke played what its coach called the toughest schedule ever, which included 15 games against nationally ranked opponents. It was the youngest squad since '83, featuring five freshmen and three sophomores. Three senior starters had to be replaced.

Only Laettner and Hurley were returning regulars. They were the only players who started all 39 games in '91. No less than eight other players started games. Clay Buckley got a ceremonial slot

(FROM LEFT) CHRISTIAN LAETTNER, BOBBY HURLEY AND GRANT HILL LED DUKE TO BACK-TO-BACK NCAA CHAMPIONSHIPS IN '91 AND '92.

for his senior day, but the other seven all were in the opening lineup at least eight times.

The final statistics revealed the depth and balance. While Laettner averaged almost 20 points, four others—Bill McCaffrey, Thomas Hill, Hurley and freshman Grant Hill—averaged between 11.2 and 11.6. Brian Davis and Koubek got extensive minutes, as did another freshman, Tony Lang.

Duke was well-regarded because of its past history, but began the year at No. 6, fell to as low as 14th, and never was rated higher than fourth. Although the Blue Devils would get crushed in the ACC tournament finals by a North Carolina team it had beaten twice, after it entered the NCAAs as the No. 2 seed in the Midwest, it never had a game closer than 14 points until it reached the Final Four.

The championship campaign began with the preseason NIT, with Duke winning home games against Marquette and Boston College. In the semifinals in New York against No. 2 Arkansas, the team it had upset in the Final Four eight months before, the Blue Devils led early by 11 points behind Laettner before the Razorbacks took advantage of fouls and turnovers to score 31 points in the last 10 minutes of the half.

Duke never threatened in the second half and lost, 98-88, as the bench scored only eight points. In the third-place game, the Devils rebounded to defeat Notre Dame, 85-77, as McCaffrey scored 21.

After thrashing East Carolina and UNC Charlotte, coached by Duke alum Jeff Mullins, the Blue Devils were defeated at Georgetown by the No. 6 Hoyas, led by twin towers Alonzo Mourning and Dikembe Mutumbo. Laettner was limited to 14 points and fouled out.

After a home win against Michigan and a romp at Harvard, Duke traveled to Oklahoma, which had won 51 straight home games. Bad weather caused the Blue Devils to arrive five hours late for their Saturday afternoon game.

THOMAS HILL PLAYED ON THREE FINAL FOUR AND TWO NATIONAL CHAMPIONSHIP TEAMS.

Duke trailed 50-45 at halftime, only because Grant Hill scored 10 of the final 17 points. After the break, Thomas Hill took over, stifling Sooner star Brent Price and scoring 16 points himself with his father, an assistant athletic director at Oklahoma, watching.

The Devils shot 59 percent and ended Oklahoma's streak, 90-85, with Grant Hill and Laettner each scoring 19.

Two easy home wins set the stage for the pivotal game of the season, the ACC opener at Virginia. Until the previous year, when UVA finally ended Duke's 16-game streak, the Blue Devils had dominated the series. But it was the Cavaliers who did the dominating in astonishing fashion, 81-64.

Duke shot poorly (26.9 percent) and had 24 turnovers. As the silent bus ride ended in Durham after midnight, Krzyzewski ordered an immediate practice. "I tell them we have practice, and I get no response. I tell Max (trainer Crowder) and he says, 'OK.' Max really knows what it takes to win."

The early-morning practice was so spirited that Grant Hill suffered a badly broken nose after colliding with Lang, his roommate. He ended up at the hospital again, having his nose re-broken and set again, and missed the next two ACC games.

But the team responded. Duke demolished nationally ranked Georgia Tech by 41 points, 98-57, won easily at Maryland by 16, and at home against Wake Forest by 22 and The Citadel by 33.

North Carolina came to Cameron as the nation's No. 5 team, but after trailing early by 10 points and 28-24 at halftime, Duke rallied after intermission. The Blue Devils grabbed the lead at 35-34 before Thomas Hill scored nine points during an 18-8 outburst that put the Heels away, 74-60. UNC was limited to 27.6 percent shooting and eight baskets in the last half.

Now 15-3, Duke stumbled at State's Reynolds Coliseum again, 95-89. The defense showed none of the intensity of the Carolina game and the Devils were torched by Rodney Monroe's 35 points.

But the next three road games were all wins at Clemson, Georgia Tech and Notre Dame, and Duke had won five straight when LSU visited Cameron with man-mountain Shaquille O'Neal going against Laettner in a battle of big men.

This one was no contest. O'Neal couldn't stay with Laettner on the perimeter, or driving for the basket. The Duke star had 24 points, many from Hurley's school-record 14 assists, and 11 rebounds. Two late dunks allowed Shaq to finish with 15 as the Devils won, 88-70.

After rolling past Davidson, Duke stumbled at Wake Forest, 86-77, as Laettner was the only of-

fense with 29 points. "I didn't think we were hungry," said an unhappy Coach K. "It may have been because we already had won 22 games."

The Hills made sure Duke got back on track, combining for 32 points in a home win over N.C. State, before a trip to Arizona. Duke had now played the Wildcats, Georgetown, Oklahoma and Notre Dame on the road, Arkansas and Notre Dame (again) in New York and LSU at home. The schedule made the team tougher.

At Arizona, Duke lost 103-96 in double overtime after leading with 12 seconds left in regulation on two Laettner free throws.

The Blue Devils came home to rout Clemson and complete their first-ever 16-0 season in Cameron, then beat UNC for the second time, 83-77, at the Dean Dome as Laettner, Hurley and Grant Hill starred.

Duke entered the ACC Tournament in Charlotte as the top seed. After a first-round bye, the Devils eliminated State, 93-72, with Laettner, Hurley and McCaffrey shooting brilliantly.

Carolina awaited in the finals. Things started going badly for Duke almost immediately. Coach K stood to yell at Grant Hill in the first two minutes, and was hit with a technical by referee Lenny Wirtz. The Blue Devils never led. They were down 13 at halftime and 26 points with nine minutes left. UNC locked up the No. 1 seed in the NCAA East with a 96-74 blowout.

After the game, the Duke team had dinner in a Charlotte restaurant and watched the NCAA pairings on TV. Instead of screaming at his team, Krzyzewski told them forcefully, "We're going to win the national championship."

The team responded as Coach K wished after heading to Minneapolis and the Metrodome, where it would win two future titles. Northwest Louisiana fell, 102-73 (Laettner and T. Hill combined for 40), and Iowa was bounced, 85-70, as the same two players tallied 36. Duke shot 59.7 and 51.7 percent in the two games.

The Midwest Regional was held at the Silverdome in Pontiac, Michigan. After being edged in the previous tournament by Duke on Laettner's last-second bucket, Connecticut was looking for revenge. The Huskies never had a chance. The Devils grabbed a 17-point lead by halftime and won easily, 81-67, while continuing their hot shooting with 55.6 percent. Koubek nailed three treys and had 18 points.

The Midwest finale was almost identical. The foe was also from the Big East (St. John's). Duke led big at halftime (13 points), shot 52.1 percent and forced 26 turnovers. Hurley won the Most Outstanding Player award with 20 points, a team-high seven rebounds, four assists and just one turnover. "His game has risen to a new level," Coach K said.

Duke was off to another Final Four, this time in Indianapolis. Awaiting was the same UNLV team that had beaten the Devils by 30 points the previous year. The Rebels were undefeated, had been tested just twice, and were being measured for immortality.

Nobody thought Duke had a chance—except Coach K and his players. "There were about 30 people in the whole world who thought we had a chance to win," Laettner said. "The players, the coaches, and the people who work with the team."

Krzyzewski showed his squad tape of the '90 final, pointing out that the Blue Devils were sick as well as tired. "Everybody just looked hollow," he said. "It was hollow watching hollow."

The message to the team was pointed. "If it's close at the end, it will be new for them. They haven't been there. You have. Keep it close and the advantage is ours."

Duke wasn't intimidated, leading early 15-6. UNLV rallied and took a 43-41 lead, but it was close, as Krzyzewski wanted. The Rebels led 74-71 with 3:51 left when Vegas point guard Greg Anthony charged into Brian Davis and collected his fifth foul.

After a UNLV basket, Duke came down the court and Hurley confidently drained a three-pointer, what was then, and remains, the biggest basket in school history. The Blue Devils had shown they weren't going away.

The defense took over, forcing a 45-second shot clock violation, the first all year on UNLV. With 1:02 left, Grant Hill hit a driving Davis for a layup and a subsequent foul. Brian made the free throw and Duke had the lead, 77-76. Davis scored 15 points, double his average.

By now UNLV was panicked. All-American Larry Johnson was fouled on a rebound. He missed both free throws with 50 seconds left, but T. Hill stepped in the lane on the second and Johnson got a third try. He made it for a 77-77 tie.

Duke held the ball until 15 seconds remained. Thomas Hill missed on a drive, but Laettner corralled the rebound and was fouled with 12.7 sec-

THOMAS HILL REBOUNDS AGAINST IOWA IN AN NCAA TOURNAMENT VICTORY.

onds left. UNLV coach Jerry Tarkanian called timeout.

"After Christian makes these free throws," Coach K said, looking at his star, "don't let (Anderson) Hunt get the ball." Hunt had scored 29 points. Laettner swished both foul shots.

The pass went to Johnson, the National Player of the Year. He wouldn't try what could have been the winning three. Instead, he passed toward center court, where Hunt had to run it down. His desperate heave didn't come close and the Blue Devils had pulled off the shocker, 79-77.

As the team was leaving the court, Hurley was riding on Buckley's back. But Krzyzewski had his hands palms down, yelling, "We have one more."

Hurley got the message immediately. He jumped down and began screaming, "One more game. One more game."

Nobody had shot better than 47 percent on Vegas all season. Duke hit 51.8, its fifth straight time of making more than half its shots. Laettner provided all kinds of defensive problems and scored 28 points. "He's really a forward," Tarkanian said. "It changed our whole defense. It was really difficult for us."

The upset sent Duke into the championship game against Kansas, which had pulled off a stunner of its own, eliminating North Carolina as UNC alumnus and longtime assistant Roy Williams got the best of Dean Smith. More embarrassing to the Tar Heels, Smith was ejected by official Pete Pavia in the closing minute when he was given a second technical foul.

Coach K was concerned about his team's emotional status after Vegas. Before practice on Sunday, he told them, "I don't like the way you're walking, the way you're talking or the way you're dressing. You guys are acting like you're big time, and, right now, you haven't done anything big-time yet."

"He got our attention," said Koubek, the lone senior starter. "After that, we weren't thinking about Saturday any more."

Duke led from start to finish against the Jayhawks. Koubek started it with a three-pointer and added another basket for his only points of the game. Grant Hill followed with an astonishing dunk, as he somehow grabbed Hurley's high pass and slammed it home for a 7-1 lead. The shot made the cover of *Sports Illustrated*.

The team was tired after the emotional UNLV game. Laettner, who had played 40 minutes, had no legs and required brief rests throughout. He did score 18 points by going 12 for 12 from the foul line.

A three by Thomas Hill gave Duke a 42-34 lead at halftime and the advantage grew to 61-47. Kansas fought back, cutting the margin to 70-65,

BOBBY HURLEY AND DUKE TOPPLED CONNECTICUT IN THE 1991 SWEET SIXTEEN.

with 35 seconds left. The Jayhawks pressed, and Thomas Hill called a timeout just before there would have been a halfcourt violation.

On the inbounds pass, Grant Hill caught Davis's eye. "I gave him a look," Grant said, "and he just nodded." Hill lofted a pass to the breaking Davis, who dunked, and Duke had secured its first NCAA championship, 72-65. Once again Duke shot well, hitting 56.1 percent.

"I'm so happy for our guys," Coach K said. "I am not sure anyone has ever played harder to work for a national championship."

Hill's pass was accurate and symbolic. A year later, he would make an even more important heave.

The next year, 1992, the challenge for Duke was far different. Although Krzyzewski never talks about defending anything—"You've won, they can't take it away from you"—the fact is that Duke, with almost everybody returning, started the season No. 1 and the team that everybody was shooting to beat.

Some 36 games later, after a very difficult schedule, injuries and other obstacles strewn along the way, the Blue Devils still were No. 1. Even in their two defeats, they never fell from the top.

Duke won the NCAA championship, and it was the first time since UCLA ended its remarkable seven-year run in 1973 that any team ever had won back-to-back titles.

From history's perspective, that was 12 years before the NCAA field was expanded to 64 teams and the teams bracketed all across the country. As great as UCLA was, the Bruins never had to do that. They always played out of the NCAA West, and only had to win two games to reach the Final Four.

Krzyzewski considered this his best team. When Duke won in '91, he said, "It was a tre-

mendous achievement, but we always were building for 1992. We knew we would have a great team then."

These Blue Devils were led by three players whose jerseys would be retired—Laettner, who posted the greatest NCAA statistical career of any player; Hurley, who would become college basketball's all-time assists leader, a mark he still holds; and the multitalented Grant Hill.

CHRISTIAN LAETTNER SEALED THE GAME WITH TWO FREE THROWS AGAINST UNDEFEATED UNLV.

The Blue Devils overcame a variety of injuries, including a broken foot by Hurley, to win. In doing so, they became only the third team ever—UCLA and Cincinnati ('59-63) were the others—to go to five consecutive Final Fours. Laettner would become the first player ever to start in the Final Four every season during his career.

There was tragedy to deal with as trainer Max Crowder, who had been on the bench for 30 years and 899 consecutive games, was diagnosed with lung cancer on December 12. He never returned

CHRISTIAN LAETTNER REBOUNDS IN THE 1991 NCAA CHAMPIONSHIP VICTORY OVER KANSAS.

scored 26 points. It was the first game for trainer Dave Engelhardt, who replaced the ailing Crowder.

Duke started the ACC season with five consecutive wins, with the only close game at Virginia, 68-62. Ahead by just two at 61-59, Hurley made the shot of the game, a three-pointer that gave the Devils the breathing room they needed. The junior guard was one for 11 before that critical shot.

The Blue Devils beat Florida State, Maryland, Georgia Tech and N.C. State, all by at least 13 points. Laettner had a season-high 33 points and 11 rebounds against Georgia Tech, which came into the game unbeaten in the ACC.

The ACC schedule was unbalanced with FSU in the league for the first time. Duke actually played the Seminoles a second time before meeting UNC for the first time. After beating Notre Dame 100-71 for the 500th win in Cameron (Laettner

to the bench, and a month after being inducted into the Duke Sports Hall of Fame, he died on May 28.

All five starters, led by Laettner's 21.5 average, increased their scoring average over the previous season. Both Hills averaged better than 14 points, Hurley more than 13 and Davis more than 11.

The season opened against East Carolina, the only game Laettner missed in his career with a bruised foot. Cherokee Parks replaced him, didn't miss a shot from the floor, and Duke won 103-75.

In their fifth game, the Blue Devils were carried into overtime by Michigan's Fab Five at Ann Arbor. Duke had a 12-point halftime lead but Michigan rallied to take a five-point margin into the last 1:28. Hurley made a three-pointer and later three foul shots as regulation ended ended in a 76-all tie.

Laettner and Chris Webber fouled out in the extra period, but Duke won 88-85 as Hurley

BRIAN DAVIS'S SIGN SUMS UP DUKE'S FIRST NATIONAL CHAMPIONSHIP.

LONGTIME TRAINER MAX CROWDER PASSED AWAY IN MAY OF 1991.

29 points), the Blue Devils were 17-0 when they played at Chapel Hill.

Hurley broke his foot midway in the first half, but played 37 minutes anyway. Seven-footers Eric Montross and Kevin Salvadori dominated inside for the No. 9 Tar Heels. Laettner had two shots roll off the rim in the closing minute of the 75-73 defeat.

Minus Hurley, Duke had a tough assignment at LSU, with All-American O'Neal. Grant Hill, at 6-8, played point guard and was spectacular. He had 16 points and six assists. The Tigers were ahead 60-59 when Laettner made back-to-back three-pointers to once again get the best of O'Neal (25 points, 12 rebounds) as Duke won a critical road game, 77-67.

Hurley missed five games, including at Georgia Tech and N.C. State. Without him, Duke struggled to edge Maryland at home, 91-89.

At Wake Forest, Duke suffered its second loss, 72-68. Missed free throws doomed the Devils. In the closing seconds, Grant Hill tried a three-quarter court pass to Laettner, but the ball went

FEBRUARY 8, 1992

Duke brought its No. 1 ranking to Baton Rouge to play LSU and its mammoth center, Shaquille O'Neal, who had been outplayed the past season at Cameron by Blue Devil center Christian Laettner.

And the Blue Devils were without point guard Bobby Hurley, who had broken his foot in Duke's first loss in the previous game at Chapel Hill against Carolina, 75-73. That defeat snapped a 23-game winning streak.

O'Neal, 7-1 and 295 pounds, had marked the game against Duke on his calendar. And the Blue Devils needed a new guard. Coach K selected 6-8 sophomore Grant Hill.

"I was a little nervous coming in here," Hill said. "Not after the game started, but at the hotel and on the bus coming over here. I played point guard before when Bobby was out against Boston U. and Canisius. I played it in high school. It was just a matter of starting."

Against No. 22 LSU and its hulking big man, Hill wound up with 16 points, nine rebounds, six assists and only three turnovers. "We slowed things down and were very patient in the halfcourt," said Hurley, who tried to watch the game with a coach's eye. "Grant's so tall, he can see over things. I told him once he should shoot the open 17-footer, but mostly I just encouraged him. He was on his own."

Duke led at halftime, 34-28, thanks to balanced scoring although O'Neal had tallied 16 points. But after another Shaq attack, the home team took a 54-49 lead midway in the second half. That was when Duke All-American Laettner took over.

The 6-11 Laettner scored 12 of his 22 points in the final 9:06 as Duke closed on a 28-13 run to win going away, 77-67. The biggest shots were a pair of three-pointers that he made after the Tigers had grabbed a 60-59 lead. O'Neal paid a price for not defending on the perimeter.

"For him to step up then, that was the turning point," said Coach K.

Meanwhile, LSU helped out by missing 10-of-13 free throws down the stretch. "It's a mental game more than it is execution," said LSU coach Dale Brown. "That's why they are No. 1 and we're striving to get there."

"He knows when we have to have it," said Duke senior Brian Davis of Laettner, his best friend and roommate. "We never worry about Christian. His shot is going to come."

Because LSU couldn't expect O'Neal to guard Laettner on the outside, the Tigers went into a zone. "We were in a 2-3 matchup and when he shot those two, I was like 'Man, who's got him?' That's how the game goes," O'Neal said.

O'Neal outscored Laettner with 25 points, and had 12 rebounds to Christian's 10, plus seven blocked shots to none. "But we got what we wanted," Laettner said.

"I was proud of the way we came together with Bobby (Hurley) out," Krzyzewski said. "I never saw a head down in the last two days. We really got together to play a terrific game."

out of bounds. The same tandem would succeed a month later in what has become one of the most improbable baskets in the history of the sport.

The night before Duke met Virginia, when Laettner's jersey was to be retired, Grant Hill sprained an ankle. But Hurley had gotten permission to suit up. He played 28 minutes in the 76-67 victory and recorded nine assists. Laettner matched his jersey number, with his parents watching, with 32 points.

Without G. Hill, Duke rallied in the second half to win at UCLA. "Laettner wouldn't let us lose," Coach K said.

That was followed by a game at Clemson, and four minutes into the second half, Coach K pulled all his starters with Duke trailing 66-51 and playing little defense. The reserves outscored the Tigers 8-2, and the starters returned to pull

out a 98-97 victory as Davis had a career-high 30 points.

Typically of the way the entire year went, the Duke bus had to pull into the bowels of Littlejohn Coliseum to enable the players to avoid the crowd gathered outside. Numerous cars followed the bus to the Greenville-Spartanburg airport some 50 miles away. Because of the popularity of Laettner, Hurley, Grant Hill and others, traveling with Duke that season had all the aspects of being with the Beatles.

In other road games, the Duke team had to be sneaked out the back of buildings, so fanatic was the following. The Blue Devils weren't just No. 1 in the polls, but also with fandom.

The regular-season finale at home against North Carolina featured 35 points by UNC's Hubert Davis, but Duke turned the tables on the

CHRISTIAN LAETTNER LED DUKE TO TWO VICTORIES OVER SHAQUILLE O'NEAL AND LSU.

Heels as an 18-6 run in the closing minutes produced an 89-77 win. Laettner scored 26 in his farewell, Hurley was 100 percent healthy, and Hill returned to the lineup for 21 minutes.

The Cameron Crazies rushed the court, after which Laettner and Davis said their thank-yous. In their careers, Duke was 58-2 at home.

The ACC Tournament began with a tough 94-87 win over last-place Maryland. Laettner continued his scoring with 33 points, while Hurley had 16 points, 13 assists and one turnover.

The Blue Devils advanced to the finals by building an 18-point halftime lead on Georgia Tech in winning 89-76, after which they crushed North Carolina, 94-74, for the championship. Laettner had 25 points, including five of eight from three-point range, plus 10 rebounds and seven steals. Grant Hill made all eight shots, while Hurley handed out 11 assists.

"I didn't think they could play better than they did against us in Durham," said Dean Smith. "But they did. They were just remarkable."

All eyes were on No. 1 Duke as the NCAAs began. After blitzing outmanned Campbell in the opener, 82-56, the Devils advanced to the Sweet 16 with a 75-62 victory over Iowa. The score was deceiving; Duke led at halftime, 48-24.

The first game of the East Regional in Philadelphia was an emotional one for Hurley, who played head to head against brother Danny of Seton Hall. It was the first time they had played on opposite sides in a game that counted. It was a difficult struggle for Bobby, who scored four points with seven assists, but six turnovers.

The other five Devils who played significant minutes all were in double figures as Duke rolled into the

Elite Eight, 81-69. "I'm just glad it's over and we won," said a relieved Hurley.

That sent the Blue Devils into the regional finals against Kentucky, a meeting of basketball bluebloods—not to mention similar school colors. Duke's scintillating 104-103 overtime victory was called then—few dispute it now—"the greatest college game ever played."

The Blue Devils were favored, but the seniors on the Kentucky team were equally accustomed to winning big games, and they weren't about to be intimidated. The quality of the game was extraordinary. Duke shot 65.4 percent, making 34 of 52 shots plus 28 of 34 free throws, and needed every one. Kentucky shot 56.9 percent and forced 20 turnovers.

There also was controversy, with Laettner putting his foot squarely on the chest of a fallen Aminu Timberlake, for which he was assessed a technical foul.

The Blue Devils led 50-45 after one half, pushed that to 12 points, and then were harassed by an effective UK press. The Wildcats took the lead, 89-87, before Davis tied it. With 1:03 left,

BOBBY HURLEY AND MIKE KRZYZEWSKI ALWAYS SEEMED TO BE IN SYNC.

CHRISTIAN LAETTNER FIRES "THE SHOT" AGAINST KENTUCKY IN WHAT MANY CONSIDER THE GREATEST GAME EVER PLAYED.

Thomas Hill scored to make it 93-93 and the game went into overtime.

Tied at 98, Duke took the lead when Laettner somehow avoided two defenders and made a jumper as the time clock expired. With 19.6 seconds left, Jamal Mashburn made a layup, was fouled, and the three-point play gave the 'Cats the lead, 101-100. It was merely setting the stage for the dramatic ending.

Laettner was fouled with 7.8 seconds to play and made them both on what was to be an amazing night of shooting. But Kentucky wasn't dead. After a timeout, guard Sean Woods drove by Hurley, hooked the ball up over the leaping Laettner, and it banked in for a 103-102 lead. There were 2.1 seconds to play and Duke's chances of another title appeared dead.

As the team came to the bench after the time-out called by Hurley, Coach K greeted his players with this positive response, "We're going to win this game, and here's how we're going to do it." Did he believe it? It doesn't matter. He knew his players required confidence.

Actually, THE PLAY had been tried before, at Wake Forest, and failed. It was to be a pass by Grant Hill to Laettner, who was to flash to the foul line, some 70 feet away. Unlike the Wake game, Kentucky left Hill uncovered, and he had a clear view of his objective.

Laettner was guarded by John Pelphrey and Deron Feldhaus, each 6-6. They actually backed off, making sure there was no foul, knowing that Laettner hadn't missed.

The pass was on target. Laettner actually had time to dribble left, then spin and shoot an 18-

foot jumper that was on target all the way as the clock hit 0:00. It has become the most famous shot in collegiate history, shown again and again on television and in countless newspapers and magazines.

For the game, Laettner was perfect—10-10 from the floor, the same from the foul line, for 31 points. Nobody in the history of the game ever made so many critical NCAA tournament shots—outplaying Mourning as a freshman, the buzzer-beater against UConn as a sophomore, and the winning free throws against UNLV as a junior. Now he had even outdone himself.

The Philadelphia Spectrum was a madhouse. Coach K immediately went on the Kentucky radio network with Hall of Fame announcer Cawood Ledford and praised the Wildcats for their play and their spirit.

Louisville columnist Rick Bozich penned, "The game ends. The story never will. The dream wilts. The legacy blossoms. The moment fades. The memories multiply. Ship the videotape to the Basketball Hall of Fame. This is the game's centennial season. We may dribble 100 years more before we see another game that fills an arena with more energy."

According to Boston columnist Bob Ryan, "There have been noted upsets. There have been countless games played at a high level and for great stakes. But no other college game has ever combined, in one package, this much meaning, this much expertise and this much drama. Duke-Kentucky was the greatest college game of them all."

In reality, however, the victory just sent the Blue Devils back to the Final Four, where awaiting would be Indiana, coached by Bob Knight, Krzyzewski's mentor.

Coach K was fearful, accurately as it developed, that Laettner would be emotionally drained for the Final Four. He told Hurley, who had fresh legs because of his injury absence, that he would have to accelerate his offense.

In the first half, had it not been for Hurley, the Blue Devils would have been blown out. They trailed by as much as 12 points, 39-27, but Hurley's five three-pointers got his team to within 42-37 at the break.

Duke started the last half with a surge, outscoring the Hoosiers 21-3 to make it 58-45. It was 69-61 with less than two minutes to play when Indiana began fouling reserve Marty Clark, who was playing because Davis had sprained his ankle. Clark hit five of six shots in the clutch.

For Indiana, the hero was sophomore Todd Leary, so obscure that he had not been mentioned in the scouting report. He made three consecutive three-pointers and suddenly it was 78-75. A Duke turnover gave the Hoosiers a chance to tie, but Thomas Hill's defense forced Leary to pass the ball to Jamal Meeks, who missed from the corner.

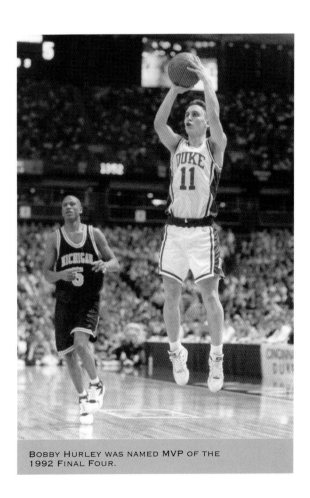

BOBBY HURLEY WAS NAMED MVP OF THE 1992 FINAL FOUR.

CHRISTIAN LAETTNER HELPED DUKE BECOME THE NCAA'S FIRST BACK-TO-BACK CHAMPION SINCE UCLA.

an easy basket, got 12 more points and no turnovers, and wound up as the leading scorer with 19 points.

Duke limited Michigan to 20 second-half points and 29-percent shooting. The Devils scored on their final 12 possessions, punctuated when G. Hill drove under the basket, spun, and hit a monster slam. The score was 71-51, and the repeat championship, the only one ever in the era of the 64/65 team field, was achieved.

"This is the greatest year I've ever had in coaching," said Krzyzewski. "To be ranked number one all year, to do all the things these guys did, they deserve this."

According to losing coach Steve Fisher, "What Mike has done, given the way the tournament has changed, must compare favorably with what John Wooden did at UCLA. You just can't do what they have done. Yet they have done it. It is an incredible achievement."

USA Today's Steve Weiberg opined, "This is what 100 years of basketball evolution has produced: Duke—The Perfect Program."

Duke closed it out 81-78 on free throws by Tony Lang and Cherokee Parks. Hurley, spurred on by his coach's request, had 26 points, including six baskets from beyond the arc. Laettner played 39 minutes, but was two for eight from the floor and four for seven from the foul line, a dead giveaway that his tank was running on empty. It was the only game all season that the National Player of the Year didn't score in double figures.

Michigan's freshmen, the Fab Five, were the other finalists. They had no fear of Duke, having carried the Devils into overtime in December.

Grant Hill returned to the lineup for Davis. Laettner still was missing offensively. He had seven turnovers and five points in the first half as the Wolverines led, 31-30.

Krzyzewski told Hurley to get Laettner involved immediately in the offense. He scored

BACK-TO-BACK PLAQUES REFLECT DUKE'S UNCOMMON SUCCESS.

CHAPTER

11

CHANGE AHEAD

Things were different in 1993. Laettner, holder of numerous NCAA records, was gone to the pros. But Duke still would be good, especially with All-Americans like Hurley and Grant Hill.

In search of its sixth consecutive Final Four, the Blue Devils instead fell apart at the end of the season following an injury to Hill. When Duke was beaten by California and Jason Kidd in the second round of the NCAA, the streak of Sweet 16 appearances ended at seven.

By any other standard other than the one it had developed, the Blue Devils had a fine season. They finished 24-8 and ranked 10th in the polls. That was the low mark in a year in which Duke again had been No. 1 for five weeks.

For those who had grown accustomed to the winning, the season began normally enough—a sixth straight win, 79-68, over No. 1 Michigan in the second game. And Duke won the Maui Classic en route to a 10-0 start.

Almost every defeat in a season in which the ACC had five teams rated in the top 18 ended a lengthy streak for the Blue Devils. Even as their Sweet 16 skein stopped, the league sent four teams into the third round and eventually North Carolina would win the championship.

It was a bad year to have any flaws, which Duke did. But the critical problem was an injury to superstar Grant Hill late in the campaign. He

GRANT HILL SCORES AGAINST CALIFORNIA IN THE 1993 NCAA TOURNAMENT.

missed six games before returning for the ACC Tournament. But he wasn't ready, and neither were the Blue Devils. They lost in the opening round to sixth-seed Georgia Tech, which went on to win the title.

For Duke, the problem was "Never on Sunday." The unbeaten Devils carried a 23-game winning streak to Atlanta and lost to Georgia Tech, 80-79. The game was played on Sunday.

By the time Virginia, the nation's last undefeated team, visited the next Sunday, Duke also had played at Wake Forest on Wednesday and No. 13 Iowa had come to Durham on Saturday. Although Duke won, both games were grueling, especially the one with the Hawkeyes.

UVA took every advantage of Duke's fatigue. The Cavaliers led the entire game, won 77-68, and ended a streak of 36 consecutive home wins. Duke had not lost in nearly three years in Cameron. "I never thought I'd lose another home game," said Hurley, who lost three in his career.

One week later, again on Sunday, Duke lost again. This time it was in overtime at Florida State, 89-88, as reserve Byron Wells, playing because starter Doug Edwards had fouled out, hit a three-pointer from the corner with 3.7 seconds left for the victory. "It was our biggest victory ever," said FSU coach Pat Kennedy, "because that was the one team we hadn't beaten."

Duke regained form and won six straight, hiking its record to 19-3, including an 81-67 belting of UNC and a 10-point revenge win over Georgia Tech. That set up a home game against Wake Forest, a team it had beaten by 27 points in Winston-Salem.

Duke was ahead early when Grant Hill went down with an injured big toe. Duke's hopes for a third national championship went with him. Without Hill to guard him, the Deac's massive Rodney Rogers went wild, scoring a career-high 35 points as Wake Forest won, 98-86.

The Blue Devils never recovered. They lost their next game at Virginia, and the finale at UNC, 83-69, a virtual reversal of the first match. Duke finished the regular season 10-6 and 23-6 in an ACC in which five teams won at least 21 games and tournament champ Georgia Tech won 19.

Hill played in the ACC Tournament after missing six games and scored 14 points, but neither he nor any of his teammates could slow down James Forrest. The eventual MVP (he scored 80 points in three games) made 13 of 15 shots and had 27 points as the Blue Devils were eliminated, 69-66. Tech shot better than 55 percent; Duke hit 40 percent.

The Devils were the No. 3 seed in the NCAA Midwest. After beating Southern Illinois, 105-70, the injury bug struck again. Parks sprained his ankle in the first half against California and didn't return. Hill was still hobbled. Hurley had a career night in his collegiate finale, scoring 32 points with seven threes, but it wasn't enough. Kidd carried the Bears to an 82-77 victory.

The '94 season certainly promised to be different. In a program where the point guard—Dawkins, Amaker, Snyder, Hurley—had been prominent, suddenly Duke didn't have one.

GRANT HILL RETURNED FROM INJURY TO PLAY IN THE 1993 ACC TOURNAMENT.

IN 2011 JEFF CAPEL RETURNED TO DUKE AS AN ASSISTANT COACH.

from a team that had gone to the NCAA finals on consecutive years.

The Wolverines were rated fourth nationally, just ahead of Duke.

The Blue Devils shut down everybody except Jalen Rose (31 points) and Juwan Howard (20) and won, 73-63, by shooting better than 55 percent.

The day after the Michigan game, Krzyzewski learned of the near-fatal accident of Hurley, a rookie with the Sacramento Kings, whose truck had been slammed on a lonely road after a game. The other truck didn't have its lights on, and Hurley was ejected into a pool of water.

Only the appearance of teammate Mike Peplowski and immediate medical service at a nearby hospital saved his life. It shook the Duke community, and Coach K flew to California to see his former star player. Although Hurley eventually recovered and returned to the NBA, his career was effectively prematurely ended as he never regained the quickness that was the six-foot guard's primary physical attribute.

Duke took a 10-day break, won at Iowa, and then was off another week for Christmas. By the time the Devils opened ACC play at Clemson, they had played only seven games.

The Iowa game, coming as it did after Hurley's accident, was a bonding of programs. Two days after the Hawkeyes lost at Duke the previous year, forward Chris Street was killed in an accident. It served as a reminder that even basketball stars were not invulnerable.

As the ACC season began, Coach K said he'd still continue to experiment. "We'll be experimenting until the season is over," he said. With Capel and Collins in the backcourt, Hill played more often up front, and, as Collins said, "Ball handling is done by committee."

The first stumble came at home against Wake Forest, when a three-point play by Randolph Childress with nine seconds left gave the Deacs a 69-68 victory.

But the Blue Devils made do, with All-America 6-8 senior Grant Hill playing the role that Bobby Hurley had vacated. He did it so well that, after a year's absence, Duke returned to the Final Four again, this time in Charlotte, with President Bill Clinton on hand to cheer on homestate Arkansas.

It was the sixth Final Four in seven years and the seventh in nine for the Blue Devils, completing a remarkable run that knew no peer in the post-1985 era of 64 team NCAA fields and balanced regionals, rather than geographic placements.

Coach K was uncertain at the beginning, using a big lineup that included Hill, Cherokee Parks, Eric Meek and Tony Lang along with sophomore Chris Collins. After six games, freshman Jeff Capel replaced Meek to provide more balance.

Duke started well with 10 straight wins. The most important came at Michigan. The Fab Five had been reduced by one as Chris Webber turned pro, but there were still four veterans remaining

Grant Hill forces Wake Forest's Randolph Childress to adjust his shot.

Duke won its next five games, running the record to 15-1, and became the sixth team to be ranked No. 1 in the polls. UNC was second, and for the first time in the long rivalry, the teams were 1-2 when they played. Considering that they had won the three previous NCAA titles, that was surprising.

The first half was a shootout. Duke hit 64 percent and led 40-38 over the Tar Heels, who made 54.5 percent. In the second half, the Devils missed 19 of their first 24 attempts, fell behind by 13, and lost 89-78.

Three games later, Duke lost at Wake Forest, 78-69. In a series in which the Devils have a 150-74 lead, they would lose nine in a row to Tim Duncan, then win the next 14 after he graduated. Hill had to do it all. He played 40 minutes and guarded Childress for 37 of them. He scored 24 points, had a career-high 13 rebounds, six assists, three steals and two turnovers. He also tired and shot poorly in the second half as Wake rallied to win.

But the team rebounded to win five straight, making its record 22-3, including a 59-47 victory over No. 8 Temple when Hill's jersey was retired.

Duke clinched the regular-season title with a win at Maryland, 73-69. Playing before family and friends, Hill had 19 points, six rebounds, eight assists and four blocks. "I'm still working on the play where he can pass the ball to himself," Coach K said.

North Carolina came to Cameron for the finale and won again, 87-77. The Heels shot 60 percent in the second half with two turnovers. "We aren't really this good," claimed Dean Smith.

The ACC Tournament in Charlotte thus began with Duke the top seed and Carolina as the favorite. It was accurate. After beating Clemson, the Blue Devils were upset in the semifinals by a Virginia team it had beaten twice, once by 30 points.

There was little emotion, and a weary Hill missed shots and turned the ball over in the final four minutes of the 66-61 defeat. Duke's 36 percent shooting was its worst of the season. "Today

Chris Collins was an emotional leader for the Blue Devils.

I tried and failed," Hill said. "You just have to accept it and move on."

"Sometimes we try to put everything on Grant's back," said freshman Capel. "We can't continue to do that."

Hill got help in the first two rounds of the NCAAs at St. Petersburg, Florida. In an 82-70 win over Texas Southern, Collins hit four three-pointers in the first half and five overall with 20 points. Lang had 18, Hill a modest 11.

Hill came back with 25 points against Michigan State, but Parks (24) and Lang (16) came up big as Duke won 85-74 on a night when Boston College upset Carolina and Marquette beat Kentucky, which had been anticipating a rematch of '92 with the Blue Devils.

Against Marquette, "It seemed there were 10 Grant Hills out there," said Marty Clark. The Warriors scored the first nine points, after which Hill dominated in the 59-49 defensive struggle. He had 16 of his 22 points in the last half, including a couple of monster dunks that sent the Devils into the regional final against top-seeded Purdue.

JEFF CAPEL WAS A FOUR-YEAR STARTER.

Purdue featured the National Player of the Year (Hill was second) in Glenn "Big Dog" Robinson, who scored 44 points against Kansas in the Sweet 16 and was averaging nearly 31. He got 13 against Duke, including two in a six-minute span when Hill had to sit with four fouls.

Capel was the offensive spark with 19 points, but this was a game in which Hill showed the Big Dog didn't have enough bark. "We knew we could get to the Final Four," he said. "We went out there and we did it."

In Charlotte, No. 6 Duke squared off with No. 14 Florida while Arkansas, top-rated most of the season and No. 2 in the last poll, played No. 9 Arizona.

The big news was that Clinton attended, causing a logistical nightmare and metal detectors at every entrance. The first president ever at a Final Four saw his Razorbacks upend Arizona, 81-72.

Duke advanced to its fourth championship game in five years with a rally against Florida. The Gators led by 13 in the first half and 39-32 at in-

DUKE RETURNED TO THE NCAA CHAMPIONSHIP GAME IN 1994.

termission. "Grant decided his career wasn't over," said Coach K. With Hill scoring 25 points, the Blue Devils came back to win, 70-65.

Two nights later, Clinton was smiling in the hallway of the Charlotte Coliseum after Arkansas won its first title, 76-72. Ten players deep, the Hogs had to fight every inch of the way. Duke used just seven men, including Meek, who played sparingly.

The Blue Devils, down 34-33 at halftime, took a 10-point lead early in the second half as Collins hit a couple of his four three-pointers. But Duke couldn't hold on. Despite 15 points from Lang and 14 rebounds from a fatigued Hill, it came down to a final shot.

Scottie Thurman swished a three from the wing with the score tied 70-70 in the closing seconds. Lang was a mere inch or so away from blocking the shot. After Collins missed a three at the other end, Arkansas rebounded, got fouled, and won the crown, 76-72.

"We went absolutely as far as we could," Krzyzewski said.

"I thought we did a lot for a team that didn't have a point guard, a power forward or much depth," said Hill. Later, Coach K would say that Grant was his greatest player. Lest there be controversy, "Laettner and Hurley told me that Grant was better than they were."

In the summer of 1994, Krzyzewski believed that he had suffered from a pulled hamstring. For three months, that's what he was treated for by medical people. But it didn't get any better, and as he details in his book, *Leading with the Heart* with Donald Phillips, wife Mickie finally persuaded him to go to his doctors because pulled hamstrings don't last that long.

Coach K was told he had a disk problem in his back and that the exercises he had been doing for the hamstring were only making it worse.

But a few weeks later, the disk ruptured on a recruiting trip to Kansas City. Prescriptions and a series of shots didn't help, and when Coach K went to see a neurosurgeon, when he stood on his toes with his weight on his left leg, he collapsed to the floor. He had lost his left calf muscle, and two days later, on October 23, eight days into fall practice, he had surgery to repair a severely herniated disk.

As he began to feel better, Krzyzewski explored the possibility of returning to practice. He told the doctors he was feeling pretty good—and he was determined. The physicians agreed, if the coach would get a special chair and proceed on a limited basis.

Within 10 days of the surgery, he was back at practice. It was the wrong decision. Coach K lost weight. He couldn't sleep. He was exhausted all the time. But he refused to stop working.

On the lengthy flight home from the Rainbow Classic in Hawaii, the problems became over-

ANTONIO LANG FIGHTS FOR A REBOUND AGAINST ARKANSAS IN THE NATIONAL CHAMPIONSHIP GAME.

MIKE KRZYZEWSKI SAT OUT THE FINAL 19 GAMES OF THE 1994-95 SEASON WITH EXHAUSTION AND BACK PROBLEMS.

whelming. He couldn't get comfortable. His back was killing him. He got no sleep. He coached two more games, the second being a home loss to Clemson. Physically, he was feeling worse. He insisted he was going to the game at Georgia Tech, but Mickie issued a mandate. Her husband, who could barely walk, needed help. She made an appointment with Dr. John Feagin at Duke Sports Medicine. The time was to be 2:30—the start of practice.

Krzyzewski protested, but Mickie insisted. And she won. Feagin told him he was going straight to the hospital. Coach K asked to be allowed to tell his coaches. Feagin agreed, "But make it quick." The military background came to the forefront as he apologized for not making the upcoming Georgia Tech game. "I feel like I'm deserting you guys," he said. But they understood. He was in no condition to continue to work.

Coach K underwent a battery of tests. He didn't have the cancer that had killed his friend Jim Valvano the previous year. The team of doctors agreed it was a case of a man trying to do too much, too soon. He wanted to rejoin his team;

the five doctors collectively told him he had to take two weeks off. It was January 8.

Things did not improve. As he reported in his book, the doctors told him the problem was that he wasn't trying to get better, he was trying to get back to his job. The team had lost five straight games, including a double-overtime at home against Virginia when it blew a 25-point lead.

His medical crew told him, "You're just making things worse. We have to reverse this process right now. You're out for the whole year. We don't want you to think about coming back until next year." The ex-Army captain was shocked—and relieved. Somebody had told him what he needed to hear, not what he wanted to hear.

Krzyzewski went to see Butters, the man who had hired him. "If you want me to resign, I'll understand completely," he said. Butters listened, then told him, "Mike, this is your job whenever you're ready to come back. I don't want anybody else as Duke's basketball coach."

It was then Coach K began to get better, but as he recuperated, he realized he would have to change, and that would be difficult. But the man who went to five straight Final Fours (seven of nine) and won two national championships had been attempting to do too much. As difficult as it would be, he had to learn to say no.

There were so many requests—of all kinds—that time management, something Krzyzewski always emphasized with his players, had gotten out of whack. He wrote, "If I teach it, I'd better be able to do it myself." He knew he couldn't do it alone, so much of the burden of managing his schedule fell on sports information director Mike Cragg (now head of the Legacy Fund) and executive assistant Gerry Brown.

The team, even with eventual first-round draft picks Cherokee Parks and Trajan Langdon, never recovered the lost momentum. It lost close game after close game—two in double overtime, including a classic with North Carolina, 102-100;

CHEROKEE PARKS RANKS THIRD AMONG THE SCHOOL'S ALL-TIME BLOCKED SHOTS LEADERS.

another by one point; two others by two points; and one by three.

The program that played for the national championship in 1994 finished in last place in the ACC in 1995 with a 2-14 record, 13-18 overall. Duke had fallen from the top to the bottom with Krzyzewski sidelined.

"With Coach K not there, it was very easy for us to fragment and become individuals," said senior Chris Collins on the eve of the 1995-96 season. "It was a tough experience. It really makes you grow up a lot."

"It's not just me being back," Krzyzewski said. "You have to have one leader. It's just that these kids need one leader for an entire year. Whenever a leader goes down, there is some chaos." The coach was back. His program wasn't. Duke was selected sixth in the preseason by one publication and fifth by another. And the work days still were long; they just weren't unreasonable.

"Even as I was allowing myself to be conned into thinking he was Superman," Mickie said,

"then I finally realized he's not handling it. He's falling apart."

The changes included no meetings at the Krzyzewski home after games to watch film until the wee hours. The game reviews were completed earlier and the coach got needed rest. A special phone line was installed at Mickie's urging so that family members were always able to communicate, and they hired a time-management counselor to ensure some type of normalcy in their lives.

Coach K scaled back his speaking engagements and appearances. He accommodated some interview requests while in the car, or in conference-call settings. "I feel like I have better balance for it now," he said.

But '96 proved to be a difficult year. Langdon, a double-figure scorer as a freshman, had not recovered from a summer leg injury and had to be redshirted. Starting forward Tony Moore, a senior, was ruled academically ineligible after the first semester. Duke's depth suddenly went from suspect to non-existent.

The team would make it back to the NCAAs, a Krzyzewski priority. It finished 18-13, including 8-8 in the ACC after a 4-7 start. A five-game winning streak was propelled by a scoring outburst from Collins, who then was injured against UNC. Duke would lose in the first round of the ACC Tournament to Maryland and the first round of the NCAAs to Eastern Michigan.

The season began upbeat.

Krzyzewski resisted the rebuilding tag people wanted to place on Duke. "That gives you an excuse," he said. "But we're not a very big team. We're not a very strong team. There's more insecurity in our program right now than there has been in over a decade."

As if to prove the point, Illinois came to Cameron and ended Duke's streak of 95 straight wins against non-ACC foes, something that had lasted 12 years, 10 months and 20 days. "I never paid any attention to that streak," Coach K said.

"The most important streak for us was two national championships in a row."

Duke started the ACC season by losing its first four games. Depth was a problem; there were just eight recruited players and seven played. The Devils led by 14, 15 and 12 points in the first three games and in all four at halftime. At Virginia, they were ahead 62-57 with six and a half minutes left and got outscored 20-4. They missed 10 straight shots. "I can definitely remember what it's like to win," Collins said. "We realized coming into this season it wasn't going to happen overnight."

The losing streak finally ended at N.C. State with a fortunate bounce. Collins took a 30-footer with five seconds left that bounced three times off the rim and fell through for a 71-70 victory. But, after a win against Florida State, Duke dropped one-pointers to Temple and UNC.

A two-point defeat in overtime at Georgia Tech and the eighth straight loss to Tim Duncan and Wake Forest left the Devils at 13-10, including 4-7 in the ACC. Any postseason hopes appeared attached to the NIT.

Coach K went to Collins, his only senior, and said, "For the rest of the season, I want you to play without thinking. I want you to follow your instincts. If you've got a shot when you cross half-court, I want you to take it. Don't be afraid to fail. Act like it's impossible to fail."

In the next five games, Collins played like a man possessed. He scored 23 points against Virginia, 12 against N.C. State, 27 against Florida State, 27 against UCLA and another 27 against Maryland. He had 18 points in 25 minutes against Carolina, then hurt his foot again and had to sit as Duke lost. But the 8-8 ACC record, even with a first-round ACC Tournament loss, got the Devils that elusive NCAA bid.

Without Collins, they had no chance in the NCAAs, but at least that goal had been achieved. The road to recovery had begun.

CHRIS COLLINS HELPED LEAD DUKE BACK TO THE NCAA TOURNAMENT.

The 1996-97 team was a vast improvement over the previous year, finishing first in the regular season. But the failure to finish strong spoiled the comeback, as Duke lost four of its last six games, including at UNC, in the opening round of the ACC Tournament to play-in survivor N.C. State, and to Providence in the second round of the NCAA Tournament.

The record was 24-9, with an eighth-place finish in the polls. But the real excitement was provided during recruiting. Duke landed the No. 1 class in the nation with Shane Battier, Elton Brand, William Avery and Chris Burgess. For once, the recruiting gurus were close to correct. This wasn't the Fab Five, they said. In that respect they were wrong—it was better.

For the first time in history, a school signed two performers who would win National Player of the Year honors. Brand was a unanimous choice in

St. John's transfer Roshown McLeod became an All-American.

1999, and Battier won every award in '01 except one, which went to teammate Jason Williams. Avery was to become a first-round NBA draft pick.

Still, it was a class that established another first—Duke players going early to the NBA. And, following a sophomore season in '99 in which the team finished 37-2 after losing to Connecticut in the NCAA final, only Battier remained in Durham. Burgess transferred to Utah, was injured much of his career, and never came close to the projections that made him the nation's top recruit according to some experts in the fall of 1996.

No matter what eventually happened, however, the Blue Devils were on the way back to dominance. They made progress in '97, but injuries, lack of quality big men and the absence of a superstar doomed the finish. By the end of the season, the Blue Devils were starting four perimeter players and 6-8 transfer Roshown McLeod.

Duke's inability to handle an opposing power forward—or to rebound well as a team—was exposed in the preseason NIT finals, when the Blue Devils were ahead by six at halftime against Indiana—and Bob Knight—and then were taken apart by Andrae Patterson. The 6-8 Patterson scored 15 points in a row in the second half (39 overall) as the Hoosiers won, 85-69. Krzyzewski tried five different defenders on him, and none got the job done. It was a precursor of the future.

Lineup changes were the order of the day. Some were dictated by injuries (Langdon, Ricky Price) and others by slumps (Capel, Newton). Carmen Wallace came off the bench to save Duke in its ACC opener, an overtime win against Florida State. But nobody could stop 300-pound Robert "Tractor" Traylor from dunking with 6.2 seconds left as Michigan rallied to win in Cameron, 62-61.

The Blue Devils did win at No. 4 Villanova as Price and Capel, breaking slumps, combined for five three-pointers. That was to become the weapon of choice, as Duke never developed an inside game. As the season progressed, Langdon and Capel were the most consistent, McLeod fit in nicely, and Newton's play regressed. Although Duke had nine players who appeared in 30 or more games, this was among the smallest teams ever for Krzyzewski.

As ACC play started, Duke lost at fifth-ranked Clemson in overtime, and was squashed at home by No. 2 Wake Forest and Duncan, 81-69. It was the ninth win in a row in the series for the Deacs, and Duncan was 8-0 to that point in his career against the Devils.

But Krzyzewski finally had his team where he wanted it. Duke won 11 of its next 12 games, losing only at No. 7 Maryland. The ACC had five teams in the Top 20 in one of its most competitive seasons. Following the 74-70 loss at College Park, the Devils defeated North Carolina at home and ran off seven straight victories.

RICKY PRICE WAS A FOUR-TIME LETTERWINNER.

17 threes on 34 tries. Steve Wojciechowski hit six of seven.

Langdon was All-ACC but slumped at the end. Wojo came on strong to make second team and Krzyzewski was the ACC Coach of the Year. None of that saved Duke in the league tournament, where the Blue Devils became only the second No. 1 seed to lose to No. 8, N.C. State, 66-60.

The season that had looked so good only three weeks before ended in the second round of the Southeast Regional at Charlotte. After squeaking past No. 15 seed Murray State by three points, Duke couldn't handle Providence forward Austin Croshere and was eliminated, 98-87. The lack of a go-to superstar was an obvious problem.

But help was on the way. Their names were Elton Brand and Shane Battier.

The most impressive was at Wake Forest, 73-68. Coach K went with a lineup switch, benching Newton and using 6-6 freshman Chris Carrawell as the defacto center to guard Duncan. Wake's All-American made 11 of 13 shots and had 26 points, but only seven rebounds. Meanwhile, the defense negated everybody else. Duke led most of the game, fell behind briefly at 62-60 but regained the lead for good when McLeod broke a tie with a three-pointer. Five Langdon free throws gave the Devils their best win since Krzyzewski returned to coaching.

Duke ran its record to 22-5 before losing at UCLA, but beat Maryland at home to clinch the regular season title, a game ahead of UNC and Wake Forest.

The loss at UCLA, where Duke was killed on the boards, was a sign of things to come. In the finale at UNC, the Blue Devils couldn't match Carolina's height and got outrebounded, 49-18. Duke lost 91-85 despite making a school-record

STEVE WOJCIECHOWSKI WAS A SECOND TEAM ALL-ACC SELECTION.

CHAPTER 12

CHANGING TIMES

The three-year period from 1998 until 2000 was perhaps the most tumultuous—and among the most successful—in Duke basketball history.

In the middle season, three Duke players, two of them unexpectedly, defected early to the NBA. Although the process had been going on for years, this was the first time it had impacted the Blue Devils. Until then, all the Duke superstars—Gminski, Dawkins, Ferry, Laettner, Hurley and Hill—had remained four years and graduated with their class.

But when sophomore center Elton Brand, the unanimous 1999 National Player of the Year, announced he was leaving, he became the first Duke player to do so. Brand, who left with Coach K's blessing, was the top pick in the NBA Draft.

Shortly, sophomore William Avery and freshman Corey Maggette also said they were leaving school early. And sophomore big man Chris Burgess transferred to Utah. All of this occurred as Krzyzewski was restricted to his house following hip replacement surgery.

Senior Trajan Langdon also was selected in the '99 draft, and Duke became the first school ever to have four players picked in the first round,

TRAJAN LANGDON WAS A TWO-TIME ALL-AMERICAN.

three of them (Brand, Langdon and Maggette) lottery selections.

The projection that Duke would fall dramatically in 2000 because of the loss of personnel never was realized. That team, led by senior Chris

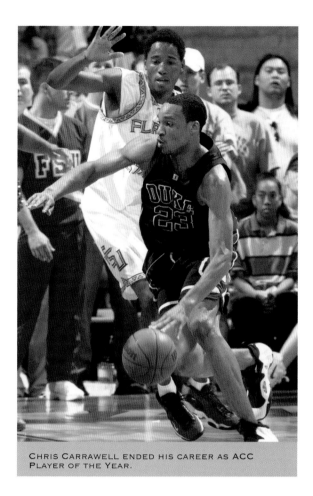

CHRIS CARRAWELL ENDED HIS CAREER AS ACC PLAYER OF THE YEAR.

rated No. 1 for seven weeks. The next year, Duke started as No. 1, fell to No. 4 following its only regular-season defeat at the hands of Cincinnati in Alaska, but regained the No. 1 ranking for the final five weeks of the poll.

After the departure of all the underclassmen, Duke started the 2000 campaign ranked 10th and dropped immediately to 18th after losing a pair of games in Madison Square Garden to begin the schedule. By the time the poll concluded at the end of the regular season, the Blue Devils had made a stunning surge to No. 1. They have remained nationally ranked in every poll from the start of the 1997 season until now, a period of 148 weeks over eight consecutive years.

The Blue Devils held their first Midnight Madness, October 18, 1997, for ESPN and with Dick Vitale on hand. "I'm about as excited as I've ever been," Coach K said. "There's a lot more to work with." It was the 18th season for Krzyzewski, who became the dean in the ACC when the other Dean, UNC's Smith, suddenly re-

Carrawell and junior Shane Battier, won the ACC regular season and tournament championships and advanced to the NCAA Sweet 16.

In the years 1998-2000, Duke won more games than ever before in a similar period. The team finished 98-11, lost only two ACC regular-season games in 48 tries and won a pair of league championships. The '98 team went to the South Regional finals and the '99 squad was ranked No. 1 and played for the national championship against Connecticut.

At home, Duke won 39 consecutive games in Cameron (the streak reached a record 46 games, including a seven-game carryover from '97). The Blue Devils had reestablished themselves as the nation's preeminent basketball program, a status they continue to hold.

The '98 squad started the season ranked No. 3 and never fell below that. The Blue Devils were

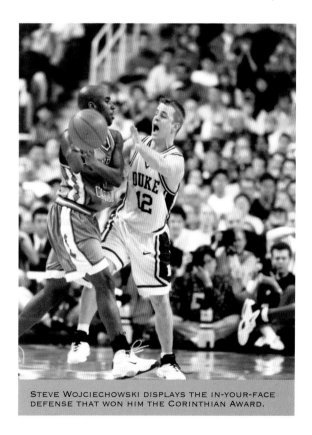

STEVE WOJCIECHOWSKI DISPLAYS THE IN-YOUR-FACE DEFENSE THAT WON HIM THE CORINTHIAN AWARD.

If you, the fan, assume that Duke games will be on television every time, you are correct. At least that was the case in 2003-2004, when all 29 regular-season contests were on TV. Plus the ACC Tournament and the NCAAs.

Duke is the darling of the networks, a fact that does not sit well with its critics. Here's why:

No basketball team on any level in the history of American sports ever has had a higher percentage of its games carried on national TV as Duke did in its 99th season (90 percent). The lone games not on ABC, CBS, Fox, ESPN or ESPN2 were the Detroit opener (Fox Sports South), Fairfield and the home game with N.C. State (Raycom/Jefferson Pilot).

"Duke is the Yankees," CBS senior vice president for programming Mike Aresco told *USA Today*. "When they play a competitive game, ratings soar."

To give you some comparison, the five teams that trailed Duke in the most TV appearances in '03-04 were all from the NBA (where they play 82 games and the season runs until late April)—Dallas Mavericks 23, Los Angeles Lakers 22, Houston Rockets 22, Sacramento Kings 21 and the San Antonio Spurs 19.

The most regular-season appearances on national TV among college teams wasn't even close. After Duke's 26 games came Arizona (16), North Carolina (16), Michigan State (15) and four schools tied at 14.

That's coast-to-coast coverage, from Alaska to New York, from Florida to Chicago. If you are a Duke supporter who doesn't live in North Carolina and is fortunate enough to have a ticket into Cameron, you always can follow the Blue Devils.

This is not a recent phenomenon. ESPN is most closely associated with college basketball—like him or not, thanks, Dick Vitale—and that network just loves Duke basketball.

And why not? More people watch Duke games than any other college.

Since 1990, a period during which Duke has won three national championships and gone to six Final Fours, the Blue Devils have been participants in some of the most-watched games ever.

The Duke-Maryland game of January 17, 2002, remains ESPN's most-viewed regular-season college game ever. The Blue Devils won, 99-78, which means that despite the blowout, the fans didn't switch channels.

What is even more significant is that this is a recent contest, after the proliferation of networks on cable has dramatically lowered individual ratings. For example, ESPN's highest-rated games ever come from the 1983 through 1985 time frame, when there were not nearly the number of available choices for the viewing audience.

The second highest ranked regular-season men's game on ESPN was Duke-Kentucky in the Jimmy V Classic on December 22, 1998. The Blue Devils won 71-60. Duke-Maryland attracted 2,971,520 homes, just 6,000 more than watched the Devils and the Wildcats.

Obviously, it helps when the teams are highly ranked. Duke was No. 1 and Maryland No. 3 before their meeting. The Blue Devils were No. 2 and Kentucky No. 3 when they met at the Meadowlands.

When ESPN2 was born, the cable giant utilized Duke basketball to attract viewership. Obviously, it has been a good decision.

The highest-rated college games ever on the Deuce have been Duke at North Carolina on February 5, 1998, followed by Carolina at Duke on

February 1, 2001. (The third highest rated game on ESPN2 was the Duke-Connecticut women's game from Cameron on February 1, 2003).

Among ESPN2's most-viewed men's basketball games ever, Duke sweeps the first three positions. The two Duke-Carolina games ranked first and second and in third was Duke at Wake Forest on February 13, 2003. If you want to compare all games, either gender, the Blue Devils have the first four slots, with that UConn game checking in at No. 3.

When it comes to the postseason, and NCAA games on CBS, Duke has the most-viewed games of all time. There were 20,910,000 homes when the viewers watched the Blue Devils complete their back-to-back championship against Michigan's Fab Five, 71-51, on April 5, 1992.

Duke-Arkansas for the NCAA championship in 1994 from Charlotte is third on the all-time list with 20,350,000 homes where the game was being viewed. The Duke-UNLV game for the 1990 NCAA title is seventh, and Duke-Kansas in 1991, when the Devils won their first national championship, is 10th.

Duke-Louisville in 1986 currently ranks 12th on the most-viewed list, while Duke-Connecticut from 1999 is 16th. Overall, national ratings have dropped significantly in recent years, but Duke-Arizona, the 2001 finals, still checks in at 21st. The top 20 games were all played in the 20th century.

The final Duke game to make the most-watched list was the Duke-Indiana semifinal in 1992, Mike Krzyzewski against Bobby Knight. It ranks 23rd, and every game above it on the all-time list was an NCAA championship.

Add it up, and seven of the top 23 most-viewed games ever featured the Blue Devils—six of them for the championship. Michigan, North Carolina, Kentucky and Georgetown each have three games. Syracuse, Arizona and Kansas have two games each.

The highest-rated games, for the most part, come from the '70s and '80s, when viewers had far fewer choices. All-time, No. 1 is Michigan State (Magic Johnson) versus Indiana State (Larry Bird) in 1979, which got a 24.1 rating and 38 (percent of TV sets tuned in) share. However, among total viewers, that game is listed at No. 11.

The Duke-Michigan game from '92 is rated third (22.3) and second in TV share (35). Duke-Arkansas from '94 checks in at No. 6 and Duke-Louisville from '86 is 10th. Duke-UNLV in '90 is No. 14, one place ahead of Duke-Kentucky from '78. That means five Blue Devil games are in the top 15 highest-rated of all-time. Duke-Kansas in '91 is No. 20, giving the school six of the top 20. Again, nobody else has more than three appearances on this list.

If you are a Duke fan, you can accurately say the Blue Devils are the most watched team on an annual basis. And No. 1 historically. No other schools among the 326 that play Division I basketball are close.

tired less than 10 days before practice began and the Tar Heels elevated longtime assistant coach Bill Guthridge.

The Duke coach was experienced, but his 11-man roster included four freshmen, three sophomores and just two seniors, Steve Wojciechowski and Roshown McLeod.

The Blue Devils were dominant immediately. They won the Maui Classic when they defeated No. 1 Arizona, 95-87. The Wildcats were the defending NCAA champs and had their top eight players back. Duke rolled to a 60-36 lead, but had to hold off a late comeback. Wojo was voted tournament MVP after blanketing Arizona star Mike Bibby.

For nine outrageous wins, Duke looked the part of No. 1, defeating its foes by an average of more than 35 points. A 44-point victory over Virginia in the ACC opener was the greatest margin in 32 years in a conference game.

Then came Michigan. The Wolverines were the first genuine road test. Duke failed. The Blue Devils led by 17 points early in the second half, then came unglued and eventually lost, 81-73. "It's not like I thought it would be," Brand said of his first collegiate loss. "You have to give them respect. They played a lot harder than us."

In the first practice after Christmas, Duke took a major hit when Brand broke his foot. The big freshman, who was leading the team in scoring and rebounding while shooting better than 64 percent, was declared out for the season. "I've never had a player have as big an impact as Elton's had in such a short time period," Coach K said. His numbers were better than Laettner, Ferry or Hill posted as rookies.

The first game without Brand was at Maryland. Instead of an inside attack, the Blue Devils took four three-pointers in the first 1:19 and made them all. They wound up winning 104-72 over a team that had won at No. 2 Kansas. That would be the start of an unbeaten January, in which

Duke won 10 games and only was threatened once, by Clemson.

Without Brand, and with Nate James sidelined a week later with a bad ankle and headed for a redshirt season, Krzyzewski began juggling his lineups. Burgess got the first shot at center, but couldn't make a free throw. Then Taymon Domzalski got his chance. Battier and Carrawell started coming off the bench and being productive.

Clemson was the only scare until No. 1 Duke took a 20-1 record to Chapel Hill to meet No. 2 UNC, which was 22-1. In their previous 50 meetings, there had been a No. 1 team 13 times, and in half of the games, at least one of them was ranked in the top three. This game was perhaps the most hyped of them all.

It ended as a blowout. Thanks to 23 points by Antawn Jamison, Carolina led 50-34 at halftime

ELTON BRAND RETURNED TO THE LINEUP AFTER SUFFERING A BROKEN FOOT.

The Cameron faithful storm the court after Duke rallied to defeat North Carolina, giving Coach K his 500th career win.

against the smaller Blue Devils. Duke rallied, helped by a six-point play set up by a technical on Makhtar Ndiaye, and it was 73-69. But UNC's Ed Cota led a 24-4 outburst in the final six minutes for a 97-73 victory, the worst loss for the Devils since they were beaten by UNLV in the 1990 NCAA finals by 30.

Duke didn't hang its head after the crushing loss. The Blue Devils won their next seven games—the 70-66 win at Clemson was the only close one—before Carolina came calling to Cameron. "I thought we could get back here because I've traveled this road before," Krzyzewski said.

UCLA, still a magical name and No. 12 nationally with a 20-5 record, came to Cameron, where a stranger awaited. Brand had been declared ready to return to the lineup. Ultrasound and an orthotic in his shoe, plus his determination, had the big freshman chafing to play after missing 15 games.

It was if he never had left. Elton scored 14 points and collected seven rebounds in only 16 minutes. Duke rolled, 120-84, the most points ever allowed by the Bruins. Langdon had a career-high 34 points, making six of 10 three-pointers. "We knew UCLA was talented, but we wanted to step it up," said McLeod, who scored 23.

"I'm not in basketball shape," Brand acknowledged, "but it was just so good to get back out there. I never gave up on the thought of coming back."

On a Tuesday night of the week that Duke would play Carolina to determine the No. 1 team in the ACC Tournament, Tar Heel guard Shammond Williams paid a visit to the tenting Duke students in Krzyzewskiville. Some UNC female students dared Williams, the Heels' No. 2 scorer, to visit the campers. He accepted the challenge. "They treated me great," Williams said. "They didn't ask anything about the game. They just asked me how I was doing. It was really a good conversation."

For almost three-quarters of the game, Carolina shredded Duke's defense again and took a 64-47 lead with 10:29 to play. Coach K took a time-out. "I just asked them to be themselves," he said. "Our man-to-man defense down the stretch was terrific."

Duke held Carolina to two baskets the rest of the way. The Blue Devils pulled into contention behind Brand, who had 13 of his 16 points in the second half. He also limited Jamison to one tap-in basket in the final 11 minutes. McLeod's driving goal gave Duke its only lead of the game, 77-75, and then three Carolina turnovers kept the Tar Heels in arrears. The win was Krzyzewski's 500th as a coach, and Duke became the first team ever to win 15 ACC games.

The ACC Tournament in Greensboro involved a new format, with the coaches having argued successfully against the 8-9 play-in. So top-seeded Duke went against No. 9 Virginia on Thursday, with the winner getting a bye to the Saturday semifinals. The only problem was the media kept pointing out that the last-place team only had to win three games for the championship, while Nos. 7 and 8 would have had to win four.

Duke beat the Cavaliers, 63-41, a game significant only because Langdon went scoreless for the only time in his career. Not only did he miss seven shots from the field, but the 90-percent foul shooter went zero for two at the line.

The win sent the Devils against tough Clemson, a team they had beaten by one and four points. This one was no different. It took Avery's rebound of his own missed shot with 0.3 seconds left to eliminate the Tigers, 66-64, and send Duke into the title game against No. 1 Carolina.

The Blue Devils had won the regular season by two games over UNC, but it made no difference to the basketball committee after the Tar Heels hammered Duke again, 83-68, behind 22 points from Jamison. It was 57-57 when Carolina scored 13 in a row to win the tournament.

The committee, headed by Kentucky AD C.M. Newton, did Duke no favors. Or Carolina, either. Both were awarded No. 1 seeds, but UNC in the East and Duke in the South didn't go to Washington, D.C., and Atlanta. Instead, they were sent to Hartford and Lexington, Kentucky, a move that incensed Coach K.

At Rupp Arena, where the Kentucky fans still hadn't forgotten Laettner's shot in '92, Duke hammered Radford, 99-63, and then struggled past Oklahoma State, 79-73, to advance to the Sweet 16 in St. Petersburg. There the Blue Devils would face Syracuse, while Kentucky met UCLA.

While veterans Wojo, McLeod and Langdon all struggled, it was the freshmen who carried Duke past Syracuse, 80-67. Brand, in his best game since returning to the lineup, had 20 points and 10 rebounds. Battier scored 14 points coming off the bench, making six of seven shots. Avery, also a reserve, scored 11, including the clinching layup with 1:51 remaining.

AFTER PLAYING ONE OF HIS FINEST GAMES, WILLIAM AVERY'S 35-FOOTER WAS OFF THE MARK IN THE REGIONAL FINAL.

That set up the dream matchup, the Blue Devils against Kentucky, for the right to go to the Final Four. Midway in the last half, Duke led by 17 points, and it appeared that Krzyzewski was going to win his eighth regional championship game without a defeat. But Kentucky staged a miraculous rally, making a trio of three-pointers in less than a minute to reduce the deficit to eight points.

Finally, Kentucky grabbed the lead, 80-79, on a three by former walk-on Cameron Mills. Duke tied the score at 81, but Scott Padgett's three with 39 seconds to play gave the Wildcats their winning margin. With time running out, Avery's 35-footer banged harmlessly off the glass and Kentucky had the comeback victory, 86-84. It remains the only Elite Eight loss for Coach K, who is 10-1 in NCAA regional finals.

Even with all its youth, and Brand missing half the season, Duke finished with a 32-4 record. But the Blue Devils regretted letting this one get away, just as Kentucky fans will never forget '92 and the Laettner shot.

Because the '99 team lost in the NCAA championship game to Connecticut, it is impossible to call it the best team in school history. It was, however, the most dominant.

Those Blue Devils finished with 37 victories, tying their own NCAA record. The only other loss was to Cincinnati in the finals of the Great Alaska Shootout, when the Bearcats scored at the buzzer for a 77-75 triumph. After that, Duke rolled to 32 consecutive victories before losing to UConn in the title game.

And it wasn't just winning—but the margins in the games. The Blue Devils outscored their opponents by 24.7 points, an ACC record. The only other league team ever to outscore the opposition by more than 20 points was N.C. State's undefeated team in 1973, where the Wolfpack won by an average of 21.8 points. That team was on probation and did not play in the postseason.

TRAJAN LANGDON WAS THE LONE SENIOR STARTER ON THE 1999 SQUAD.

Since 1972, only the 1991 UNLV team (which Duke beat in the NCAA semifinals) had a wider victory margin (26.7). Ironically, neither team won the championship. The Blue Devils were hurt because '99 was one of the weakest ever for the ACC. There were just three NCAA bids—Duke, Maryland and North Carolina. They were the only teams with winning league records, and

FRESHMAN COREY MAGGETTE SCORED WELL COMING OFF THE BENCH.

the Tar Heels lost in the opening round of the NCAA to Weber State.

Things were so one-sided that only four times during the season was the winning margin in single digits (Michigan State twice, St. John's in overtime, and an eight-pointer at Georgia Tech). The team simply never had an opportunity to develop a competitive edge. Everything came so easily.

Even more remarkable, and in direct contrast to UNLV's veteran team of '91, this was a particularly young Duke squad. The starters included one senior, Langdon; a junior, Carrawell; and sophomores Brand, Battier and Avery. A freshman, Maggette, was the sixth man and fourth-leading scorer. Sophomores James and Burgess were the leading contributors off the bench.

What Duke did during the season, and what happened to this powerhouse after the NCAA, was indicative of the changing world of college basketball. For the first time, the Blue Devils lost players to the NBA—three of them—and Burgess transferred.

Since Jason Williams and Mike Dunleavy signed before the season began, there is no telling how good this team might have become. But, with their coach rehabilitating a hip replacement, the basketball world changed dramatically. No longer would schools be able to stockpile enormous talent and keep it for four years. While players had been leaving for many years, no school ever had been impacted the way Duke was in the spring of 1999. It appears highly unlikely that it will ever occur again. With high school players and college freshmen now routinely defecting to the NBA, it would be extremely difficult for any program ever to have that many quality players at the same time (Carlos Boozer signed after the season, when it was presumed Brand was turning pro.).

Brand became the National Player of the Year. Battier won the award two seasons later. Williams, who won awards in consecutive years (2001-02), would have been a freshman playing with Brand,

Avery and Maggette. It is mind-boggling even to think about it.

Duke defeated Virginia by 46 points. Twice. The Devils whipped Carolina by 12, 20 and 23 points, the last in the ACC title game. Maryland, which finished fifth nationally with a 28-6 record, was decisively handled twice by 18-point margins. The victories became so routine that the Cameron Crazies had a difficult time remaining involved.

It was talent against experience. Maryland, selected second in the ACC's preseason poll, started three seniors and junior college transfer Steve Francis. Meanwhile, the only concern for Duke was who would replace Wojciechowski, the emotional point guard and floor leader. Avery played the point and led the team in minutes while averaging almost 15 points. He wasn't a typical Duke point guard, but it scarcely mattered.

"This year's team has a chance to be a special basketball team," said Coach K, never one to shy away from high expectations. "I'm very comfortable with that," he said. "I have high expectations for myself and the team all the time."

Duke was No. 1 in both preseason polls, which were remarkably prescient. UConn was rated second, Stanford third, Kentucky fourth, Michigan State fifth and Maryland sixth. In actuality, Michigan State finished No. 2 in the last poll, with UConn third, Maryland fifth, Stanford seventh and Kentucky eighth. Never before or since have the polls been that accurate.

After three opening routs, Duke headed to Alaska and a homecoming for local hero Langdon. The Blue Devils hit 15 of 20 threes in ripping Notre Dame by 36, but needed 21 points and as many rebounds from Brand and 16 more rebounds from Burgess to defeat Fresno State, 93-82.

In the finals, Cincinnati caught Duke flatfooted. The Bearcats at one time led by 19 points, the only time Duke trailed by double figures all year. The Devils rallied to tie at 75, but Cincinnati scored on a home-run pass to Kenyon Martin, who flipped to Melvin Levett for a dunk with one second left. Duke tried its own baseball pass, with Brand tipping the ball to Avery. The guard, who scored 30 points, made the basket, but the officials ruled it came after the buzzer. "I have no trouble with that call," Coach K said. "Certainly they played better than we did."

It would be a long time before Duke lost again.

The next game was at Michigan State in the Great Eight, played in Chicago. Unlike the Cincinnati game, when Duke was left at the starting gate, the Devils scored the first 13 points and eventually led 21-4. Michigan State got 25 offensive rebounds and had a 41-25 edge on the boards, but never could overcome that early deficit as the Devils held on, 73-67. "We got worn out in the second half," said Coach K, still experimenting with his lineup.

After that came the ACC opener against N.C. State, in which Duke pressed its way to a 40-14 lead in the first half and eventually won by 20 in what would become a typical pattern for the rest of the season. Brand, who had been quiet for two games, had a career-high 26 points.

The schedule appeared daunting, with games against Florida and Michigan. Duke won by 30 and 44, scoring 224 points. Next was the rematch with Kentucky, the defending NCAA champs, at the Meadowlands. Unlike the previous March, Duke got a 16-point lead and held most of it to win, 71-60. The No. 3 Wildcats, who had thumped Maryland and Georgia Tech, couldn't control Brand, who made nine of 12 shots. It wasn't the thriller that previous Kentucky games had been, "but it feels so good to win," Avery said. "Now we've got to get better." They did.

Maryland was 13-1, rated fourth nationally and playing in Cole Field House. Duke scored 13 straight early in the second half, Carrawell shut

down Steve Francis, and the Devils romped 82-64 on a night when they didn't shoot well. It was to be a typical ACC contest.

Things became so lopsided that when Duke won by a mere 10 points at Wake Forest, Coach K had to point out that he wasn't disappointed, that "every road win in the ACC is a good win." Still, after beating Florida State by 25, all the Devils could talk about was how poorly they played.

The major concern was Krzyzewski's health. He scheduled an April 5 hip replacement four months in advance, but by late January, he was limping badly. The hip caused back problems, then a pain in the shoulder for which he went to Duke Hospital before the trip to Clemson. In Littlejohn, with four minutes left in a 22-point rout, Coach K left the bench and walked off to the locker room.

Later, he explained the journey. "I had to go to the bathroom. I didn't have a diaper. There wasn't a bed pan. When you're over 50, you can't pass that up."

In the next game, against No. 8 St. John's in Madison Square Garden, nobody was laughing. Duke couldn't slow down Bootsy Thornton, who scored 40 points. Brand and Avery fouled out, as did Nate James. But the Blue Devils made their free throws and won in overtime, 92-88. "Emotionally, it had to take a lot out of both teams," Krzyzewski said. And next for Duke was a home game with Carolina.

UNC led by three points with less than nine minutes left. But Duke's defense took over, forcing turnover after turnover, and the Devils won, 89-77. It was their 20th win, and the January 27 date was the earliest in history for such a mark. "We're a tired team right now," Coach K said. But his tired team shot 51 percent against the Heels, who had been holding opponents to 37.3.

There was only one close game in February. At Georgia Tech, a team they had beaten by 41, Duke trailed 57-49 in the second half. But Langdon got hot, hitting four three-pointers, and the Blue Devils pulled it out, 87-79. Langdon scored 23 points to snap a personal slump.

Carrawell said it was all about the shoes. He had convinced Trajan to change them. "He had gone back to an old brand and he'd been missing ever since," Carrawell said. "I was like, 'Look, you need to switch shoes.' He switched, and the shots started falling again. I'm not going to say it was the shoes; it's Trajan. But switching them didn't hurt."

Duke closed out the regular season with a 20-point blowout at Carolina and headed for Charlotte and the ACC Tournament as the overwhelming favorite. Virginia was first on the list. "I took a vote of the team," said UVA coach Pete Gillen. "The seven walk-ons voted to play; the six scholarship players said no. Since it was 7-6, we'll play." Maybe it wasn't a good idea; Duke led by 38 at halftime, 59-21. UVA actually won the second half by a point and lost 104-67.

Against N.C. State in the semifinals, the Devils were without Langdon, who sprained a foot against UVA. He had started a school-record 121 straight games. The Wolfpack went into a zone, figuring that Duke couldn't shoot as well from outside. But freshman Maggette shot from everywhere in his first start, scoring 24 points. Duke won by 15.

Even without Langdon, the title game was another blowout as the Devils won their first ACC Tournament championship since '92. Avery had 29 points and Brand scored 24 as Duke blitzed North Carolina, 96-73. "I don't remember a team dominating the league the way they have," said UNC coach Bill Guthridge.

The domination continued in the East Region, helped along by upsets that knocked seeds two through five out before the Sweet 16. As No. 1 seed in the NCAAs, Duke returned to Charlotte to meet Florida A&M (12-18). The result was predictable, 99-58, again without Langdon.

Tulsa was supposed to be stronger. The spread was the same—41 points, 97-56. Langdon returned and scored a dozen. Mike Ruffin, Tulsa's star, was held scoreless. "I've never seen defense like that," he said.

Duke had won its last 11 games by an average margin of 31 points. According to Coach K, "It might be difficult to keep them at this level." The Devils were headed to the Meadowlands, one of their favorite sites, to face 12-seed Southwest Missouri State. The other teams were No. 6 Temple and No. 10 Purdue.

"This better be a wakeup call," Carrawell said after a methodical 78-61 win against SMS. It was the first time in three months that Duke had scored fewer than 80 points. The Bears swarmed all over Brand, but left Langdon open. He made four of six threes and 24 points overall. "Trajan is our leader," Coach K said. "He gives us strength through his maturity."

ELTON BRAND WAS THE TEAM'S LEADING SCORER.

Next was Temple, with its famous 1-3-1 zone. Again, Langdon was given opportunities to shoot. He made five of six three-pointers and was the Most Outstanding Player as Duke breezed, 85-64. The Blue Devils worked the ball and made 16 of 23 first-half shots. Overall, they hit 61 percent. "If you're going to beat Duke, you better have a lot of faith in God," said Temple coach John Chaney. "And you'd better bring along Frank and Jesse James."

The Final Four in St. Petersburg was Krzyzewski's eighth, and the field was imposing. Only fourth-seed Ohio State was any sort of outsider. The others were No. 1 seeds Michigan State and Connecticut, ranked 2-3 in the nation. It was the first time since 1985 that three top seeds had advanced. Duke's first task was MSU, a team it had struggled against in December, winning a defensive struggle, 73-67, despite getting clobbered on the boards.

The Spartans were every bit as strong defensively the second time around. But the Duke "D" was even better. The Blue Devils claimed a 26-14 rebounding edge in building a 32-20 halftime lead as each team struggled to score.

MSU coach Tom Izzo turned to a zone defense in the second half, and cut into the deficit as Duke had to sit Brand with four fouls. With the Blue Devils clanking free throw after free throw—they were merely 11 for 23 in the last half—the Spartans got to within three at 51-48. That was a situation they wanted. "They've played a lot of close games and won most of them," Langdon said. "We haven't played many."

Langdon had been having problem getting a shot. He had been smothered and was two for eight from the field. But he came through in the clutch, swishing his only three of the game to make it a six-point lead. Avery followed with his own three-pointer and a driving basket and Duke was in command. It ended 68-62, with Avery flinging the ball high at Tropicana Field as the buzzer sounded.

It was Duke's lowest scoring game of the season. "It was really as fulfilling a victory as we've had all year because they're so good," Krzyzewski said.

Refuting the debate over whether or not it was a poor performance, Battier said, "I don't think it was a bad game for us. We had a heck of a game defensively and on the boards. We're never going to judge ourselves on whether or not our shots go down."

Duke had a chance at history, to become the first team ever to win 38 games. But UConn got in the way. The Huskies came up huge defensively, especially in the final minute, and upset the Blue Devils, 77-74.

Langdon carried Duke offensively, scoring 25 points, including five three-pointers. But he had two critical turnovers in the closing seconds. He was guarded by Ricky Moore, a native of Augusta, Georgia, who grew up 10 houses away from Avery. When the game was on the line, Moore won the battle.

Duke led 39-37 at halftime, thanks to Langdon's sniping from long range. But Duke didn't stop Moore, who had all of his 13 points before intermission. In the second half, Richard Hamilton got hot as he finished with 27 points, and the Blue Devils couldn't get the ball inside to Brand. Elton finished with 15 points and a game-high 13 rebounds. "I give those guys credit," he said of his defenders. "They were just fighting for possession every time I touched it."

UConn led 73-69, when Battier grabbed an offensive rebound and passed to Langdon, whose three cut the deficit to one point. Khalid El-Amin scored for the Huskies, after which Avery made two free throws to make it 75-74. After an El-Amin airball, Duke came down the floor with 24 seconds left. The play was for Langdon, the fifth-year senior. Guarded tightly by Moore, he was called for traveling.

"Moore was on me the whole game," Langdon said. "It was no different through the entire game. So I'm not going to hang my head on that play."

With 5.2 seconds left, El-Amin was fouled and made both shots for a three-point lead. Duke had pulled out miracles before, and Coach K wasn't going to take a timeout. "That's the way we play," he said. "I think it's aggressive, and it's winning, and you know we're going for the win.

Langdon couldn't get off the shot, losing the ball as the game ended. "They did a good job of funneling me toward the sideline," he said. "I got tripped a little bit. I tried to get the shot off and it was stripped."

"It was clean. Everything about the game was clean," Krzyzewski said. So the season was over. Duke finished 37-2 because it shot just 41 percent and the Huskies shot 52.5. "We had a great year," said Carrawell. "Sometimes, it doesn't work out."

Duke returned to Durham without the championship that had appeared ordained. Krzyzewski had his hip replaced. And then, for the first time,

came the defections to the NBA. First Brand, then, surprising everybody and without Coach K's blessing, Avery and Maggette.

Even at Duke, the college basketball world was changing rapidly. Only the strong would adjust. In the summer of 1999, Coach K held his first media conference since his hip replacement—and the NBA defections. "When they all decided to leave, it hurt my feelings a little bit. I was sorry to see them go because you can't establish as strong a relationship in one or two years as you can in four. I could understand Elton's situation. He had missed a lot of time as a freshman with a broken foot, and the risk of something like that happening again was hanging over him. But there was no way I could have forecast that the other three would leave.

"Realistically, I'm not shocked by anything that happens in sport. It's a changing time and things like this will happen. I think it will turn out pretty good for the individuals involved. Whether it will be for the best, I don't know." He pointed out that the team received notoriety for going 69-6 the previous two years that might not have happened in the past. "If Antawn Jamison and Vince Carter don't leave UNC (early), there's no way Elton's picture is on all the preseason magazines. Kids are widely publicized before they've had a chance to do very much.

"None of our kids expected to be gone after one or two years. But when they're talented and have had extreme success like we had, they feel like it might be the best time to take advantage of their notoriety and move to the next level."

Duke was faced with an enormous task. Only three veterans had much experience—Carrawell, James and Battier. One senior and two juniors. Collectively, they averaged 24 points in '99. They were joined by six freshmen. Of those, only Jason Williams, Carlos Boozer and Mike Dunleavy played meaningful minutes. Williams and Boozer, who broke his foot in the summer but who returned for fall practice and played all 34 games, were starters. Dunleavy became the sixth man.

He actually averaged more minutes (24.1) than Boozer (23.7). Nobody else averaged double-figure minutes.

That team without a bench went 15-1 in winning the ACC regular-season title for the fourth straight year. Duke finished four games ahead of runnerup Maryland. It won the ACC Tournament with ease and finished No. 1 in the polls, moving up in the last week. It lost its first two games and the doomsayers had their way. Then the Blue Devils won 18 consecutive games, four of them in overtime. They were weakened when Dunleavy missed four games near the end of the year with mononucleosis, and with no depth at all, were eliminated from the NCAA Tournament in the Sweet 16 by Florida. They finished a remarkable 29-5.

Krzyzewski was the ACC and National Coach of the Year. Carrawell was a consensus All-American. Battier was consensus second-team All-American. Not bad for a predicted "off" year.

It had been 41 years—before Vic Bubas began Duke's path to greatness—since the Blue Devils lost their first two games. They shot 28.2 percent and lost to Stanford in overtime, 80-79, despite leading by six points with a minute to go. It was the worst shooting for a Krzyzewski team in his 20 years at Duke. Against No. 1 UConn, Duke improved its shooting to 34 percent but lost again, 71-66. Matt Christensen started at center for the still-recovering Boozer and was one for 12 in the two games. Williams, the rookie point guard, was eight for 32. "There were a lot of good things," Coach K said. "We just didn't score, and we will score." He was correct. The team averaged 88 points and led the ACC.

After a couple of easy home wins, the Devils faced a killer stretch in which they played Southern Cal in Anaheim, Illinois in Chicago, DePaul at home and at Michigan during a 12-day stretch. They won all four.

The Blue Devils were in search of a new ACC record for consecutive wins. They started January

with 22 league victories in a row. N.C. State held the mark with 27. By the end of the month, Duke had 29 and counting.

The league opener was at Virginia, where Duke trailed by 10 points with seven minutes left in regulation before rallying to win, 109-100, in overtime. Staying on the road, Duke won at Maryland, 80-70, as Battier blocked seven shots and stifled Terps' star Terrence Morris. Carrawell scored 45 points in the two wins.

Then the Devils turned into a second-half dynamo. They led Georgia Tech by five at halftime and won, 82-57. That was nothing compared to what occurred at Florida State. Down 34-32 at intermission, Duke turned it on to outscore the 'Noles 53-20 in the second half to make it a laugher.

Next was N.C. State, in Cameron, as Duke tried to match the Pack's mark of 27 ACC wins, set in '73-74. Duke led by five with 31 seconds left, before State had a miracle finish. Trailing by two points with 0.8 seconds left, Justin Gainey intentionally missed a Wolfpack free throw. Marshall Williams grabbed the rebound and made a tying basket that counted. Overtime. "I think we were shocked when it went into overtime," Battier said. "But the great thing was we were able to keep going to the next play. We had a firm resolve." Duke won, 92-88, for No. 27.

The record was broken on the road at Wake Forest, 75-61. It was the fifteenth straight league road victory, tying a record. "If you ask me," Carrawell said, "15 straight road wins is more impressive than the other record. Road wins are hard to come by in this league."

The road record was broken—happily for the Blue Devils—at Chapel Hill. Again it went into overtime, Duke's fifth of the season and fourth straight OT win. Leading 41-24 at halftime and by 19 with 14 minutes left, Duke saw UNC guard Ed Cota lead a sizzling rally. The Tar Heels eventually tied the game at 73 on a three-pointer by freshman Joe Forte with five seconds left. But Duke con-

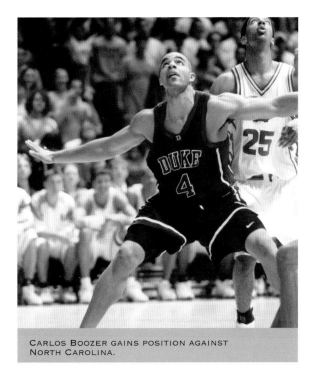

CARLOS BOOZER GAINS POSITION AGAINST NORTH CAROLINA.

trolled the extra period, getting the ball to Boozer for three layups, and won 90-86. "It seems like overtimes are old hat," Battier said. "In overtime, we decided it was our time."

Only 38 hours later, Duke overcame fatigue to outscore Virginia 65-33 in the first half and went on to a 106-86 victory. But Coach K and Carrawell knew all the record streaks were deceiving. Noting the overtime victories, Krzyzewski said, "That's a tribute to your toughness, but it doesn't mean that you're great. Last year we had a great team. We're a good basketball team that has been playing well."

Carrawell all but predicted a 98-87 home loss to Maryland that ended Duke's 18-game win streak, 31-straight ACC streak, and 46-game Cameron streak. Asked if he thought the Devils would go unbeaten in the ACC again, he said, "No, I think somebody is going to get us. We're not the overpowering team we were last year."

Maryland proved him correct. Juan Dixon scored 31 points, mostly against a weary Carrawell, and Terrence Morris made two critical threes after the game was tied at 83. "All streaks have to end. Any team can be beaten on a given day. It's been a great run and it's sad it had to end on our court, but Maryland deserved to win. All we can do is try and start a new streak," Carrawell said.

The Devils did just that, clinching the ACC for the fourth straight regular season by winning their last six. There were two negatives—St. John's upset Duke 83-82 in Cameron on a jumper by Bootsy Thornton with 11.9 seconds left, and, much more damaging, Dunleavy developed mononucleosis and missed four straight games. Suddenly, the six-man rotation was down to five. Freshman Nick Horvath got most of Dunleavy's minutes, and scored a career-high 13 points against Wake Forest. But the Devils no longer had any options or versatility coming off the bench. Dunleavy had been averaging nearly 10 points in 25 minutes. He was a de facto sixth starter.

At Clemson, Duke won 92-78 as Battier and Williams each played 40 minutes and Carrawell logged 39. The Devils closed out the regular season by crushing UNC, 90-76, with Battier making six three-pointers in a 30-point outing and Carrawell getting 21. The senior was named the MVP in the ACC.

How good had Krzyzewski been after all the personnel problems? "I think almost everybody would agree it's one of the great coaching jobs that's taken place in college basketball," said Clemson coach Larry Shyatt. "I don't think what they've been able to do has ever been mirrored before, because I'm not sure anybody else has ever had as many players go into the draft and go as high as theirs did."

Just before the ACC Tournament, Battier announced he was returning for his senior year. "I saw last year what it could do to a team. The focus was not on the team. It was on the future individual projects. I'm definitely coming back. There's a lot for this team to accomplish next year."

The Blue Devils cruised to the 2000 ACC Tournament title, while welcoming Dunleavy back into action. Against Clemson, Duke made a record 17 of 29 threes in a 31-point win. Dunleavy played 20 minutes and was four for four on threes. He made three of three in a victo-

SHANE BATTIER EMERGED AS A STAR DURING HIS JUNIOR SEASON.

bound. Duke won, 69-64, as Battier scored 21 points, had eight rebounds and eight blocks, most of them against somebody else's man. "They didn't think I could block shots," he said. "They took it to me, so I tried to play old-fashioned defense."

Duke was headed to Syracuse to play Florida in the Sweet 16. There had been a danger warning. In two games, Dunleavy scored five points. He didn't score in 14 minutes against the Jayhawks. He was back, but he wasn't completely healthy. He had no energy.

Florida was the worst kind of opponent for the depth-shy Devils. Billy Donovan played 10 players regularly. Duke was down to six, and Dunleavy was ailing. Duke led 78-74 with 3:19 left, and didn't score again. Florida had the last 13 points of the game for an 87-78 victory, including eight foul shots in the last minute. The Florida bench outscored the Duke bench (Dunleavy), 35-6.

"It's great motivation not to lose next year at all," Dunleavy said. "It's going to make us want to win even more." A year later, he made good on that statement.

ry over Wake Forest, but the hero was James, who had 14 points in the last 11 minutes. The Devils made 13 more threes. Against Maryland in the title game, the offense changed. Duke got the ball to Boozer inside for 21 points, while Williams outscored Steve Blake 23-7, including 18-0 in the last half as the Devils pulled away from a 37-36 edge.

The Devils were the No. 1 seed in the NCAA East at Winston-Salem. They finally put away No. 16 Lamar, 82-55, but not without working hard. That sent Duke against Kansas, a matchup neither Coach K nor Roy Williams liked. "What are they doing as an eight-seed?" Krzyzewski asked. "I thought we were seeded low," Williams agreed.

With 1:18 left, Duke trailed 64-63. Carrawell missed, but Boozer dropped in the rebound for the go-ahead goal. He then anticipated a pass, stole the ball and Carrawell was fouled. He made them both for a three-point lead. Kirk Hinrich missed for Kansas, and Carrawell grabbed the re-

FRESHMAN MIKE DUNLEAVY AND DUKE FACED FLORIDA IN THE SWEET SIXTEEN.

CHAPTER 13

THIRD TITLE

When the 2001 season began, Duke was the national favorite. There were four starters returning, plus sixth man Mike Dunleavy. Freshman Chris Duhon came with high expectations. Reserves Nick Horvath, Casey Sanders and Matt Christensen all were expected to contribute. David Henderson, who left for the Delaware head coaching job, had been replaced by another former player, Chris Collins.

"We have high expectations—we always have high expectations—and I never poor-mouth my team," Mike Krzyzewski said. "I don't ever want them to hear me say that I don't think we're going to be really good."

Coach K pointed out that his team had led the nation in scoring the previous two years and "my feeling is that we'll score maybe a little bit more because we have depth."

MIKE KRZYZEWSKI MONITORS THE GAME WITH HIS ASSISTANT COACHES WHO WERE ALL DUKE TEAM CAPTAINS: CHRIS COLLINS (LEFT), STEVE WOJCIECHOWSKI (SECOND FROM LEFT) AND JOHNNY DAWKINS (RIGHT).

He was correct about most things. The scoring increased almost three points per game to 90.7. The team started out No. 2 nationally, just behind Arizona. It wound up tied for the ACC regular-season championship with North Carolina after winning the previous four years outright. It was an overwhelming favorite to win the ACC crown, which happened in a blowout of the Tar Heels.

And the Devils made Dick Vitale look good. He picked them to win it all, which happened in Minneapolis, where Duke won its second NCAA crown in 1992.

The only area where Coach K, and the pundits, were wrong, concerned the depth. Horvath got hurt and was redshirted. Freshman Andre Sweet played seven games before becoming academically ineligible. Sanders didn't play much until Carlos Boozer broke a foot in late February. Christensen was a reserve player all year. The depth consisted primarily of Duhon.

But this team finished the season No. 1, advanced easily to the Final Four, and staged the greatest rally in NCAA Tournament history in coming from 22 points down in the first half to eliminate Maryland in the semifinals. Every NCAA game was won by double figures.

The first three losses—at Stanford, in Cameron to UNC, and at Virginia—all occurred at the buzzer. In the other defeat, at home to Maryland 91-80, Boozer broke his foot. Despite all the problems, this was one of Duke's greatest teams. Before the season, Coach K told ESPN (and former Duke star Jay Bilas) that "We will take the attitude that the championships is not ours, we must win it. But, can we win it? Absolutely."

Duke began the season by winning the preseason NIT. Battier broke the school record with nine three-pointers in the opening rout of Princeton. Then, with Krzyzewski going for his 500th win at Duke, the floor at Cameron was christened Coach K court before the game with Villanova, in which Boozer was the leading scorer. In New York, the Devils crunched Texas 95-69

as Nate James had a career-high 26, and rallied to beat Temple 63-61 on some late heroics by Williams. It was that kind of balance that carried the team to No. 1 in the polls.

The tough early schedule continued with an ACC/Big Ten Challenge game against No. 9 Illinois in Greensboro and a quick rematch with Temple, this time in Philadelphia. "I set up the schedule to improve your team and see styles you'll have to play against different people," Krzyzewski said.

Illinois definitely was a challenge, but Duke stole one, 78-77. The Devils had a dozen steals, half by freshman Duhon. They led by nine with three minutes left, turned it over three times, and saw the Illini climb to within a point with 3.5 seconds left. But Duke held until less than a second remained, and when James was fouled, he intentionally missed as the clock ran out. Temple, so tough just nine days before, was no test. Duke made 17 of 30 three-pointers in a 93-68 blowout. Williams scored 30 points and Temple coach John Chaney raved, "He is absolutely the best point guard in the country. He can probe a defense, penetrate a defense, like nobody else. He's just outstanding."

Michigan came to Cameron, and in the first eight minutes, fell behind 34-2. It was 59-18 at halftime as Duke won 104-61. Then came the first loss. The Devils were upset by unbeaten, No. 3 Stanford in Oakland. Lack of depth caught up to Duke—along with missed free throws. The Blue Devils led by 11 with 3:30 left, but Boozer already had fouled out, and Battier soon followed him. That left the inside open to the Collins twins, who dominated. The Devils still led 83-82 and had Dunleavy at the foul line with 14 seconds left. He missed two. "I'm a man," he said. "You can say I choked, but I just missed them." Casey Jacobsen scored for the Cardinal with 3.6 seconds, and when Williams's 94-foot sojourn to the basket ended when his shot rolled off the rim, Duke had lost, 84-83.

CARLOS BOOZER DRIVES IN A HOME VICTORY OVER BOSTON COLLEGE.

It will forever be known as the "Miracle Minute."

With 1:15 to play, homestanding Maryland led Duke 89-77. When Drew Nicholas made a foul shot with 61 seconds left, the Terps were still ahead by 10 at 90-80 and the boisterous Terp students were screaming, "Over-rated, over-rated" at the second-ranked Blue Devils.

Then Duke staged a rally for the ages. With 54 seconds left, Jason Williams made a layup. Until then, Williams had not made a three-pointer, and, guarded by nemesis Steve Blake, he had committed 10 turnovers.

But Williams stole the inbounds pass and made a three, and eight seconds later, he hit another three. Suddenly, it was 90-88, and Jason had scored eight points in 14 seconds.

Nate James then stole the ball from Maryland star Juan Dixon, and was fouled when he tried to follow a Mike Dunleavy shot. The two free throws by James tied the score at 90, and the game went into a shocking overtime after Drew Nicholas missed a jumper for the Terps.

In the extra period, Shane Battier gave Duke the lead for good at 95-92 with a three-pointer, and the Blue Devils made five-of-six foul shots to win, 98-96. Maryland's last chance was a 10-foot jumper by Dixon, but Battier blocked it.

Mike Krzyzewski thought the key play was Williams's steal of the inbounds pass and subsequent three-pointer. "That was a monster shot. He shot it almost sitting on our bench." It was his first three of the game and he would wind up with 25 points after playing poorly for 39 minutes.

Maryland's fans didn't take kindly to the collapse. Carlos Boozer's father stormed into the media room where the press was waiting for Coach K and said that his wife had been hit in the head by a water bottle. Chris Duhon's mother said water bottles twice hit her.

Despite the postgame reaction, Duke had the victory. "That was an amazing win for us," Coach K said. "Down 10 with a minute left, we just hung in there. Our kids made winning plays to win."

When the ACC season started, the league had five nationally ranked teams, a major improvement over the previous two mediocre seasons. Virginia and Wake Forest were unbeaten. But Duke was in charge. The Blue Devils went 8-0 in January, including four wins over nationally ranked opponents.

After Williams scored all 22 of his points in the second half at N.C. State, No. 10 Virginia came to Cameron. And played like Michigan. Duke went on a 23-0 run, led 39-9 and 60-20 early in the second half. "We got shook," said UVA coach Pete Gillen. "They do that to you." It ended 103-61. When No. 25 Boston College came to Durham, Williams scored 34 points in a 97-75 romp. He, Boozer and Battier combined for 78 points. They outdid themselves at Georgia Tech, collecting 82 points in a 98-77 win.

But the story was Battier. He scored 30 of his 34 points in the last half, including 20 in a row. "I felt like I was outside myself looking in," he said. "For a while there I didn't know what the score was, I was just playing ball." The Big Three against No. 9 Wake Forest had Dunleavy substituting for Boozer. He scored 21, Williams had 27 and Battier 22 in an 85-62 romp in which the Devils made another 14 three-pointers.

The month ended at Maryland, where Duke staged a rally for the ages. Down 12 points with 1:15 left, the Blue Devils came back to send the game into overtime. Williams, who had 10 turnovers in the first 25 minutes, scored eight points in 13 seconds and two free throws by James sent it into overtime. Duke led the entire extra period, and sealed the 98-96 victory when Battier swatted away a shot by Juan Dixon.

The euphoria lasted only a few days. As good as Duke was in January, it was unfortunate in February. The Blue Devils lost three times, including at home to North Carolina in their next game. Down 78-71, the Devils staged another comeback and tied the score on a Dunleavy jumper with 3.6 seconds left, 83-83. On the inbounds pass to beyond midcourt, Battier fouled Brendan Haywood going for the ball, and two free throws by the seven-footer gave Carolina its 15th straight win. Duke shot a season-low 39 percent, and was inaccurate from the foul line, missing 14 of 27.

Rebounding from the setback, Duke won its next three games, including a win in Cameron against N.C. State, 101-75, when the Devils honored their '91 NCAA championship team. Duke attacked the entire game. "I saw it I their eyes," said State's Damien Wilkins. "I've never seen them that aggressive." Battier, the erudite student, saw it a different way. "Basketball had become a big, hairy monster, and we were scared to disturb it. When we're attacking, we're Lancelot, slaying the monster."

The monster arose in the next game. Playing at Charlottesville against a team it had beaten by 42 in Cameron, Duke saw an end to its greatest streak. Desperate Virginia, ranked 12th but slumping, beat the Devils 91-89 when Adam Hall picked up a loose ball after James had blocked Roger Mason's attempt and scored at the buzzer. The Blue Devils had not lost an ACC road game in three years and two days. They were outshot and got killed on the boards, 41-25. "The team that should have won the game did win," said Coach K.

The loss left Duke two games behind North Carolina as it sought to win the ACC regular season for the fifth straight year. "It puts us in a very lousy position," Williams conceded.

Two games later, against Georgia Tech in Cameron, Battier had his jersey retired as Duke rolled 98-54. "We had a game befitting the kid who had his jersey retired," said Krzyzewski. "To me, he is the consummate winner."

Williams and Boozer came up big as the Devils started another road streak at Winston-Salem, beating Wake Forest, 82-80. But the winner came from the rookie, Duhon, who hit a floater at the buzzer. "I practice that shot primarily to get it over the big men, but never thought I'd have to use it to win a game." With last-place Clemson upsetting UNC, Duke was now within a game of the ACC lead with two to play.

Maryland wouldn't concede, however, in what turned out to be the most critical game of the season. Boozer scored 16 first-half points as Duke led 50-43, but early in the second half, he heard a "pop" as the third metatarsal bone broke in his right foot. Maryland took control and defeated the Devils on Senior Night, 91-80. It was the only game that Duke lost that didn't go to the buzzer.

Casey Sanders replaced Boozer and had four fouls in as many minutes. "This is not the way I envisioned playing my last game in this building,"

CASEY SANDERS, REPLACING THE INJURED CARLOS BOOZER, WAS INSTRUMENTAL IN DUKE'S WIN AT NORTH CAROLINA.

scorer, but he could run, and he did. The jet-quick Duhon gave Duke more speed. Ahead was Carolina, playing at home. The Devils had to win to tie for the title at 13-3.

Everything went Duke's way in the Dean Dome, including small ball. Sanders played 11 minutes and fouled out. Reggie Love, a 6-4 football player, guarded seven-footer Haywood for awhile. And the Devils took three after three after three, making 14 of them. Ahead 42-40 at half-time, the speedier Blue Devils ran to a 14-point lead that forced UNC coach Matt Doherty to bench Haywood and 6-11 Kris Lang. Nothing helped. Duke won going away, 95-81.

Before the game, Coach K had scorned the idea of being an underdog. "No way," he said.

SHANE BATTIER BLOCKED JOSEPH FORTE'S BREAKAWAY SHOT IN A KEY MOMENT IN THE VICTORY AT UNC.

James said. "We'll just have to circle the wagons and get tougher," said Coach K.

That's exactly what happened, as Krzyzewski made some stunning lineup adjustments and led his team to 10 consecutive victories in search of another NCAA crown.

At practice, the day after the Boozer injury, Coach K said to his battered team, which essentially had played with six men all season, "If you do what I say, we'll win the national championship." They listened—and they won.

Sanders, who had barely played all year, would replace Boozer, but the dramatic move by the staff was to move Duhon into the starting lineup and place James, the fifth-year senior who only two games before had a career-high 27 points at Clemson, on the bench. Sanders was not a

"We're beyond underdog. We're Duke. You've still got to beat Duke." Carolina couldn't come close. The instructions on offense? "Shane, run around and make plays," Battier said. He had 25 points, 11 rebounds, five blocks and four steals. Williams made seven three-pointers and scored 33. Duhon had 15 points, four assists and no turnovers.

"We easily could have come out and folded and hid behind the excuse that Boozer was out. But now we have new blood, new life, and it's time to fight and go for it," Battier said. Two days later, he was the leading vote-getter on the Associated Press All-America team and Williams was second, the first time teammates ever had been so honored.

The ACC Tournament was played in the Georgia Dome in Atlanta, the first time the league ever had played in such a facility. The crowds were over 40,000 for each of the final four sessions. When Duke left for its game with N.C. State, it was discovered that the managers had left the home white uniforms and the warm-ups in Durham. The team played in road blacks and wore blue t-shirts on the bench. "I felt a little naked," Dunleavy said.

The Devils played like the good road team they were. Behind 19-16, they went on a 15-0 tear, inspired by the defense of Love, who had just entered the game. The Duke run actually went to 41-14 and the 76-61 win was deceivingly close. Defense was the difference. State had 15 turnovers in the first half and never threatened again.

The semifinals matched the bitter rivals, Duke and Maryland. With Boozer out, the Terps owned the boards, 51-30. But 12 Duke three-pointers kept the Devils in the game. With 16 seconds left, Dunleavy made two free throws for an 82-79 lead, but with 8.1 seconds to play, Steve Blake tied it with a three. Williams rushed the ball down the floor, missing a tough jumper in the lane. James, who came off the bench to score 14, leaped over Sanders and tapped in the ball for a two-point lead with 1.3 seconds left.

Maryland had one chance, and came close. Dixon caught a long pass, whirled and took a 40-footer that looked good all the way. But it hit the rim, bounced off, and Duke had won. "When I saw it go off the rim, I wanted to drop down and cry," Williams said. Battier hugged Dixon and told him, "See you in the Final Four." He was clairvoyant.

The Blue Devils played one of the more remarkable tournament games ever in thumping Carolina, 79-53, for the third straight championship. It vindicated James, who 10 days before, right after Boozer's injury, said, "I still think we're the better basketball team." They twice went out and proved it decisively.

This was never a contest as Duke won by the second-widest margin in ACC history. Down 12-10, the Devils went on a 32-9 tear, led 50-30 at halftime, and the margin never was below 20 in the last half. Williams sprained an ankle and missed the final 13 minutes and it didn't matter. Smaller, depth-shy Duke outrebounded the Heels, 54-47, and forced 20 turnovers while making only seven themselves. "This was one of those games where you could see the look of doubt, hesitancy and defeat creep into their eyes," Battier said. "It invigorated us."

The road to the Final Four began in Greensboro. Duke, No. 1 in the final polls, dispatched 16th seed Monmouth, 95-52, grabbing a 62-29 halftime lead as Williams scored 20 of his 22 points. The Blue Devils made 18 three-pointers, second all-time in NCAA history, and established an NCAA mark for the most three-point attempts in a season.

In the second round, Krzyzewski didn't enjoy going against his former player and assistant coach, Quin Snyder, now of Missouri. The Tigers stayed close behind the 29 points of Kareem Rush, but Duke shot 54.2 percent and won, 94-81. Williams scored 31 points as Duke used just seven players, including footballer Love, who played 16 minutes.

JASON WILLIAMS SLAMS ONE HOME AGAINST
MARYLAND IN THE FINAL FOUR.

In the Sweet 16 in Philadelphia, Duke went against a pair of teams from Los Angeles. It was the Jason Williams show in both contests. Against UCLA, Williams went on a tear in the second half, scoring 19 consecutive points to tie his career high of 34 as Duke won, 74-63. Battier had 24 points and 10 rebounds. The big news for the Devils was that Boozer was cleared to play, three weeks after his injury. He played 22 minutes, had a field goal and six rebounds in a reserve role.

That sent the Blue Devils against Southern Cal in the regional final. Williams (28) and Battier (20) were the offensive stars again. Duke led 43-38 at halftime, and that pair had all but 10 of the points. The final was 79-69 as the defense held the Trojans to 40 percent shooting. The key in the second half was a trio of three-pointers from Duhon, who was left open as USC ganged up on Williams.

Duke arrived in Minneapolis to be greeted by an old adversary, Maryland. The two ACC foes would meet in one Final Four game, while Arizona went against defending champion Michigan State. No teams ever had met for a fourth time at this stage, but when it came to the Devils and Terps, anything was possible.

Duke got left at the starting gate. With 6:55 left in the half, Maryland was ahead 39-17 and the Blue Devils were zero for eight on threes, their favorite weapon. Coach K called timeout. "You're losing by so much, you can't play any worse," he said. "What, were we going to lose by 40? We're already losing by 20. I'm not calling any more plays. Just go play."

By halftime, the deficit was reduced to 11 points, 49-38. Midway in the second half, the Blue Devils took the lead, 73-72, when cold-shooting Williams made his first three-pointer. Duke pulled away after that and won, 95-84. It was the greatest comeback in NCAA Final Four history. Battier had 25 points and Williams finished with 23, but the big story was Boozer, who came off the bench to tally 19, making seven of eight shots. "It was the best our inside people have played all year," Krzyzewski said.

That set up a meeting with Arizona, also a No. 1 seed. This was Battier's night, as he played all 40 minutes in the 82-72 victory, the 131st of his career (tying Wayne Turner of Kentucky). He scored 18 points and grabbed 11 rebounds. Williams again didn't shoot well, but scored 16. Boozer, continuing his comeback from injury, had 12 points and as many boards.

But the guy who provided the killing baskets was Dunleavy, who shook off a slump with 18 second-half points and a total of 21. In a span of 45 seconds, he hit three consecutive threes to break the backs of Arizona's hope of a comeback. Duke held the Wildcats to four for 22 on threes, and 39.4 overall shooting.

2002 Blue Devils had similar success to the national champs.

Duke won its fourth consecutive ACC championship in a 30-point blowout of N.C. State. It also finished No. 1 in the polls for a record fourth consecutive year. The Blue Devils were ranked first for 14 of the 18 weeks by The Associated Press. Williams was the consensus National Player of the Year, making him the first repeat winner since UVA's Ralph Sampson in 1983. Dunleavy was consensus second-team All-America and Boozer made the third team.

The Blue Devils finished 31-4, and, again, depth became an issue. Duke had a six-man rotation all season, with transfer Dahntay Jones joining Williams, Dunleavy, Boozer and Duhon in the starting lineup and freshman Daniel Ewing was the sixth man. The starting lineup rarely changed. Nobody else averaged more than eight minutes.

"It's complete," Battier said of his career. "All that's left for me is to ride off into the sunset on a white horse. We fought, we fought. It was a great year, and this is just the perfect way for us to end it." He was named Most Outstanding Player.

The championship was the third for Krzyzewski. Only John Wooden (10) and Adolph Rupp (four) have more. Battier was the consensus National Player of the Year. The NABC award went to Williams. It's the only time two players from the same team have won such awards in the same season.

Duke established a similar record the following season, when Williams, Boozer and Dunleavy made the All-ACC team, the first time that had been achieved. In fact, up until a stunning second-half rally by Indiana in a Sweet 16 game, the

MIKE DUNLEAVY NAILS ONE OF HIS THREE-POINTERS VS. ARIZONA IN THE TITLE GAME.

By the time the season began, Krzyzewski had been installed into the Naismith Memorial Basketball Hall of Fame in his first year of eligibility, being enshrined along with Temple coach John Chaney and Moses Malone. Duke also signed the nation's best recruiting class, six players

JASON WILLIAMS WAS DUKE'S ONLY TWO-TIME NATIONAL PLAYER OF THE YEAR.

headed by Shelden Williams, Shavlik Randolph and J.J. Redick. Meanwhile, Jason Williams was a unanimous pick for preseason All-America and Duke was No. 1 in the polls, with Maryland second.

Krzyzewski agreed to a long-term contract extension, ostensibly to 2011, when he would be 65, but in reality a lifetime deal that gave him the title of special assistant to the president, a posi-

tion he said he intended to hold after he retires as coach. His program, meanwhile, was considered the nation's finest.

"I don't know that I would call them the model," said Colorado coach Ricardo Patton. "They're the exception. There always are a select few programs that just have more of an edge versus the others in the country, and Coach Krzyzewski has built one of the great programs ever."

Duke started the season in the Maui Classic, a long way from home, knowing that Williams and Boozer, both juniors, were headed to the NBA after this year, and searching for the leadership provided to the championship team by the departed Battier.

The initial scare came immediately. Duke couldn't throw the ball in the Pacific Ocean and trailed Seton Hall at halftime by seven. Things didn't improve much after that, but Williams did find a way to score 21 of his 27 points. The last one was a free throw with seven seconds left—he missed the first, barely drawing iron. Jason then stole a pass to clinch the victory.

Duke played more like No. 1 in whipping South Carolina and upset-minded Ball State to win the tournament, but still was playing indifferently until it met No. 7 Iowa in Chicago in the ACC/Big Ten Challenge. Williams, Boozer and Dunleavy combined for 65 points, three more than the Hawkeyes, in a blowout. "There's a reason they are No. 1," said Iowa star Luke Recker.

The other big scare in December came at the Meadowlands, that favorite home away from home. Against No. 8 Kentucky, the Blue Devils were so sluggish that Coach K benched the starting unit in the second half with Duke down 10. The subs, including Love, outscored the Wildcats 5-4 in three minutes. After that, Duke turned the offense over to Williams, who had a career-high 38 as the Devils won in overtime, 95-92. "We've got to quit taking things for granted, but I'm glad

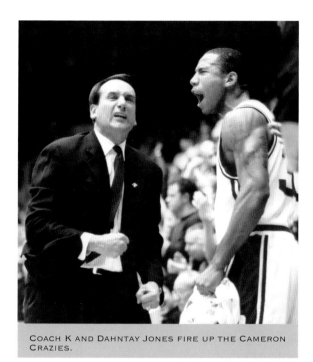

COACH K AND DAHNTAY JONES FIRE UP THE CAMERON CRAZIES.

we didn't have to learn with a loss," Dunleavy said.

But the defeat was coming. The Blue Devils were 12-0 when they went to Florida State, yet they weren't playing well. All of their shortcomings showed as FSU pulled off a 77-76 shocker, with the winning basket coming with 7.4 seconds left. Duke had nobody to blame but itself. Williams scored 26 points, including eight threes, but was 0-6 at the foul line in the last 5:40. Dunleavy missed two free throws in the last 30 seconds. The team was a woeful seven for 19 from the line. "We have a lot of work to do," said Coach K.

When the team arrived at its locker room for its next practice, the nameplates were gone, as were the individual chairs. There were no pictures on the walls. "We're starting over," Krzyzewski said. "The first 12 games coach was laid back and let us control the intensity," Jones said. "After a while, he got ticked off."

That resulted in a 25-point demolishing of Georgia Tech, but even then Duke slacked off in the second half. Maryland brought its No. 3 ranking and ACC lead to Cameron, where it had

won the previous two years. No such luck over the rededicated Devils. With Williams scoring 34 points and Dunleavy getting 19 of his 21 in the second half, it was a 99-78 rout in this battle of what had become the nation's best rivalry. Williams added eight assists, seven rebounds and three steals to his point total. Dunleavy had nine boards, seven steals, and just one turnover. Duke finally had played a game like No. 1.

Duke closed January on a roll, and in Chapel Hill, where UNC was headed for its worst season in modern history. The good news for the Heels was their bench outscored the Blue Devils, 30-4. The bad news was they lost, 87-58, for the worst defeat in Smith Center history. It could have been worse. Carolina scored the final eight points.

It was Duke's fourth straight win in the Dean Dome. "Coming here and dominating them like we did, that means quite a lot to us," Dunleavy

MIKE DUNLEAVY PLAYED A BIG PART IN HANDING MARYLAND ITS ONLY ACC LOSS.

said. "I never imagined, when I was being recruited by Duke, to ever do that."

The Blue Devils got their revenge against Florida State, although it took them a half to get started. They led only 27-24 at intermission, but shot 60 percent in the second period to romp, 80-49. By the time Duke got to Maryland, it had won 11 straight since that initial loss, by a margin of nearly 23 points. In fact, since losing at home to the Terps the previous season when Boozer broke his foot, the Devils had won 33 of 34.

But it was never close in Cole Field House as Duke suffered its worst loss in nearly four years, 87-73. Steve Blake took Williams out of the game as the Blue Devils' star shot six of 22. Chris Wilcox, at 6-10, stifled Dunleavy, and Maryland dropped Juan Dixon off Duhon to double-team Boozer, who had made 13 of 14 shots against State in his previous game. "We got a little bit flustered," Krzyzewski said. "The team that should have won, in convincing fashion."

What Maryland had done was strip away Duke's aura as an unbeatable team. Two easy wins didn't restore it. After that, a shocking 87-84 loss at Virginia had the Blue Devils shaking their heads. Boozer was unstoppable, scoring a career-high 33 points on 12-for-13 shooting with 8:47 left to play. Duke was ahead by 15. UVA gambled, and won. It doubled-down on Boozer, leaving Jones alone. Boozer didn't score again and got just three shots. The Cavaliers went on a 21-1 run to take the lead.

Williams finally warmed up and scored seven points in the last 28 seconds. His basket with 12 seconds left cut the lead to 85-84, but he missed a free throw that would have tied it. That would be repeated later in the season under more dire circumstances. Roger Mason made two free throws, Williams suffered his eighth turnover, and Maryland had clinched the ACC regular season title, snapping Duke's streak at five straight.

Even an easy win over Carolina in the finale didn't help matters. Duke went into the ACC

Tournament knowing that Maryland, which had finished 15-1 to win by two games, was the favorite.

In an unusual twist, the Blue Devils were matched against seventh-seed Carolina in the first round. Twice before in the 211 games of the nation's greatest rivalry, the Tar Heels had tried to hold the ball. Both times the strategy failed. It failed against in this third effort in Charlotte. Beaten by 29 and 25 points by Duke, Matt Doherty elected to stall until the end of the shot clock. To an extent it worked. But it only kept the game close. "It was our only hope," he said.

The Heels trailed 28-22 at halftime and couldn't get ahead in the last half. With time running out, they continued to hold the ball even as they trailed by five. Duke made most of its foul

CARLOS BOOZER HELPED HAND NORTH CAROLINA ITS WORST DEAN DOME DEFEAT.

shots and won, 60-48. UNC never did get out of the stall.

Wake Forest used a different strategy. The Deacs played a zone, and dropped off Jones, using Darius Songaila to help double up on Boozer. But the Devils made over half of their shots. Boozer got just eight, but he made seven and collected 16 rebounds. Dunleavy hit four threes, scored 18 points, and Duke won comfortably, 79-64. "The zone helped us," said Wake coach Skip Prosser. "But ultimately they're going to make their shots."

Going for its fourth straight title, the Blue Devils were surprised to meet State in the finals. The Wolfpack shot 59 percent in upsetting Maryland. Against Duke, it was no contest. Boozer made 11 of 12 shots (20 of 24 in the tournament) and won MVP honors. Williams scored 24, Dunleavy had 18 and Duke cruised, 91-61, shooting 64 percent. "We connected," Coach K said. It was the second-largest winning margin in ACC history. In winning the record four championships, the Devils had triumphed by 23, 13, 26 and 30 points—total domination.

Once again, on the last weekend of the season, Duke moved up to No. 1 in the polls. Nobody else ever had finished first in four straight years. "I'm surprised," Krzyzewski said. "I would have thought UCLA must have done it 100 times."

Seeded first in the Southeast, Duke went to Greenville, S.C., where it predictably demolished Winthrop, 84-37. The second-round game, against Notre Dame, would be far more difficult. The Irish were coached by longtime Duke assistant Mike Brey, and he knew all about the Blue Devils.

With 6:24 left, the Irish led 71-64. They had gambled by defending on Duke's trio of scorers, Williams, Boozer and Dunleavy. "We weren't going to let them beat us," Brey said. "I can live with Ewing and Duhon." It was the latter pair who led the comeback. A three-pointer by Ewing and two foul shots by Duhon tied the score at 71. Ewing

had a career-high 18 points; Duhon scored 13, his highest total in 13 games.

Boozer's basket gave Duke the lead, and the Devils closed out the 84-77 victory by making their free throws. The Devils had missed seven of their previous eight, but this time Williams hit four in a row to clinch the game. "It just helps me to buckle down," he said. "Their lives flashed before their eyes when they got down seven and they really locked us down defensively," Brey said. "That's why they're Duke."

The Blue Devils advanced to the Sweet 16 for the fifth straight year, the only team to achieve that during that time period. The regional was in Lexington, Ky., perhaps Duke's least favorite arena. Normally, Indiana, Duke's opponent, would have been greeted with jeers in Rupp Arena. But not when the opponent was the Blue Devils. Kentucky fans had not forgotten '92 and "the greatest game ever played."

Duke led for 39 minutes but was unable to put away the underdog Hoosiers in what would be one of the biggest Sweet 16 surprises ever. After taking an early 17-point lead by causing turnover after turnover, the Devils still led by 42-29 at halftime. Indiana rallied by hitting the offensive boards. Jarrad Odle scored five times on stickbacks as the Hoosiers collected 28 rebounds in the second half.

Duke still led 70-64 with less than three minutes to play, but went ice cold. A free throw by Tom Coverdale and a three-point play by Jared Jeffries made it 70-68, and, after a Duke miss, Coverdale made two free throws with 1:54 left to tie the score for the first time. After a Duke turnover, Coverdale rolled in a basket with 58 seconds left to give the Hoosiers their first lead, and two foul shots by A.J. Moye with 11 seconds left made it 74-70.

Duke appeared dead, but the closing seconds were filled with drama. Ewing missed a three-pointer, but Williams grabbed the rebound and

MIKE DUNLEAVY WAS PART OF THREE ACC CHAMPIONSHIP TEAMS.

Duke's successful season had ended in an unfathomable fashion. "Last year things went our way," said Dunleavy. "This year, they didn't."

It was the last game for Williams and Boozer. Six weeks later, Dunleavy joined them in leaving early for the NBA. His father, NBA coach Mike Dunleavy Sr., had seen his son move up the draft list. "He'll leave $15 million on the table if he doesn't come out," he said.

Dunleavy was drafted third behind Williams. The No. 1 pick was 7-6 Chinese center Yao Ming. It was the first time that college teammates ever had been the top two Americans selected by the NBA.

POINT GUARDS JASON WILLIAMS (LEFT) AND CHRIS DUHON OFTEN FOUND THEMSELVES ON THE COURT AT THE SAME TIME.

drained a three of his own. Indiana coach Mike Davis fell to the floor in agony as a foul was called on Dane Fife on the play. Williams had a chance to make the tying free throw.

He missed—"sometimes the ball bounces your way, sometimes it doesn't," he said—but Boozer leaped to grab the offensive rebound away from Jeffries. "When he was going up, I figured, 'Well, he ain't going to hit this shot,' so I grabbed him and the ball rolled off the rim and we won," Jeffries said. Referee Bruce Benedict didn't whistle a foul, and the Hoosiers had their shocking upset, 74-73.

While losing three players early to the NBA resembled what happened in 2000, circumstances were far different for the 2003 team. There were only two returning starters, and Jones, the lone senior, was a transfer who had played just one season for Duke. While Duhon was a two-year veteran, he had more pressure than he could handle after the unexpected departure of Dunleavy, who also had been named a co-captain.

There were six touted freshmen, including walk-on Lee Melchionni, whose father, Gary, paid his way because of the NCAA's 5/8 rule. Unknown to Duke, indeed to himself, the most hyped of those rookies, Raleigh's Shavlik Randolph, was suffering from a high school injury that wasn't diagnosed and fixed by surgery until after the season ended. He rarely played much in the final six weeks.

Unlike most previous years under Kzryzewski, the starting lineup remained in flux throughout the season. Nobody started in every game (Duhon was benched once). Six players had as many as 15 starts and eight had at least eight. Freshmen Shelden Williams, Randolph and Sean Dockery shared minutes with Sanders and Horvath as Duke had a nine-man rotation. The depth was deep, if unsettled. Jones, Duhon, Ewing and freshman J.J. Redick got the most minutes, although Williams usually started as Ewing came off the bench.

Despite all the uncertainty, this team was undefeated at home (15-0), tied for second in the regular season and won the fifth straight ACC Tournament, extending the Duke record. The Blue Devils actually reached No. 1 in the polls for two weeks in January and finished seventh, highest among league teams. They reached the Sweet 16 for a sixth consecutive year and finished with a 26-7 record. "It was a very good year," Krzyzewski said.

Duke got off to an unusually early start—one that surprised almost everybody. The Blue Devils became the first team to play overseas in the fall, after school started. It was typical of why this is the nation's best program; the Duke staff discovered it wasn't illegal to make a trip if no classes were missed. So the team used its October fall break to play four games in London against pro teams.

What differed from foreign trips taken regularly in the summer is that the freshmen got to go. Duke didn't have enough players without the six rookies, but Coach K was anxious for this trip to give them additional game experience. Under existing NCAA rules, the move was legal, and controversial. In fact, that loophole was closed in April, 2004, when it was decreed no fall excursions could be made. But on Sept. 28, 2002, the Blue Devils began 10 days of practice, more than two weeks before anybody else could start drills. Other coaches agreed they would do the same thing, had they just known it was possible.

SHAVLIK RANDOLPH WAS ONE OF SIX KEY FRESHMEN FOR THE BLUE DEVILS.

J.J. Redick broke Duke's single-game freshman scoring record against Virginia.

in 18 minutes. But it was mostly downhill for him after that, as his problems with a cranky hip grew worse as the season went along. More telling was a 95-80 win over Davidson, in which the Devils didn't pull away until the closing minutes.

The Devils won their first 12 games, but only UCLA (No. 14) and Wake Forest (17) were nationally ranked. But it was enough to get the Blue Devils ranked No. 1, making the sixth straight season in which they topped the polls at some time. Only one of the wins, at Clemson, was on an opposing team's floor, so there were still some uncertainties.

Win No. 12 was against Virginia, and homestate (Roanoke) boy J.J. Redick established a new record for a Duke freshman, getting 34 points to surpass the mark of Johnny Dawkins. "He was amazing tonight," said Duhon.

Not so amazing was the effort against Maryland in the next game. The Blue Devils fell apart defensively in the second half, getting outscored 50-29, and lost, 87-72. So much for the top billing. "I've coached No. 1 teams before, and this is not one of them," Coach K said. "We're far from going on Broadway."

The pattern was much the same in the next outing, at N.C. State. Duke led 39-34 at halftime because Redick had 20 points against a Wolfpack zone. But State switched to a man for man, Clifford Crawford and helpers held Redick to four points, and nobody else helped offensively for the Devils. State won, 80-71, only Herb Sendek's second win in 17 starts against Duke.

A pattern had been established. The Blue Devils won at home and lost on the road. They were upset again at Florida State, 75-70, and fell by 14 points in double overtime at Wake Forest to make it four road defeats in succession, something that hadn't happened since '96. There were

Despite its youth, Duke was the preseason choice to win the ACC. "I could think people are setting us up," Coach K said. Maryland, which won the NCAA title the previous season, was second although the Terps returned more experienced players. "I know who's been picked highest," said Maryland coach Gary Williams. "So I guess they are." Duhon was the preseason ACC Player of the Year. Wake Forest, which actually finished first, was selected sixth.

Duke opened with a 48-point win over Army and Randolph, on his 19th birthday, had 23 points

home victories against Carolina, Maryland and N.C. State, and with six wins in seven outings, it appeared Duke (20-4) was peaking when it played at St. John's.

Instead, the Devils were peeking ahead. They gave one away in the Garden. Ahead 71-60 with 4:05 left, Duke didn't score again. The Red Storm made four shots in a row and a free throw to tie the score. Duke had missed three straight shots, but had the ball with 10 seconds left and a chance to win. Instead, Marcus Hatten stole the ball at midcourt from Ewing and headed for the basket. Ewing fouled him. Hatten made the first one and the fans went crazy.

"The coaches tried everything," Duhon said. "We had them worried the whole game because they were worried about us instead of worrying about the game. The whole game there was an intensity issue."

The road woes came to a conclusion in the finale at Chapel Hill against a UNC team that was 15-14 and struggling mightily. The Heels, led by Rashad McCants and Raymond Felton, shot 61 percent in the first half and led, 42-36. Jones scored 20 of his 22 points after intermission as the Devils tied it. But Duke couldn't get the lead.

Krzyzewski was so unhappy with the defense he did the unthinkable—going to a zone. That didn't work either. McCants drained another three. "They have the talent to break you down," Coach K said. "And they did. I just didn't think we had the intensity defensively to match that."

It was 82-79 as the clock ran down. Jones hit from 30 feet for what would have been the tying

SHELDEN WILLIAMS DEVELOPED INTO ONE OF THE ACC'S TOP POST PLAYERS.

In the semifinals, it was an all-Big Four look, with Duke taking on UNC again and top-seeded Wake Forest against State. This time, the Duke "D" was ready. The Blue Devils led early, 24-12, and never looked back, spoiling Sean May's return to the UNC lineup after a broken foot in December. The Devils were red hot in the first half, taking a 54-33 lead that was never challenged. Duke was never threatened in a 75-63 victory that set up a meeting with State for the title.

Duke's string of ACC titles appeared over when State, led by Julius Hodge, held a 15-point lead with 10:05 left. But then freshman Redick got hot. And hotter. In that time, Redick scored 23 points. He hit four straight from beyond the arc. He made two clinching free throws with 12 seconds left and his team ahead, 80-77. He had outscored the 'Pack 23-22 down the stretch.

With five seconds left, Duhon walked to midcourt and held up five fingers, representing the five straight championships. Redick made two more free throws for 84-77, and got a bear hug from Krzyzewski. Coach K said the title was the most special of the five. "Other years we've had more veteran players, and a couple of times we had the most talent. This year, it was wide open. I felt so good for them."

The Blue Devils were sent West by the tournament committee, the No. 3 seed in a bracket that included Arizona and Kansas. At Salt Lake City, Duke struggled in its opener against Colorado State before Shelden Williams rescued them. Williams had just one basket until 1:21 remained with his team holding a two-point lead. Then he scored on an offensive rebound and added two free throws for a 67-57 victory. "It's not the Duke team we wanted to show," he said. "We've still got some things to work on."

goal, but Duke didn't wait for the officials to look at the TV monitor. "We just walked off," Krzyzewski said. "It was like an alarm clock went off. I said, 'The game's over, they won. Let's quit fooling around.'"

Duke entered the ACC Tournament as the third seed, its lowest since '96, and hardly on a roll. Krzyzewski said the team was still a work in progress. He started Ewing for the first time in more than a month, and the sophomore guard responded with a career-high 32 points, including five three-pointers, in an 83-76 win over Virginia. "I just wanted to be a sparkplug," Ewing said, "especially on the defensive end, and that carried over to my offensive game."

Obviously, everything was worked out against Central Michigan. Jones had a career-high 28 points; Redick, who had been sick, recovered in time to net 26 more in the 86-60 blowout. Duke shot 62 percent and made 10 of 15 three-pointers. "They're growing up," Krzyzewski said. "That's the thing not many people have allowed them to do."

The West Regional was in Anaheim, Duke against Kansas, a battle of heavyweights. The Blue Devils stuck with their four guards. It opened up the inside to the Jayhawks' All-American, Nick Collison. Kansas won, 69-65. Collison had 33 of the points and 19 rebounds. His team trailed 54-53 when Collison scored 12 consecutive points. Duke never could catch up.

Duhon did a defensive number on the other Kansas All-American, guard Kirk Hinrich, who was held to two points. But Hinrich played defense, too. His man, Redick, shot just 2-for-16, including 1-for-11 on threes. Some of them were wide open. "I had the shots. I felt good," Redick said. "They just didn't fall."

By any standards, especially considering what had happened the previous season, it was a great year. That's what Krzyzewski thought. "We were so young. We had some growing pains, but overall they did a great job. I'm happy with what we did."

Chris Duhon became the second-winningest player in ACC history.

CHAPTER

14

WHY WE'RE STILL WATCHING

Cameron Indoor Stadium looked young in old age. This was in October of 2009, a few months before the hallowed arena's 70th birthday, during an event called Countdown to Craziness, the first such season-opening spectacle Duke had hosted in five years. The stadium was dressed for the occasion. The seats in the upper bowl, once the color of an overcast morning, had been painted dark blue. The buttresses between sections were powerwashed to look less like cement. Only the year before, a video monitor had replaced the scoreboard suspended over midcourt. With all of the lights out, it gleamed in the dark. The arena even sounded unfamiliar, with the announcer Michael Buffer asking a capacity crowd if it was ready to rumble. The 9,314 fans roared the only possible response. Not long afterward, Jon Scheyer, Kyle Singler, and Nolan Smith strutted out to personalized music introductions with the rest of Duke's players before their glorified scrimmage. There was even a slam-dunk contest.

It may not sound like much now—other programs have held lavish Midnight Madness events for years—but it seemed like the start of something new. That's because Duke's basketball program is one that prides itself on status and tradition. For everything that remained and still remains the same—the size of Cameron, the winning percentage of Mike Krzyzewski, the decibel level of the Crazies—so much more was about to change.

The event marked Krzyzewski's 30th year at Duke, but the time between his 2001 national championship and the 2009-2010 season was perhaps stranger than any other stretch of his career. In short, Duke was winning just as much as ever but only made one Final Four.

This was when the Blue Devils featured J.J. Redick and Shelden Williams, whose No. 23 joined Redick's No. 4 in Cameron's rafters. Redick wasn't only the country's top guard as a junior and senior. He was also the most ostentatious character on the court. His 40 points on 13 shots, or his 41 points in the Meadowlands, became that much more legendary because of the way he acted. Redick was the best, and he knew it. He ended up winning numerous Player of the Year awards on his way to 2,769 points, the most of anyone who has ever played in the ACC. He also was despised more than any college-basketball star since Christian Laettner.

179

In the four-year period with Redick and Williams—who left Duke with the most blocked shots and rebounds in school history—Duke accomplished as much as possible without actually winning a national championship. The Blue Devils reached the Final Four in 2004 and they were expected to return in 2006, when they lost just three times all year. That was until the cruelest ending of Redick's college career: a Sweet 16 loss to Louisiana State. The leading scorer in school history was hounded so ferociously that he might have exited the arena with more scratches than points in his last time in a Duke jersey.

The departures of Redick and Williams, whose jerseys were retired before the next class even graduated, left Duke with its youngest team since World War II at a time when Krzyzewski also was busier than any coach in United States. In the summer of 2005, the West Point graduate became the head coach of Team USA with the ultimate goal of leading the Americans back to the gold-medal stand at the 2008 Olympics in Beijing. The U.S. had limped to a sixth-place finish at the 2002 World Championships and a bronze medal at the 2004 Olympics. At the 2006 World Championships, Krzyzewski's first at the helm, the Americans still lost in the semifinals.

He was spending his summers draped in red, white, and blue, but Krzyzewski's 2006-2007 team at Duke faced an even bigger problem: It lacked scholarship seniors. The Blue Devils' go-to scorer was junior DeMarcus Nelson, who had started just nine games. He was complemented by a pair of touted sophomores, Josh McRoberts and Greg Paulus, and a freshman class that, eventually, would usher in a new era. At the time, though, they were overwhelmed and overmatched, like a freshman math major in a graduate-level game-theory seminar. In the first two weeks of February, the Blue Devils lost four straight games. That seemed like the nadir until a month later, when Duke endured

an identical stretch: a home loss to Maryland, a road loss to North Carolina, a first-round ACC Tournament loss to N.C. State, and, worst of all, a first-round NCAA Tournament loss to No. 11 seed Virginia Commonwealth. The brutal fall capped the school's worst season since the mid-1990s.

The next season arrived with promise in October, peaked in early February, and still ended all too early in March. With essentially the same roster—plus Singler and Smith, two more freshmen thrown into a tamer fire—Duke actually climbed to No. 2 in the polls by February and knocked off North Carolina and Maryland a week apart. Nelson, Singler, Gerald Henderson, Scheyer, and Paulus all averaged double-figure scoring totals, forming a team with the balance that was impossible with the virtuosic Redick filling up box scores.

But for the second year in a row, and not yet the last, Duke's slide coincided with the arrival of warmer weather. The Blue Devils lost five of their last eleven games, including a home matchup with UNC with the ACC title at stake. It was almost worse than that, too. In the first round of the NCAA Tournament, Henderson was forced to coast down the floor and convert a finger-roll to lift Duke over Belmont, a mid-major seeded 15th. Two days later, West Virginia sent Duke home on the big dance's first weekend. The schadenfreude arrived immediately in thick and steady doses. Whether or not Duke's basketball team was actually dead didn't stop anyone from dancing on its grave.

In a way, however, the summers of 2007 and 2008 proved more worthwhile than any midseason adversity. In 2007, after the loss to VCU, Krzyzewski convened a staff meeting to solicit ideas for changing the public face of the program. This conference resulted in the launch of DukeBluePlanet.com, the expansion of Duke's recruiting pamphlet into a multimedia empire with behind-the-scenes access, interactive videos, and, eventually, a popular Twitter feed. If the goal was humanizing Duke's players, making it that much harder to blindly despise a bunch of teenagers and twentysomethings, then it worked. Krzyzewski did his part the next year. He took Team USA, ultimately dubbed the Redeem Team, to Beijing and came back to the United States on top of the world. In China, he was so famous, yet faceless, that he was greeted on the streets with a simple salutation: "Duke!"

At home, Duke inched closer to a gold medal of its own. Henderson turned himself from a violent dunker with freakish hops into a well-rounded threat. He had backup in Singler, the floppy-haired sophomore who looked and played like Larry Bird, and Scheyer, who assumed point-guard duties and turned the ball over as often as he missed open jumpers. All three contributed to a rollicking 41-point win over Maryland in late January that catapulted Duke to the top of the polls for the first time in three years. The midseason swoon arrived yet again—the Blue Devils lost four of six games—but Duke recovered to win the ACC Tournament in Atlanta, where Henderson, Scheyer, and Singler combined for 70 of Duke's 79 points in the championship. The season ended in a Sweet 16 blowout against Villanova, but the losses didn't stop in March. The next month, Henderson announced that he was leaving Duke one year early for the NBA Draft. Later in the summer, a promising freshman transferred closer to home.

That's how Duke opened the 2009-2010 season: as the No. 9 team in the country and the No. 2 team in the Triangle. The Blue Devils got out to a 6-0 start with all the flair of an unranked mid-major. At one point, an ESPN analyst described Duke as "alarmingly unathletic"—and that was during a winning streak. This time, the see-saw was tipping back and forth earlier than ever. Duke lost its first ACC/Big Ten Challenge game at Wisconsin

and responded with a 35-point thrashing of Gonzaga in Madison Square Garden, the team's home away from home. A pounding of Clemson was negated by a loss at Georgia Tech. Two wins over Boston College and Wake Forest, then a somber trip back from North Carolina State. Two more wins over Clemson and Florida State, then rock bottom: a 12-point loss that never felt that close at Georgetown with Barack Obama and Joe Biden, not to mention many more Cabinet appointees, watching from the front row. When the rout was mercifully over, Durham had been coated with a carpet of snow, layering over the past and setting a fresh foundation for what would come next.

Then something simultaneously familiar and unfamiliar happened: Duke started winning and barely stopped. The Blue Devils avenged a loss by trouncing Georgia Tech at home. Then they drove to Chapel Hill, where Scheyer, Singler, and Smith combined for 53 points in a 64-54 win over the Tar Heels. By this time, it was clear that the senior and two juniors were the team's backbone. The only thing the triumvirate was missing was a decent nickname.

Scheyer, a co-captain with Lance Thomas, arrived at Duke as a freshman known for scoring 21 points in 75 seconds in high school. He was reliable from the day he stepped into Cameron. First, he was a starting shooting guard. As a sophomore, he embraced the role of sixth man. Toward the end of his junior year, Scheyer assumed ball-handling responsibilities, carving out his own unconventional spot in the backcourt. And now, as a tested senior, he was hailed as a National Player of the Year candidate, pouring in 18.2 points per game while making the Duke offense go. Somehow, he had turned himself into not just a serviceable point guard, but a superb one.

The reinvention of Smith was more impressive. After he considered transferring as a freshman, he earned a starting spot as a sophomore, in 2009, only to be benched midway through the season. Adding injury to insult, he ran into a hard screen and went down with a concussion a few games later. His transformation from a timid sophomore to an intimidating junior had as much to do with his personality as it did with his basketball ability. Krzyzewski advised Smith to be himself, rather than imitating any other Duke legend. For Smith, that meant interacting with fans online and saying hi to everyone on the quad. He earned the nickname "The People's Champ," in addition to "Showtime," and it wasn't long before his play reflected his carefree personality. As a senior, he was the ACC's Player of the Year.

Singler enjoyed the steady career trajectory of that rare freshman stud who stays for four years. His statistics remained remarkably similar. He averaged 13.3 points and 5.8 rebounds per game as a freshman. As a junior, his best offensive season, he posted 17.7 points and 7.0 rebounds per game. He was also at his best when Duke needed him the most: He poured in 40 points in Duke's two Final Four games in 2010.

And still Duke wouldn't have made that Final Four if another unlikely hero, Brian Zoubek, hadn't emerged just in time. The 7-foot senior had struggled through injuries in his career but chose a matinee against Maryland to score 16 points and grab 17 rebounds in a performance that seemed like a flash in the pan. In fact, it was the exact opposite. Zoubek started every game the rest of the season. Duke lost only once more but followed that defeat with an 82-50 throttling of UNC at home on senior night for Scheyer, Thomas, and Zoubek. The most lopsided rivalry victory in 46 years gave Duke all the momentum it needed to win the ACC Tournament in Greensboro and secure a No. 1 seed in the NCAA Tournament for the first time since 2006.

Duke entered March Madness having won 12 of 13 games. And yet all year long, Krzyzewski refused to describe his team as "great." The

consensus at the time, at least among the pundits, was that Duke would continue its habit of bowing out in the NCAA Tournament. This wasn't the glitziest Duke team—there were no Redicks, let alone Laettners, Hills, or Battiers—and if anything, it reeked of an early exit. The Blue Devils were good, but just how good they were wouldn't become clear for six more games.

Duke cruised through its first three opponents, looking nothing like the team that struggled with N.C. State in January or even the teams that crashed in previous Marches. The Blue Devils weren't tested until the Elite Eight. They were effectively tasked with a road game, against Baylor in Houston, with a Final Four spot on the line. Duke passed with flying colors. Smith scored a then- career-high 29 points to send his team to the Final Four in Indianapolis, the same city where his late father, Derek, won a national championship with Louisville thirty years earlier. With less than five minutes left in the game, and potentially the season, Smith canned a three-pointer to give Duke a 60-59 lead. Then he tied the score again with a free throw. Finally, another Smith three-pointer gave Duke the lead at 64-61, and the game was never again that tight.

Around 1 a.m. on Monday morning, when they probably should have been asleep, several hundred Duke students filed out of their dormitories into the first thunderstorm of the spring and met the three Duke buses as they returned from the airport. Rain trickled down the brick exterior of the Gothic buildings and formed puddles on campus. Krzyzewski, clad in a crisp white button-down and navy tie, still knotted, followed his players into the damp night. They didn't quite know how to handle the attention. But then, this was the first Final Four for any of them. The continuous applause of ear-splitting, high-pitched hollers, peaked when Smith stepped off the bus. His toothy smile stretched from ear to ear. Next up was

Krzyzewski, with his carry-on slung over his left shoulder and a blazer resting on his arm. He walked toward the swarm and addressed the students in a tired voice, raspy from chatting loudly with referees.

"Our guys did a magnificent job," he whispered as loud as he could. "The job's not done, but we beat two hellacious teams, and you should be very proud of them."

Up to this point, in the midnight rain, it had been difficult to define this particular team. With a swarming defense and incredibly efficient offense, Duke played like a mid-major injected with steroids, not like any of the Duke teams commemorated with banners in Cameron. That history was the real problem with understanding these Blue Devils. It was tempting to equate them with their predecessors. They weren't. This was a team that won because it lost. In that way, it wasn't like any other Duke team of recent memory. It was, in fact, something else entirely. This was a team of its own.

Krzyzewski capped the short speech with two waves and then walked into Cameron, rolling his suitcase behind him. It wasn't long until Krzyzewski and the Blue Devils were on the road again. They had a game on Saturday in Indianapolis against West Virginia, the team that knocked the Blue Devils out in 2008. But in this Final Four matchup, at least, Duke played basketball that was pretty much perfect. One of their most efficient offensive performances of the past decade couldn't have come at a better time: Duke was headed for Monday's national championship game.

The final matchup of the 2010 season pitted Goliath vs. David in Duke and Butler, the upstart located so close to Lucas Oil Stadium that its players attended classes that day. The pre-game narrative was almost as entertaining as the game itself, which was maybe the oddest and also the finest title game in recent memory. There were no slam dunks and only one fast-break bucket, seven ties and fifteen lead changes. The biggest advantage, for either team, was six points.

Everything in the end—the season, the last four seasons, the revival of an entire program—came down to one defensive possession, one trip to the free-throw line, and one halfcourt heave. Butler called a timeout with 13 seconds left, trailing 60-59, and drew up a play for its star, Gordon Hayward, who had matched up all game long with Singler, the Final Four's Most Outstanding Player. Hayward dribbled around the key and, with five seconds left, lofted a jumper over Zoubek's outstretched arm. It clanged off the back rim. Zoubek grabbed the rebound and was fouled with three seconds left. He made the first. Krzyzewski told him to miss the second, fearing a Butler inbound and game-tying three-pointer, so he did. Hayward snatched the loose ball. He took four dribbles, with his team trailing 61-59, until he reached halfcourt. Leaping off his right foot, he put up the shot, which soared in line with the basket, on a direct path for the most improbable national championship ever. Who knows what would have happened had Hayward's shot dropped? It didn't. It missed by millimeters, bouncing off the backboard, then the rim, then the raised hardwood. Just like that, the game was over. Duke had won *its* most improbable national championship.

Main West quadrangle was quickly ablaze with a bonfire that burned long and bright. At the same time, in Indianapolis, Krzyzewski and his team bussed back to the Hilton, where they were greeted by a throng of Duke fans. Krzyzewski found a microphone.

"I told the team right after, in the locker room: I've said you were good, then I said you were really good, then I said you were really good and had great character. I was running out of things to say, because I always wanted the carrot in front of 'em," he said.

The crowd chuckled as a coy smile creeped over Krzyzewski's face.

"But what you have before you right now," he concluded, "is a great basketball team."

He repeated this message the next day, when the team returned to Cameron, but he left the speaking duties to someone else in May during a visit to the White House's Rose Garden. The players wore suits on a steamy day as they stood behind the president. It was the first time they had seen Obama since that snowy afternoon in Georgetown. "When I woke up this morning and saw a few hundred students camping on my lawn, I remembered that today is Duke day," the leader of the free world said.

Front and center were Scheyer, Singler, and Smith, squinting into the sun as Obama congratulated them. They came together once again the following October, on a Friday night in Cameron, for Countdown to Craziness, which Duke had adopted as tradition. Finally, after six anxious months, the most anticipated Duke season in a decade had arrived. And yet this event was as much a preview of the upcoming year as it was a gala celebration honoring the previous team. The players from the 2010 squad flashed their gaudy rings, watched a fourth banner rise to the rafters over Cameron's student entrance, and mouthed the words to "We Are The Champions." Right in the middle of the bash was Scheyer, in dark jeans, standing next to Singler and Smith, wearing warmup sweats under their championship T-shirts.

In this era of college basketball, when programs like Duke increasingly rely on precocious teenagers who spend one year on East Campus before bolting for luxury condos in NBA cities, there might never again be such a talented trio of players who stick around for four years and leave an unmistakeable legacy along the way. But then, who knows? To find out, after all, is why we keep watching.

—Ben Cohen
September 1, 2011

RECORD BOOK

Year	Overall W-L	Southern Conference W-L	Southern Tournament Finish	AP Poll	Coaches Poll	Postseason Results	Head Coach	Captains
1905-06	2-3	---	---	---	---	---	W.W. Cap Card	T.G. Stern
1906-07	4-2	---	---	---	---	---	W.W. Cap Card	T.G. Stern
1907-08	2-3	---	---	---	---	---	W.W. Cap Card	Bill Lilly
1908-09	8-1	---	---	---	---	---	W.W. Cap Card	
1909-10	4-4	---	---	---	---	---	W.W. Cap Card	P.J. Kiker
1910-11	4-3	---	---	---	---	---	W.W. Cap Card	H.G. Hendrick
1911-12	6-1	---	---	---	---	---	W.W. Cap Card	C.B. Brinn
1912-13	11-8	---	---	---	---	---	J.E. Brinn	
1913-14	12-8	---	---	---	---	---	Noble L. Clay	
1914-15	10-10	---	---	---	---	---	Noble L. Clay	
1915-16	9-11	---	---	---	---	---	Bob Doak	
1916-17	20-4	---	---	---	---	---	Chick Doak	"Hip" Martin
1917-18	10-5	---	---	---	---	---	Chick Doak	
1918-19	6-5	---	---	---	---	---	H.P. Cole	
1919-20	10-4	---	---	---	---	---	W.J. Rothensies	
1920-21	9-6	---	---	---	---	---	Floyd Egan	L.B. Hathaway
1921-22	6-12	---	---	---	---	---	James Baldwin	O.L. Richardson
1922-23	15-7	---	---	---	---	---	J.S. Burbage	James Simpson
1923-24	19-6	---	---	---	---	---	J.S. Burbage	L.E. Spikes
1924-25	4-9	---	---	---	---	---	George Buckheit	E.J. Bullock
1925-26	8-12	---	---	---	---	---	George Buckheit	Pete Moss
1926-27	4-10	---	---	---	---	---	George Buckheit	Marshall Butler
1927-28	9-5	---	---	---	---	---	George Buckheit	D.L. Kelley
1928-29	12-8	5-4	Finalist	---	---	---	Eddie Cameron	Coke Candler
1929-30	18-2	9-1	Finalist	---	---	---	Eddie Cameron	Bo Farley, Harry Councilor
1930-31	14-7	5-4	Round of Eight	---	---	---	Eddie Cameron	by Games
1931-32	14-11	6-5	Semifinalist	---	---	---	Eddie Cameron	by Games
1932-33	17-5	7-3	Finalist	---	---	---	Eddie Cameron	by Games
1933-34	18-6	9-4	Finalist	---	---	---	Eddie Cameron	James Thompson, Phil Weaver
1934-35	18-8	10-4	Semifinalist	---	---	---	Eddie Cameron	Sam Bell
1935-36	20-6	4-5	Quarterfinalist	---	---	---	Eddie Cameron	Charles Kunkle
1936-37	15-8	11-6	Quarterfinalist	---	---	---	Eddie Cameron	Ken Podger
1937-38	15-9	9-5	Champion	---	---	---	Eddie Cameron	Fred Edwards, John Hoffman
1938-39	10-12	8-8	Quarterfinalist	---	---	---	Eddie Cameron	Ed Swindell, Bob O'Mara
1939-40	19-7	13-2	Finalist	---	---	---	Eddie Cameron	Bill Parsons
1940-41	14-8	8-4	Champion	---	---	---	Eddie Cameron	Tom Connelly, Glen Price
1941-42	22-2	15-1	Champion	---	---	---	Eddie Cameron	Ray Spuhler
1942-43	20-6	12-1	Finalist	---	---	---	Gerry Gerard	
1943-44	13-13	4-2	Champion	---	---	---	Gerry Gerard	
1944-45	13-9	6-1	Finalist	---	---	---	Gerry Gerard	
1945-46	21-6	12-2	Champion	---	---	---	Gerry Gerard	
1946-47	19-8	10-4	Quarterfinalist	---	---	---	Gerry Gerard	Ed Koffenberger, John Seward
1947-48	17-12	8-6	Finalist	---	---	---	Gerry Gerard	Doug Ausbon
1948-49	13-9	5-7	---	---	---	---	Gerry Gerard	Ben Collins, Dick Gordon
1949-50	15-15	9-7	Finalist	---	---	---	Gerry Gerard	Corren Youmans, Tommy Hughes
1950-51	20-13	13-6	Finalist	---	---	---	Harold Bradley	Scott York
1951-52	24-6	13-3	Finalist	12th	---	---	Harold Bradley	Dick Groat
1952-53	18-8	12-4	Quarterfinalist	---	---	---	Harold Bradley	Bernie Janicki, Rudy D'Emilio, Rudy Lacy
1953-54	22-6	9-1 (1st)	Semifinalist	15th	20th	---	Harold Bradley	Bernie Janicki, Rudy D'Emilio
1954-55	20-8	11-3 (2nd)	Finalist	---	---	NCAA First Rd.	Harold Bradley	Joe Belmont, Ronnie Mayer
1955-56	19-7	10-4 (T3rd)	Semifinalist	17th	18th	---	Harold Bradley	Joe Belmont
1956-57	13-11	8-6 (3rd)	Quarterfinalist	---	---	---	Harold Bradley	
1957-58	18-7	11-3 (1st)	Semifinalist	10th	13th	---	Harold Bradley	Bobby Joe Harris, Jim Newcome
1958-59	13-12	7-7 (T3rd)	Semifinalist	---	---	---	Harold Bradley	Jerry Robertson, Marty Joyce

Year	Overall W-L	Southern Conference W-L	Southern Tournament Finish	AP Poll	Coaches Poll	Postseason Results	Head Coach	Captains
1959-60	17-11	7-7(4th)	Champion	18th	15th	NCAA Elite Eight	Vic Bubas	Howard Hurt
1960-61	22-6	10-4 (3rd)	Finalist	10th	9th	---	Vic Bubas	Howard Hurt
1961-62	20-5	11-3 (2nd)	Semifinalist	10th	13th	---	Vic Bubas	Buzz Mewhort, Art Heyman
1962-63	27-3	14-0 (1st)	Champion	2nd	2nd	NCAA Third Place	Vic Bubas	Art Heyman
1963-64	26-5	13-1 (1st)	Champion	3rd	4th	NCAA Finalist	Vic Bubas	Jeff Mullins
1964-65	20-5	11-3 (1st)	Finalist	10th	9th	---	Vic Bubas	Denny Ferguson
1965-66	26-4	12-2 (1st)	Champion	2nd	2nd	NCAA Third Place	Vic Bubas	Steve Vacendak
1966-67	18-9	9-3 (2nd)	Finalist	---	19th	NIT	Vic Bubas	Bob Verga
1967-68	22-6	11-3 (2nd)	Semifinalist	10th	11th	NIT	Vic Bubas	Mike Lewis
1968-69	15-13	8-6 (T3rd)	Finalist	---	---	---	Vic Bubas	Dave Golden, Steve Vacendak
1969-70	17-9	8-6 (4th)	Quarterfinalist	---	---	NIT	Bucky Waters	Larry Saunders
1970-71	20-10	9-5 (3rd)	Quarterfinalist	---	---	NIT Fourth Place	Bucky Waters	Larry Saunders
1971-72	14-12	6-6 (T4th)	Semifinalist	---	---	---	Bucky Waters	Pat Doughty, Gary Melchionni, Alan Shaw
1972-73	12-14	4-8 (T4th)	Quarterfinalist	---	---	---	Bucky Waters	Gary Melchionni, Alan Shaw
1973-74	10-16	2-10 (7th)	Quarterfinalist	---	---	---	Neill McGeachy	Kevin Billerman
1974-75	13-13	2-10 (T6th)	Quarterfinalist	---	---	---	Bill Foster	Kevin Billerman, Bob Fleischer
1975-76	13-14	3-9 (7th)	Quarterfinalist	---	---	---	Bill Foster	Terry Chili, Willie Hodge
1976-77	14-13	2-10 (T6th)	Quarterfinalist	---	---	---	Bill Foster	Tate Armstrong, Mark Crow
1977-78	27-7	8-4 (2nd)	Champion	7th	9th	NCAA Finalist	Bill Foster	Jim Spanarkel
1978-79	22-8	9-3 (T1st)	Finalist	11th	7th	NCAA Second Rd.	Bill Foster	Jim Spanarkel
1979-80	24-9	7-7 (T5th)	Champion	14th	16th	NCAA Elite Eight	Bill Foster	Bob Bender, Mike Gminski
1980-81	17-13	6-8 (T5th)	Quarterfinalist	---	---	NIT	Mike Krzyzewski	Gene Banks, Kenny Dennard
1981-82	10-17	4-10 (T6th)	Quarterfinalist	---	---	---	Mike Krzyzewski	Vince Taylor
1982-83	11-17	3-11 (7th)	Quarterfinalist	---	---	---	Mike Krzyzewski	Tom Emma, Chip Engelland
1983-84	24-10	7-7 (T3rd)	Finalist	14th	14th	NCAA Second Rd.	Mike Krzyzewski	Richard Ford, Doug McNeely
1984-85	23-8	8-6 (T4th)	Semifinalist	10th	12th	NCAA Second Rd.	Mike Krzyzewski	Jay Bryan, Dan Meagher
1985-86	37-3	12-2 (1st)	Champion	1st	1st	NCAA Finalist	Mike Krzyzewski	Johnny Dawkins, David Henderson
1986-87	24-9	9-5 (3rd)	Quarterfinalist	17th	---	NCAA Sweet 16	Mike Krzyzewski	Tommy Amaker
1987-88	28-7	9-5 (3rd)	Champion	5th	5th	NCAA Semifinalist	Mike Krzyzewski	Billy King, Kevin Strickland
1988-89	28-8	9-5 (T2nd)	Finalist	9th	7th	NCAA Semifinalist	Mike Krzyzewski	Danny Ferry, Quin Snyder
1989-90	29-9	9-5 (2nd)	Quarterfinalist	15th	14th	NCAA Finalist	Mike Krzyzewski	Robert Brickey
1990-91	**32-7**	**11-3 (1st)**	**Finalist***	**6th**	**6th**	**NCAA Champion**	**Mike Krzyzewski**	**Clay Buckley, Greg Koubek**
1991-92	**34-2**	**14-2 (1st)**	**Champion***	**1st**	**1st**	**NCAA Champion**	**Mike Krzyzewski**	**Brian Davis, Christian Laettner**
1992-93	24-8	10-6 (T3rd)	Quarterfinalist	10th	10th	NCAA Second Rd.	Mike Krzyzewski	Thomas Hill, Bobby Hurley
1993-94	28-6	12-4 (1st)	Semifinalist	6th	6th	NCAA Finalist	Mike Krzyzewski	Marty Clark, Grant Hill, Antonio Lang
1994-95	13-18	2-14 (9th)	Quarterfinalist	---	---	---	Mike Krzyzewski, Pete Gaudet	Kenny Blakeney, Erik Meek, Cherokee Parks
1995-96	18-13	8-8 (T4th)	Quarterfinalist	---	---	NCAA First Rd.	Mike Krzyzewski	Jeff Capel, Chris Collins
1996-97	24-9	12-4 (1st)	Quarterfinalist	8th	8th	NCAA Second Rd.	Mike Krzyzewski	Jeff Capel, Greg Newton, Carmen Wallace
1997-98	32-4	15-1 (1st)	Finalist	3rd	5th	NCAA Elite Eight	Mike Krzyzewski	Trajan Langdon, Roshown McLeod, Steve Wojciechowski
1998-99	37-2	16-0 (1st)	Champion	1st	2nd	NCAA Finalist	Mike Krzyzewski	Trajan Langdon
1999-00	29-5	15-1 (1st)	Champion	1st	4th	NCAA Sweet 16	Mike Krzyzewski	Shane Battier, Chris Carrawell, Nate James
2000-01	**35-4**	**13-3 (T1st)**	**Champion***	**1st**	**1st**	**NCAA Champion**	**Mike Krzyzewski**	**Shane Battier, Nate James, J.D. Simpson**
2001-02	31-4	13-3 (2nd)	Champion	1st	1st	NCAA Sweet 16	Mike Krzyzewski	Carlos Boozer, Mike Dunleavy, Jason Williams
2002-03	26-7	11-5 (T2nd)	Champion	7th	9th	NCAA Sweet 16	Mike Krzyzewski	Chris Duhon, Nick Horvath, Dahntay Jones
2003-04	31-6	13-3 (1st)	Finalist	6th	2nd	NCAA Semifinalist	Mike Krzyzewski	Chris Duhon, Daniel Ewing, Nick Horvath
2004-05	27-6	11-5 (3rd)	Champion	3rd	7th	NCAA Sweet 16	Mike Krzyzewski	Daniel Ewing, Reggie Love, J.J. Redick
2005-06	32-4	14-2 (1st)	Champion	1st	7th	NCAA Sweet 16	Mike Krzyzewski	Sean Dockery, Lee Melchionni, J.J. Redick, Sheldon Williams
2006-07	22-11	8-8 (T6th)	First Rd.	--	--	NCAA First Rd.	Mike Krzyzewski	Josh McRoberts, DeMarcus Nelson, Greg Paulus
2007-08	28-6	13-3 (2nd)	Semifinalist	9th	16th	NCAA Second Rd.	Mike Krzyzewski	DeMarcus Nelson
2008-09	30-7	11-5 (T2nd)	Champion	6th	11th	NCAA Sweet 16	Mike Krzyzewski	Gerald Henderson, Greg Paulus, Jon Scheyer
2009-10	**35-5**	**13-3 (T1st)**	**Champion**	**3rd**	**1st**	**NCAA Champion**	**Mike Krzyzewski**	**Jon Scheyer, Lance Thomas**
2010-11	32-5	13-3 (2nd)	Champion	3rd	7th	NCAA Sweet 16	Mike Krzyzewski	Kyle Singler, Nolan Smith

*National Champions

Victories (Minimum 25 years in Division I)

No.	School	First Season	Yrs.	Won	Lost	Tied	Pct.
1.	Kentucky	1903	106	1,988	653	1	.758
2.	North Carolina	1911	99	1,984	703	0	.738
3.	Kansas	1899	111	1,970	793	0	.713
4.	**Duke**	**1906**	**104**	**1,877**	**817**	**0**	**.697**
5.	Syracuse	1901	108	1,753	806	0	.697
6.	Temple	1895	113	1,711	960	0	.641
7.	St. John's (N.Y.)	1908	97	1,668	784	0	.680
8.	UCLA	1920	90	1,672	726	0	.697
9.	Pennsylvania	1897	109	1,658	949	2	.636
10.	Notre Dame	1898	104	1,651	908	1	.645
11.	Indiana	1901	109	1,641	909	0	.644
12.	Utah	1909	101	1,637	858	0	.656
13.	Illinois	1906	104	1,609	853	0	.654
14.	Western KY	1915	90	1,602	780	0	.673
15.	Oregon St	1902	108	1,594	1,180	0	.575
16.	Washington	1896	107	1,591	1,047	0	.603
17.	Louisville	1912	95	1,587	831	0	.656
18.	Texas	1906	103	1,586	945	0	.627
19.	BUY	1903	107	1,578	994	0	.614
20.	Arizona	1905	104	1,568	858	1	.646
21.	Purdue	1897	111	1,565	927	0	.628
22.	Cincinnati	1902	108	1,553	915	0	.629
23.	Princeton	1901	109	1,552	986	0	.612
24.	West Virginia	1904	100	1,550	972	0	.615
25.	Bradley	1903	105	1,537	1,006	0	.604
26.	North Carolina St	1913	97	1,534	924	0	.624
27.	Villanova	1921	89	1,505	850	0	.639
28.	Connecticut	1901	106	1,499	839	0	.641
29.	Oklahoma	1908	102	1,499	941	0	.614
30.	Missouri St	1901	97	1,498	833	0	.643
31.	Arkansas	1924	86	1,487	822	0	.644
32.	Alabama	1913	96	1,482	898	1	.623
33.	St. Joseph's	1910	100	1,477	966	0	.605
34.	Georgetwon	1907	101	1,476	924	0	.615
35.	Oklahoma St	1908	100	1,475	1,030	0	.589
36.	Iowa	1902	108	1,466	1,006	0	.593
37.	Southern California	1907	103	1,459	1,042	0	.583
38.	Washington St	1902	108	1,457	1,341	0	.521
39.	Missouri	1907	103	1,452	1,017	0	.588
40.	Michigan St	1899	110	1,449	995	0	.593
41.	Tennessee	1909	100	1,442	920	2	.610
42.	Montana St	1902	107	1,442	1,147	0	.557
43.	Illinois St	1899	111	1,440	1,036	0	.582
44.	Ohio St	1899	108	1,435	982	0	.594
45.	Kansas St	1903	105	1,434	1,039	0	.580
46.	Fordham	1903	106	1,432	1,190	0	.546
47.	Minnesota	1896	114	1,425	1,084	2	.568
48.	Dayton	1904	104	1,424	1,000	0	.587
49.	Marquette	1917	92	1,423	878	0	.618
50.	Vanderbilt	1901	107	1,423	1,015	0	.584

Percentage (Minimum 25 years in Division I)

No.	School	First Season	Yrs.	Won	Lost	Tied	Pct.
1.	Kentucky	1903	106	1,988	635	1	.758
2.	North Carolina	1911	99	1,984	703	0	.738
3.	Kansas	1899	111	1,970	793	0	.713
4.	UNLC	1959	51	1,051	429	9	.711
5.	UCLA	1920	90	1,672	726	0	.697
6.	**Duke**	**1906**	**104**	**1,877**	**817**	**0**	**.697**
7.	Syracuse	1901	108	1,753	806	0	.685
8.	Western KY	1915	90	1,602	780	0	.673
9.	St. John's (N.Y.)	1908	102	1,686	868	0	.660
10.	Louisville	1912	95	1,587	831	0	.656
11.	Utah	1909	101	1,637	858	0	.656
12.	Illinois	1906	104	1,609	853	0	.654
13.	Arizona	1905	104	1,568	858	1	.646
14.	Notre Dame	1898	104	1,651	908	1	.645
15.	Arkansas	1924	86	1,487	822	0	.644
16.	Indiana	1901	109	1,641	909	0	.644
17.	Missouri St	1909	97	1,498	833	0	.643
18.	Connecticut	1901	106	1,499	839	0	.641
19.	Temple	1985	113	1,711	960	0	.641
20.	Villanova	1921	89	1,505	850	0	.639
21.	Penn	1897	109	1,658	949	2	.636
22.	Murray St	1926	84	1,395	809	0	.633
23.	Weber St	1963	47	852	496	0	.632
24.	Memphis	1921	88	1,373	805	1	.630
25.	Cincinnati	1902	108	1,553	915	0	.629
26.	VCU	1971	39	707	418	0	.628
27.	Purdue	1897	111	1,565	927	0	.628
28.	UAB	1979	31	617	367	0	.627
29.	Texas	1906	103	1,586	945	0	.627
30.	DePaul	1924	86	1,352	809	0	.626
31.	North Carolina St	1913	97	1,534	924	0	.624
32.	Alabama	1913	96	1,482	898	1	.623
33.	Marquette	1917	92	1,423	878	0	.618
34.	Georgetown	1907	101	1,476	924	0	.615
35.	West Virginia	1904	100	1,550	972	0	.615
36.	Oklahoma	1908	102	1,499	941	0	.614
37.	Jackson St	1951	58	1,002	631	0	.614
38.	BYU	1903	107	1,578	994	0	.614
39.	Princeton	1901	109	1,552	986	0	.612
40.	Tennessee	1909	100	1,442	920	2	.610
41.	Old Dominion	1951	59	965	616	0	.610
42.	Holy Cross	1901	90	1,280	827	0	.607
43.	St. Joseph's	1910	100	1,477	966	0	.605
44.	Bradley	1903	105	1,537	1,006	0	.604
45.	Akron	1902	108	1,387	910	0	.604
46.	Washington	1896	107	1,591	1,047	0	.603
47.	Green Bay	1970	40	704	467	0	.601
48.	Providence	1921	84	1,274	847	0	.600
49.	Houston	1946	64	1,086	724	0	.600
50.	Southern Ill	1914	95	1,415	953	0	.598

ACC TOURNAMENT RESULTS

Round	Date	Site	Opponent	W/L Score	DU High Pts.
1954 • Seed: #1					
First Round	3/4	Raleigh, N.C	Virginia[8]	W 96-68	13-Mayer
Semifinals	3/5	Raleigh, N.C.	N.C. State[4]	L 75-79	21-Janicki
1955 • Seed: #2					
First Round	3/3	Raleigh, N.C.	South Carolina[7]	W 83-67	18-Lakata
Semifinals	3/4	Raleigh, N.C.	Virginia[6]	W 90-77	34-Mayer
Championship	3/5	Raleigh, N.C.	N.C. State[1]	L 77-87	19-Belmont
1956 • Seed: #4					
First Round	3/1	Raleigh, N.C.	Maryland[5]	W 94-69	27-Mayer
Semifinals	3/2	Raleigh, N.C.	N.C. State[1]	L 79-91	22-Mayer
1957 • Seed: #3					
First Round	3/7	Raleigh, N.C.	South Carolina[6]	L 81-84	20-Newcome
1958 • Seed: #1					
First Round	3/6	Raleigh, N.C.	Wake Forest[8]	W 51-44	12-Harris
Semifinals	3/7	Raleigh, N.C.	Maryland[4]	L 65-71(ot)	21-Allen
1959 • Seed: #3					
First Round	3/5	Raleigh, N.C.	Wake Forest[6]	W 78-71	28-Hurt
Semifinals	3/6	Raleigh, N.C.	North Carolina[2]	L 71-74	21-Youngkin
1960 • Seed: #4 • ACC Champions					
First Round	3/3	Raleigh, N.C.	South Carolina[5]	W 82-69	26-Kistler
Semifinals	3/4	Raleigh, N.C.	North Carolina[1]	W 71-69	30-Youngkin
Championship	3/5	Raleigh, N.C.	Wake Forest[2]	W 63-59	22-Kistler
1961 • Seed: #2					
First Round	3/2	Raleigh, N.C.	Virginia[7]	W 89-54	22-Heyman
Semifinals	3/3	Raleigh, N.C.	South Carolina[6]	W 92-75	32-Heyman
Championship	3/4	Raleigh, N.C.	Wake Forest[1]	L 81-96	26-Heyman
1962 • Seed: #2					
First Round	3/1	Raleigh, N.C.	Maryland[7]	W 71-58	22-Heyman
Semifinals	3/2	Raleigh, N.C.	Clemson[6]	L 72-77	27-Heyman
1963 • Seed: #1 • ACC Champions					
First Round	2/28	Raleigh, N.C.	Virginia[8]	W 89-70	29-Mullins
Semifinals	3/1	Raleigh, N.C.	N.C. State[5]	W 82-65	25-Mullins
Championship	3/2	Raleigh, N.C.	Wake Forest[2]	W 68-57	24-Heyman
1964 • Seed: #1 • ACC Champions					
First Round	3/5	Raleigh, N.C.	N.C. State[8]	W 75-44	21-Buckley
Semifinals	3/6	Raleigh, N.C.	North Carolina[5]	W 65-49	20-Buckley
Championship	3/7	Raleigh, N.C.	Wake Forest[2]	W 80-59	24-Mullins
1965 • Seed: #1					
First Round	3/4	Raleigh, N.C.	South Carolina[8]	W 62-60	25-Verga
Semifinals	3/5	Raleigh, N.C.	Wake Forest[5]	W 101-81	25-Vacendak
Championship	3/6	Raleigh, N.C.	N.C. State[2]	L 85-91	25-Verga
1966 • Seed: #1 • ACC Champions					
First Round	3/3	Raleigh, N.C.	Wake Forest[8]	W 103-73	29-Verga
Semifinals	3/4	Raleigh, N.C.	North Carolina[4]	W 21-20	6-Vacendak
Championship	3/5	Raleigh, N.C.	N.C. State[2]	W 71-66	18-Vacendak
1967 • Seed: #2					
First Round	3/9	Greensboro, N.C.	Virginia[7]	W 99-78	35-Verga
Semifinals	3/10	Greensboro, N.C.	South Carolina[3]	W 69-66	21-Verga
Championship	3/11	Greensboro, N.C.	North Carolina[1]	L 73-83	20-Verga

Round	Date	Site	Opponent	W/L Score	DU High Pts.
1968 • Seed: #2					
First Round	3/7	Charlotte, N.C.	Clemson[7]	W 43-40	13-Lewis
Semifinals	3/8	Charlotte, N.C.	N.C. State[3]	L 10-12	4-Lewis
1969 • Seed: #3					
First Round	3/6	Charlotte, N.C.	Virginia[6]	W 99-86	24-two players
Semifinals	3/7	Charlotte, N.C.	South Carolina[2]	W 68-59	18-Golden
Championship	3/8	Charlotte, N.C.	North Carolina[1]	L 74-85	19-Denton
1970 • Seed: #4					
First Round	3/5	Charlotte, N.C.	Wake Forest[5]	L 73-81	29-Saunders
1971 • Seed: #3					
First Round	3/11	Greensboro, N.C.	N.C. State[6]	L 61-68	16-Denton
1972 • Seed: #4					
First Round	3/9	Greensboro, N.C.	N.C. State[5]	W 73-60	16-two players
Semifinals	3/10	Greensboro, N.C.	North Carolina[1]	L 48-63	13-Melchionni
1973 • Seed: #4					
First Round	3/8	Greensboro, N.C.	Virginia[5]	L 55-59	14-Melchionni
1974 • Seed: #7					
First Round	3/7	Greensboro, N.C.	Maryland[2]	L 66-85	17-Armstrong
1975 • Seed: #6					
First Round	3/6	Greensboro, N.C.	Clemson[3]	L 76-78	16-Hodge
1976 • Seed: #7					
First Round	3/4	Landover, Md.	Maryland[2]	L 78-80(ot)	33-Armstrong
1977 • Seed: #6					
First Round	3/3	Greensboro, N.C.	Clemson[3]	L 74-82	23-Spanarkel
1978 • Seed: #2 • ACC Champions					
First Round	3/1	Greensboro, N.C.	Clemson[7]	W 83-72	22-Dennard
Semifinals	3/2	Greensboro, N.C.	Maryland[6]	W 81-69	21-Spanarkel
Championship	3/4	Greensboro, N.C.	Wake Forest[5]	W 85-77	25-Gminski
1979 • Seed: #2					
First Round	3/1	Greensboro, N.C.	Wake Forest[7]	W 58-56	20-Spanarkel
Semifinals	3/2	Greensboro, N.C.	N.C. State[6]	W 62-59	18-Spanarkel
Championship	3/3	Greensboro, N.C.	North Carolina[1]	L 63-71	19-Gminski
1980 • Seed: #6 • ACC Champions					
First Round	2/28	Greensboro, N.C.	N.C. State[3]	W 68-62	24-Banks
Semifinals	2/29	Greensboro, N.C.	North Carolina[2]	W 75-61	24-Gminski
Championship	3/1	Greensboro, N.C.	Maryland[1]	W 73-72	21-Banks
1981 • Seed: #5					
First Round	3/5	Landover, Md.	Maryland[4]	L 53-56	17-Banks
1982 • Seed: #6					
First Round	3/5	Greensboro, N.C.	Wake Forest[3]	L 53-88	17-Taylor
1983 • Seed: #7					
First Round	3/11	Atlanta, Ga.	Virginia[2]	L 66-109	17-Dawkins
1984 • Seed: #4					
First Round	3/9	Greensboro, N.C.	Georgia Tech[5]	W 67-63	20-Alarie
Semifinals	3/10	Greensboro, N.C.	North Carolina[1]	W 77-75	21-Alarie
Championship	3/11	Greensboro, N.C.	Maryland[2]	L 62-74	22-Dawkins

Round	Date	Site	Opponent	W/L Score	DU High Pts.
1985 • Seed: #4					
First Round	3/8	Atlanta, Ga.	Maryland[5]	W 86-73	27-Dawkins
Semifinals	3/9	Atlanta, Ga.	Georgia Tech1	L 64-75	21-Bilas
1986 • Seed: #1 • ACC Champions					
First Round	3/7	Greensboro, N.C.	Wake Forest[8]	W 68-60	22-Alarie
Semifinals	3/8	Greensboro, N.C.	Virginia[5]	W 75-70	24-Dawkins
Championship	3/9	Greensboro, N.C.	Georgia Tech[2]	W 68-67	20-Dawkins
1987 • Seed: #3					
First Round	3/6	Landover, Md.	N.C. State[6]	L 64-71(ot)	20-Ferry
1988 • Seed: #3 • ACC Champions					
First Round	3/11	Greensboro, N.C.	Virginia[6]	W 60-48	20-Ferry
Semifinals	3/12	Greensboro, N.C.	N.C. State[2]	W 73-71	16-Brickey
Championship	3/13	Greensboro, N.C.	North Carolina[1]	W 65-61	19-Ferry
1989 • Seed: #2					
First Round	3/10	Atlanta, Ga.	Wake Forest[7]	W 88-64	24-Ferry
Semifinals	3/11	Atlanta, Ga.	Virginia[3]	W 69-58	23-Ferry
Championship	3/12	Atlanta, Ga.	North Carolina[4]	L 74-77	16-Henderson
1990 • Seed: #2					
First Round	3/9	Charlotte, N.C.	Maryland[7]	W 104-84	24-Henderson
Semifinals	3/10	Charlotte, N.C.	Georgia Tech[3]	L 72-83	29-Laettner
1991 • Seed: #1					
Semifinals	3/9	Charlotte, N.C.	N.C. State[4]	W 93-72	18-two players
Championship	3/10	Charlotte, N.C.	North Carolina[2]	L 74-96	22-Laettner
1992 • Seed: #1 • ACC Champions					
First Round	3/13	Charlotte, N.C.	Maryland[8]	W 94-87	33-Laettner
Semifinals	3/14	Charlotte, N.C.	Georgia Tech[4]	W 89-76	17-two players
Championship	3/15	Charlotte, N.C.	North Carolina[3]	W 94-74	25-Laettner
1993 • Seed: #3					
First Round	3/12	Charlotte, N.C.	Georgia Tech[6]	L 66-69	17-Hurley
1994 • Seed: #1					
First Round	3/11	Charlotte, N.C.	Clemson[8]	W 77-64	23-Hill
Semifinals	3/12	Charlotte, N.C.	Virginia[4]	L 61-66	19-Hill
1995 • Seed: #9					
Play-in	3/9	Greensboro, N.C.	N.C. State[8]	W 83-70	19-Parks
First Round	3/10	Greensboro, N.C.	Wake Forest[1]	L 70-87	18-Meek
1996 • Seed: #4					
First Round	3/8	Greensboro, N.C.	Maryland[5]	L 69-82	21-Price
1997 • Seed: #1					
First Round	3/7	Greensboro, N.C.	N.C. State[8]	L 60-66	17-Capel
1998 • Seed: #1					
First Round	3/5	Greensboro, N.C.	Virginia[9]	W 63-41	14-McLeod
Semifinals	3/7	Greensboro, N.C.	Clemson[5]	W 66-64	17-McLeod
Championship	3/8	Greensboro, N.C.	North Carolina[2]	L 68-83	24-McLeod
1999 • Seed: #1 • ACC Champions					
First Round	3/4	Charlotte, N.C.	Virginia[9]	W 104-67	18-Avery
Semifinals	3/6	Charlotte, N.C.	N.C. State[5]	W 83-68	24-Maggette
Championship	3/7	Charlotte, N.C.	North Carolina[3]	W 96-73	29-Avery
2000 • Seed: #1 • ACC Champions					
First Round	3/9	Charlotte, N.C.	Clemson[9]	W 94-63	19-Battier
Semifinals	3/11	Charlotte, N.C.	Wake Forest[5]	W 82-73	18-Battier
Championship	3/12	Charlotte. N.C.	Maryland[2]	W 81-68	23-Williams
2001 • Seed: #2 • ACC Champions					
First Round	3/9	Atlanta, Ga.	N.C. State[7]	W 76-61	19-Williams
Semifinals	3/10	Atlanta, Ga.	Maryland[3]	W 84-82	20-Battier
Championship	3/11	Atlanta, Ga.	North Carolina[1]	W 79-53	24-Dunleavy
2002 • Seed: #2 • ACC Champions					
First Round	3/8	Charlotte, N.C.	North Carolina[7]	W 60-48	20-Williams
Semifinals	3/9	Charlotte, N.C.	Wake Forest[3]	W 79-64	18-Dunleavy
Championship	3/10	Charlotte, N.C.	N.C. State[4]	W 91-61	26-Boozer
2003 • Seed: #3 • ACC Champions					
First Round	3/14	Greensboro, N.C.	Virginia[6]	W 83-76	32-Ewing
Semifinals	3/15	Greensboro, N.C.	North Carolina[7]	W 75-63	19-Ewing
Championship	3/16	Greensboro, N.C.	N.C. State[4]	W 84-77	30-Redick
2004 • Seed: #1					
First Round	3/12	Greensboro, N.C.	Virginia[8]	W 84-74	27-Williams
Semifinals	3/13	Greensboro, N.C.	Georgia Tech[4]	W 85-71	20-Williams
Championship	3/14	Greensboro, N.C.	Maryland[6]	L 87-95(ot)	21-Duhon
2005 • Seed: #1 • ACC Champions					
Quarterfinals	3/11	Washington, D.C.	Virginia[11]	W 76-64	16-two players
Semifinals	3/12	Washington, D.C.	N.C. State[7]	W 76-69	35-Redick
Championship	3/13	Washington, D.C.	Georgia Tech[5]	W 69-64	26-Redick
2006 • Seed: #1 • ACC Champion					
Quarterfinals	3/10	Greensboro, N.C.	Miami[8]	W 80-76	25-Redickk
Semifinals	3/11	Greensboro, N.C.	Wake Forest[12]	W 78-66	20-Redick
Championship	3/12	Greensboro, N.C.	Boston College[3]	W 78-76	26-Redick
2007 • Seed: #7					
First Round	3/8	Tampa, Fla.	N.C. State[10]	W 80-85(ot)	18-Paulus
2008 • Seed: #2					
Quarterfinals	3/14	Charlotte, N.C.	Georgia Tech[7]	W 82-70	18-Scheyer
Semifinals	3/15	Charlotte, N.C.	Clemson[3]	L 74-78	17-Paulus
2009 • Seed: #3					
Quarterfinals	3/13	Atlanta, Ga.	Boston College[6]	W 66-65	26-Singler
Semifinals	3/14	Atlanta, Ga.	Maryland[7]	W 67-61	22-Scheyer
Finals	3/15	Atlanta, Ga.	Florida State[4]	W 87-95(ot)	29-Scheyer
2010 • Seed: #1					
Quarterfinals	3/12	Greensboro, N.C.	Virginia[9]	W 57-46	18-Singler
Semifinals	3/13	Greensboro, N.C.	Miami[12]	W 77-74	27-Singler
Championship	3/14	Greensboro, N.C.	Georgia Tech[7]	W 65-61	20-Singler

Round	Date	Site	Opponent	W/L	Score	DU High Pts.
1955 • East Regional						
First Round	3/8	New York, N.Y.	Villanova	L	73-74	22-Tobin
1960 • East Regional						
First Round	3/8	New York, N.Y.	Princeton	W	84-60	26-Kistler
Reg. Semifinal	3/11	Charlotte, N.C.	St. Joseph's	W	58-56	22-Youngkin
Reg. Final	3/12	Charlotte, N.C.	New York U.	L	59-74	20-Kistler
1963 • East Regional						
Reg. Semifinal	3/15	College Park, Md.	New York U.	W	81-76	25-Mullins
Reg. Final	3/16	College Park, Md.	St. Joseph's	W	73-59	24-Mullins
Nat. Semifinal	3/22	Louisville, Ky.	Loyola, Ill.	L	75-94	29-Heyman
Nat. Consol.	3/23	Louisville, Ky.	Oregon State	W	85-63	22-Heyman
1964 • East Regional						
Reg. Semifinal	3/13	Raleigh, N.C.	Villanova	W	87-73	43-Mullins
Reg. Final	3/14	Raleigh, N.C.	Connecticut	W	101-54	30-Mullins
Nat. Semifinal	3/20	Kansas City, Mo.	Michigan	W	91-80	25-Buckley
Nat. Final	3/21	Kansas City, Mo.	UCLA	L	83-98	22-Mullins
1966 • East Regional						
Reg. Semifinal	3/11	Raleigh, N.C.	St. Joseph's	W	76-74	22-Verga
Reg. Final	3/12	Raleigh, N.C.	Syracuse	W	91-81	22-Marin
Nat. Semifinal	3/18	College Park, Md.	Kentucky	L	79-83	29-Marin
Nat. Consol.	3/19	College Park, Md.	Utah	W	79-77	23-Marin
1978 • East Regional						
First Round	3/12	Charlotte, N.C.	Rhode Island	W	63-62	25-Gminski
Reg. Semifinal	3/17	Providence, R.I.	Pennsylvania	W	84-80	21-two players
Reg. Final	3/19	Providence, R.I.	Villanova	W	90-72	23-Spanarkel
Nat. Semifinal	3/25	St. Louis, Mo.	Notre Dame	W	90-86	29-Gminski
Nat. Final	3/27	St. Louis, Mo.	Kentucky	L	88-94	22-Banks
1979 • East Regional Seed: #2						
Second Round	3/11	Raleigh, N.C.	St. John's[10E]	L	78-80	24-Banks
1980 • Mideast Regional Seed: #4						
Second Round	3/8	W. Lafayette, Ind.	Pennsylvania[12ME]	W	52-42	19-Gminski
Reg. Semifinal	3/13	Lexington, Ky.	Kentucky[1ME]	W	55-54	17-Gminski
Reg. Final	3/15	Lexington, Ky.	Purdue[6ME]	L	60-68	17-Gminski
1984 • West Regional Seed: #3						
Second Round	3/18	Pullman, Wash.	Washington[6W]	L	78-80	22-Dawkins
1985 • Midwest Regional Seed: #3						
First Round	3/15	Houston, Texas	Pepperdine[14MW]	W	75-62	22-Henderson
Second Round	3/17	Houston, Texas	Boston College[11MW]	L	73-74	18-Dawkins
1986 • East Regional Seed: #1						
First Round	3/13	Greensboro, N.C.	Miss. Valley St.[16E]	W	85-78	27-Dawkins
Second Round	3/15	Greensboro, N.C.	Old Dominion[8E]	W	89-61	25-Dawkins
Reg. Semifinal	3/21	E. Rutherford, N.J.	DePaul[12E]	W	74-67	25-Dawkins
Reg. Final	3/23	E. Rutherford, N.J.	Navy[7E]	W	71-50	28-Dawkins
Nat. Semifinal	3/29	Dallas, Texas	Kansas[1MW]	W	71-67	24-Dawkins
Nat. Final	3/31	Dallas, Texas	Louisville[2W]	L	69-72	24-Dawkins
1987 • Midwest Regional Seed: #5						
First Round	3/12	Indianapolis, Ind.	Texas A&M[12MW]	W	58-51	20-Strickland
Second Round	3/14	Indianapolis, Ind.	Xavier[13MW]	W	65-60	20-Amaker
Reg. Semifinal	3/20	Cincinnati, Ohio	Indiana[1MW]	L	82-88	23-Amaker
1988 • East Regional Seed: #2						
First Round	3/17	Chapel Hill, N.C.	Boston U.[15E]	W	85-69	21-Ferry
Second Round	3/19	Chapel Hill, N.C.	SMU[7E]	W	94-79	31-Strickland
Reg. Semifinal	3/24	E. Rutherford, N.J.	Rhode Island[11E]	W	73-72	17-Ferry
Reg. Final	3/26	E. Rutherford, N.J.	Temple[1E]	W	63-53	21-Strickland
Nat. Semifinal	4/2	Kansas City, Mo.	Kansas[6MW]	L	59-66	19-Ferry
1989 • East Regional Seed: #2						
First Round	3/16	Greensboro, N.C.	S.C. State[15E]	W	90-69	22-Henderson
Second Round	3/18	Greensboro, N.C.	West Virginia[7E]	W	70-63	20-Ferry
Reg. Semifinal	3/24	E. Rutherford, N.J.	Minnesota[11E]	W	87-70	21-two players
Reg. Final	3/26	E. Rutherford, N.J.	Georgetown[1E]	W	85-77	24-Laettner
Nat. Semifinal	4/1	Seattle, Wash.	Seton Hall[3W]	L	78-95	34-Ferry
1990 • East Regional Seed: #3						
First Round	3/16	Atlanta, Ga.	Richmond[14E]	W	81-46	22-Abdelnaby
Second Round	3/18	Atlanta, Ga.	St. John's[6E]	W	76-72	22-Brickey
Reg. Semifinal	3/22	E. Rutherford, N.J.	UCLA[7E]	W	90-81	28-Henderson
Reg. Final	3/24	E. Rutherford, N.J.	Connecticut[1E]	W	79-78	27-Abdelnaby
Nat. Semifinal	3/31	Denver, Colo.	Arkansas[4MW]	W	97-83	28-Henderson
Nat. Final	4/2	Denver, Colo.	UNLV[1W]	L	73-103	21-Henderson
1991 • Midwest Regional Seed: #2 • National Champions						
First Round	3/14	Minneapolis	N.E. Louisiana[15MW]	W	102-73	22-Laettner
Second Round	3/16	Minneapolis	Iowa[7MW]	W	85-70	19-Laettner
Reg. Semifinal	3/22	Pontiac, Mich.	Connecticut[11MW]	W	81-67	19-Laettner
Reg. Final	3/24	Pontiac, Mich.	St. John's[4MW]	W	78-61	20-Hurley
Nat. Semifinal	3/30	Indianapolis, Ind.	UNLV[1W]	W	79-77	28-Laettner
Nat. Final	4/1	Indianapolis, Ind.	Kansas[3SE]	W	72-65	18-Laettner
1992 • East Regional Seed: #1 • National Champions						
First Round	3/19	Greensboro, N.C.	Campbell[16E]	W	82-56	22-Laettner
Second Round	3/21	Greensboro, N.C.	Iowa[9E]	W	75-62	21-Davis
Reg. Semifinal	3/26	Philadelphia, Pa.	Seton Hall[4E]	W	81-69	two players
Reg. Final	3/28	Philadelphia, Pa.	Kentucky (ot)[2E]	W	104-103	31-Laettner
Nat. Semifinal	4/4	Minneapolis	Indiana[2W]	W	81-78	26-Hurley
Nat. Final	4/6	Minneapolis	Michigan[6SE]	W	71-51	19-Laettner
1993 • Midwest Regional Seed: #3						
First Round	3/18	Chicago, Ill.	S. Illinois[14MW]	W	105-70	25-Hurley
Second Round	3/20	Chicago, Ill.	California[6MW]	L	77-82	32-Hurley
1994 • Southeast Regional Seed: #2						
First Round	3/18	St. Petersburg, Fla.	Texas Southern[15SE]	W	82-70	20-Collins
Second Round	3/20	St. Petersburg, Fla.	Michigan State[7SE]	W	85-74	25-Hill
Reg. Semifinal	3/24	Knoxville, Tenn.	Marquette[6SE]	W	59-49	22-Hill
Reg. Final	3/26	Knoxville, Tenn.	Purdue[1SE]	W	69-60	19-two players
Nat. Semifinal	4/2	Charlotte, N.C.	Florida[3E]	W	70-65	25-Hill
Nat. Final	4/4	Charlotte, N.C.	Arkansas[1MW]	L	72-76	15-Lang
1996 • Southeast Regional Seed: #8						
First Round	3/14	Indianapolis, Ind.	E. Michigan[9SE]	L	60-75	15-two players
1997 • Southeast Regional Seed: #2						
First Round	3/14	Charlotte, N.C.	Murray State[15SE]	W	71-68	25-Capel
Second Round	3/16	Charlotte, N.C.	Providence[10SE]	L	87-98	26-Capel
1998 • South Regional Seed: #1						
First Round	3/13	Lexington, Ky.	Radford[16S]	W	99-63	23-McLeod
Second Round	3/15	Lexington, Ky.	Oklahoma State[8S]	W	79-73	22-McLeod
Reg. Semifinal	3/20	St. Petersburg, Fla.	Syracuse[5S]	W	80-67	20-Brand
Reg. Final	3/22	St. Petersburg, Fla.	Kentucky[2S]	L	84-86	19-McLeod
1999 • East Regional Seed: #1						
First Round	3/12	Charlotte, N.C.	Florida A&M[16E]	W	99-58	17-Brand
Second Round	3/14	Charlotte, N.C.	Tulsa[9E]	W	97-56	19-Avery
Reg. Semifinal	3/19	E. Rutherford, N.J.	SW Missouri St.[12E]	W	78-61	24-Langdon
Reg. Final	3/21	E. Rutherford, N.J.	Temple[6E]	W	85-64	23-Langdon
Nat. Semifinal	3/27	St. Petersburg, Fla.	Michigan State[1MW]	W	68-62	18-Brand
Nat. Final	3/29	St. Petersburg, Fla.	Connecticut[1W]	L	74-77	25-Langdon

NCAA TOURNAMENT RESULTS
(continued)

Round	Date	Site	Opponent	W/L Score	DU High Pts.
2000 • East Regional Seed: #1					
First Round	3/17	Winston-Salem	Lamar[16E]	W 82-55	18-Williams
Second Round	3/19	Winston-Salem	Kansas[8E]	W 69-64	21-Battier
Reg. Semifinal	3/24	Syracuse, N.Y.	Florida[5E]	L 78-87	20-Battier
2001 • East Regional Seed: #1					
First Round	3/15	Greensboro, N.C.	Monmouth[16E]	W 95-52	22-Williams
Second Round	3/17	Greensboro, N.C	Missouri[9E]	W 94-81	31-Williams
Reg. Semifinal	3/22	Philadelphia, Pa.	UCLA[4E]	W 76-63	34-Williams
Reg. Final	3/24	Philadelphia, Pa.	USC[6E]	W 79-69	28-Williams
Nat. Semifinal	3/31	Minneapolis	Maryland[3W]	W 95-84	25-Battier
Nat. Final	4/2	Minneapolis	Arizona[2MW]	W 82-72	21-Dunleavy
2002 • South Regional Seed: #1					
First Round	3/14	Greenville, S.C.	Winthrop[16S]	W 84-37	19-two players
Second Round	3/16	Greenville, S.C.	Notre Dame[8S]	W 84-77	18-two players
Reg. Semifinal	3/21	Lexington, Ky.	Indiana[4S]	L 73-74	19-Boozer
2003 • West Regional Seed: #3					
First Round	3/20	Salt Lake City, Utah	Colorado State[14W]	W 67-57	23-Jones
Second Round	3/22	Salt Lake City, Utah	C. Michigan[11W]	W 86-60	28-Jones
Reg. Semifinal	3/27	Anaheim, Calif.	Kansas[2W]	L 65-69	23-Jones
2004 • Atlanta (South) Regional Seed: #1					
First Round	3/18	Raleigh, N.C.	Alabama State[16S]	W 96-61	20-Randolph
Second Round	3/20	Raleigh, N.C.	Seton Hall[8S]	W 90-62	21-Redick
Reg. Semifinal	3/26	Atlanta, Ga.	Illinois[4S]	W 72-62	18-Deng
Reg. Final	3/28	Atlanta, Ga.	Xavier[7S]	W 66-63	19-Deng
Nat. Semifinal	4/3	San Antonio, Texas	Connecticut[2W]	L 78-79	16-Deng
2005 • Austin (South) Regional Seed: #1					
First Round	3/18	Charlotte, N.C.	Delaware State[16S]	W 57-46	14-Williams
Second Round	3/20	Charlotte, N.C.	Mississippi State[9S]	W 63-55	22-Ewing
Reg. Semifinal	3/26	Austin, Texas	Michigan State[5S]	L 68-78	19-Williams
2006 • Atlanta (South) Regional Seed: #1					
First Round	3/16	Greensboro, N.C.	Southern[16S]	W 70-54	29-two players
Second Round	3/18	Greensboro, N.C.	George Washington[8S]	W 74-61	20-Redick
Reg. Semifinal	3/23	Atlanta, Ga.	LSU[4S]	L 54-62	23-Williams
2007 • Buffalo (West) Regional Seed: #6					
First Round	3/15	Buffalo, N.Y.	VCU[1W]	L 77-79	25-Paulus
2008 • West Regional Seed: #2					
First Round	3/20	Washington, D.C.	Belmont[15S]	W 71-70	21-Henderson
Second Round	3/22	Washington, D.C.	George Washington[7W]	L 67-73	18-Henderson
2009 • East Regional Seed: #2					
First Round	3/19	Greensboro, N.C.	Binghamton[15E]	W 86-62	15-Scheyer
Second Round	3/21	Greensboro, N.C.	Texas[7E]	W 74-69	24-Henderson
Reg. Semifinal	3/26	Boston, Mass.	Villanova[3E]	L 54-77	15-Singler
2010 • South Regional Seed: #1					
First Round	3/19	Jacksonville, Fla.	Arkansas Pine-Bluff[16]	W 74-44	22-Singler
Second Round	3/21	Jacksonville, Fla.	California[8S]	W 68-53	20-Smith
Reg. Semifinal	3/26	Houston, Texas	Purdue[4S]	W 70-57	24-Singler
Reg. Final	3/28	Houston, Texas	Baylor[3S]	W 78-71	29-Smith
Nat. Semifinal	4/3	Indianapolis, Ind.	West Virginia[2E]	W 78-57	23-Scheyer
Nat. Final	4/5	Indianapolis, Ind.	Butler[5W]	W 61-59	19-Singler

DUKE ALL-TIME COACHING RECORDS

Coach	Years	W-L	Pct.
W.W. "Cap" Card	1906-12	30-17	.638
J.E. Brinn	1913	11-8	.579
Noble L. Clay	1914-15	22-18	.550
Bob Doak	1916	9-11	.450
Chick Doak	1917-18	30-9	.769
H.P. Cole	1919	6-5	.545
W.J. Rothensies	1920	10-4	.714
Floyd Egan	1921	9-6	.600
James Baldwin	1922	6-12	.333
J.S. Burbage	1923-24	34-13	.723
George Buckheit	1925-28	25-36	.410
Eddie Cameron	1929-42	226-99	.695
Gerry Gerard	1943-50	131-78	.627
Harold Bradley	1951-59	167-78	.682
Vic Bubas	1960-69	213-67	.761
Bucky Waters	1970-73	63-45	.583
Neill McGeachy	1974	10-16	.385
Bill Foster	1975-80	113-64	.638
Mike Krzyzewski	1981-present	621-181	.774
Pete Gaudet	1995	4-15	.211

RETIRED JERSEYS

No. - Player	Date Retired
10 - Dick Groat	May 1, 1952
25 - Art Heyman	March 4, 1990
44 - Jeff Mullins	December 6, 1994
43 - Mike Gminski	February 20, 1980
24 - Johnny Dawkins	February 22, 1986
35 - Danny Ferry	February 18, 1989
32 - Christian Laettner	February 26, 1992
11 - Bobby Hurley	February 28, 1993
33 - Grant Hill	February 27, 1994
31 - Shane Battier	February 21, 2001
22 - Jason Williams	February 5, 2003
23 - Shelden Williams	Janruary 28, 2007
4 - J.J. Redick	February 4, 2007

National Player of the Year
1952 Dick Groat
1963 Art Heyman
1986 Johnny Dawkins
1989 Danny Ferry
1992 Christian Laettner
1999 Elton Brand
2001 Shane Battier
2001 Jason Williams
2002 Jason Williams
2005 J.J. Redick
2006 J.J Redick

National Defensive Player of the Year
1987 Tommy Amaker
1988 Billy King
1993 Grant Hill
1998 Steve Wojciechowski
1999 Shane Battier
2000 Shane Battier
2001 Shane Battier
2005 Sheldon Williams
2006 Sheldon Williams

All-America
1930 Bill Werber
1940 Bill Mock
1946 Ed Koffenberger
1947 Ed Koffenberger (2nd)
1951 Dick Groat (2nd)
1952 Dick Groat (1st)
1961 Art Heyman
1962 Art Heyman (2nd)
1963 Art Heyman (1st)
1963 Jeff Mullins
1964 Jeff Mullins (2nd)
1966 Jack Marin (2nd)
1966 Bob Verga (2nd)
1967 Bob Verga (1st)
1968 Mike Lewis
1971 Randy Denton
1978 Jim Spanarkel
1979 Jim Spanarkel (2nd)
1978 Mike Gminski
1979 Gene Banks
1979 Mike Gminski (1st)
1980 Mike Gminski (2nd)
1981 Gene Banks
1985 Johnny Dawkins (1st)
1986 Johnny Dawkins (1st)
1986 Mark Alarie
1987 Tommy Amaker
1988 Danny Ferry (2nd)
1989 Danny Ferry (1st)
1990 Christian Laettner
1991 Christian Laettner (2nd)

1992 Christian Laettner (1st)
1992 Bobby Hurley
1993 Bobby Hurley (1st)
1992 Grant Hill
1993 Grant Hill (2nd)
1994 Grant Hill (1st)
1998 Trajan Langdon
1998 Roshown McLeod
1999 Elton Brand (1st)
1999 Trajan Langdon (2nd)
2000 Chris Carrawell
2000 Shane Battier (2nd)
2001 Shane Battier (1st)
2001 Jason Williams (1st)
2002 Jason Williams (1st)
2002 Carlos Boozer
2002 Mike Dunleavy (2nd)
2002 Jason Williams (1st)
2004 Chris Duhon
2004 J.J. Redick
2004 Shelden Williams
2005 J.J. Redick (1st)
2005 Sheldon Williams
2008 DeMarcus Nelson
2009 Gerald Henderson
2010 Jon Scheyer (2nd)

All-Conference
Southern Conference
1929 Bill Werber
1930 Harry Councilor
      Bill Werber
1933 Jim Thompson
1934 Herb Thompson
      Jim Thompson
1939 Ed Swindell
1940 Bill Mock
1941 Chuck Holley
      Ray Spuhler
      Cy Valesek
1942 Bill McCahan
      Ray Spuhler
1943 Bob Gantt
      John Seward
1944 Gordon Carver
      Bill Wright
1945 Dan Buckley
      Gordon Carver
1946 Ed Koffenberger
      John Seward
      Dick Whiting
1947 Ed Koffenberger
1948 Corren Youmans
1949 Corren Youmans
1950 Corren Youmans
1951 Dick Groat
1952 Dick Groat

Atlantic Coast Conference
1954 Rudy D'Emilio (1st)
      Joe Belmont (2nd)
      Ronnie Mayer (2nd)
1955 Ronnie Mayer (1st)
      Joe Belmont (2nd)
1956 Joe Belmont (1st)
      Ronnie Mayer (2nd)
1957 Jim Newcome (2nd)
1958 Jim Newcome (1st)
      Bucky Allen (2nd)
      Paul Schmidt (2nd)
1959 Carroll Youngkin (1st)
      Howard Hurt (2nd)
1960 Howard Hurt (2nd)
1961 Art Heyman (1st)
      Howard Hurt (2nd)
1962 Art Heyman (1st)
      Jeff Mullins (1st)
1963 Art Heyman (1st)
      Jeff Mullins (1st)
1964 Jeff Mullins (1st)
      Jay Buckley (2nd)
      Buzzy Harrison (2nd)
      Hack Tison (2nd)
1965 Jack Marin (1st)
      Bob Verga (1st)
      Steve Vacendak (2nd)
1966 Jack Marin (1st)
      Bob Verga (1st)
      Steve Vacendak (2nd)
1967 Bob Verga (1st)
      Mike Lewis (2nd)
1968 Mike Lewis (1st)
1969 Randy Denton (2nd)
1970 Randy Denton (2nd)
1971 Randy Denton (1st)
1972 Gary Melchionni (2nd)
      Alan Shaw (2nd)
1973 Gary Melchionni (1st)
      Chris Redding (2nd)
1975 Bob Fleisher (2nd)
1976 Tate Armstrong (1st)
1977 Jim Spanarkel (2nd)
1978 Mike Gminski (1st)
      Jim Spanarkel (1st)
      Gene Banks (2nd)
1979 Mike Gminski (1st)
      Jim Spanarkel (1st)
      Gene Banks (2nd)
1980 Mike Gminski (1st)
      Gene Banks (2nd)
1981 Gene Banks (1st)
1982 Vince Taylor (1st)
1983 Johnny Dawkins (2nd)
1984 Mark Alarie (1st)
      Johnny Dawkins (2nd)

1985 Johnny Dawkins (1st)
      Mark Alarie (2nd)
1986 Mark Alarie (1st)
      Johnny Dawkins (1st)
1987 Tommy Amaker (2nd)
      Danny Ferry (2nd)
1988 Danny Ferry (1st)
1989 Danny Ferry (1st)
1990 Phil Henderson (2nd)
      Christian Laettner (2nd)
      Alaa Abdelnaby (3rd)
1991 Christian Laettner (1st)
      Thomas Hill (3rd)
      Bobby Hurley (3rd)
1992 Christian Laettner (1st)
      Grant Hill (2nd)
      Bobby Hurley (2nd)
      Thomas Hill (3rd)
1993 Grant Hill (1st)
      Bobby Hurley (1st)
      Thomas Hill (3rd)
1994 Grant Hill (1st)
      Cherokee Parks (2nd)
      Antonio Lang (3rd)
1995 Cherokee Parks (2nd)
1996 Chris Collins (2nd)
      Jeff Capel (3rd)
      Ricky Price (3rd)
1997 Trajan Langdon (1st)
      Steve Wojciechowski (2nd)
1998 Trajan Langdon (1st)
      Roshown McLeod (1st)
      Steve Wojciechowski (3rd)
1999 Elton Brand (1st)
      Trajan Langdon (1st)
      William Avery (2nd)
      Shane Battier (3rd)
      Chris Carrawell (3rd)
2000 Shane Battier (1st)
      Chris Carrawell (1st)
      Jason Williams (3rd)
2001 Shane Battier (1st)
      Jason Williams (1st)
      Nate James (3rd)
2002 Jason Williams (1st)
      Carlos Boozer (1st)
      Mike Dunleavy (1st)
2003 Dahntay Jones (1st)
      Chris Duhon (3rd)
      J.J. Redick (3rd)
2004 Chris Duhon (1st)
      J.J. Redick (2nd)
      Shelden Williams (2nd)
      Luol Deng (3rd)
2005 J.J. Redick (1st)
      Shelden Williams (1st)
      Daniel Ewing (3rd)

2006	J.J. Redick (1st)		
	Shelden Williams (1st)		
2007	Josh McRoberts (3rd)		
2008	DeMarcus Nelson (1st)		
	Greg Paulus (3rd)		
	Kyle Singler (3rd)		
2009	Gerald Henderson (1st)		
	Kyle Singler (2nd)		
2010	Jon Scheyer (1st)		
	Kyle Singler (1st)		
	Nolan Smith (2nd)		

Two-Time All-Conference

Bill Werber	1929-30
Jim Thompson	1933-34
Ray Spuhler	1941-42
John Seward	1943-46
Gordon Carver	1944-45
Ed Koffenberger	1946-47
Dick Groat	1951-52
Jack Marin	1965-66
Jim Spanarkel	1978-79
Mark Alarie	1984-86
Johnny Dawkins	1985-86
Danny Ferry	1988-89
Christian Laettner	1991-92
Grant Hill	1993-94
Shane Battier	2000-01
Jason Williams	2001-02
J.J Redick	2005-06
Sheldon Williams	2005-06

(first team selections only)

Three-Time All-Conference

Corren Youmans	1948-50
Art Heyman	1961-63
Jeff Mullins	1962-64
Bob Verga	1965-67
Mike Gminski	1978-80
Trajan Langdon	1997-99

(first team selections only)

ACC Player of the Year

1963	Art Heyman
1964	Jeff Mullins
1966	Steve Vacendak
1979	Mike Gminski
1988	Danny Ferry
1989	Danny Ferry
1992	Christian Laettner
1994	Grant Hill
1999	Elton Brand
2000	Chris Carrawell
2001	Shane Battier
2005	J.J. Redick
2006	J.J. Redick

ACC Rookie of the Year

1976	Jim Spanarkel
1977	Mike Gminski
1978	Gene Banks
2001	Chris Duhon
2008	Kyle Singler

ACC Tournament MVP

1960	Doug Kistler
1963	Art Heyman
1964	Jeff Mullins
1966	Steve Vacendak
1978	Jim Spanarkel
1986	Johnny Dawkins
1988	Danny Ferry
1992	Christian Laettner
1999	Elton Brand
2000	Jason Williams
2001	Shane Battier
2002	Carlos Boozer
2003	Daniel Ewing
2005	J.J. Redick
2006	J.J. Redick
2009	Jon Scheyer
2010	Kyle Singler

ACC All-Tournament

1954	Rudy D'Emilio (2nd)
	Bernie Janicki (2nd)
1955	Ronnie Mayer (1st)
	Joe Belmont (2nd)
1956	Ronnie Mayer (2nd)
1958	Bucky Allen (2nd)
	Bobby Joe Harris (2nd)
	Bob Vernon (2nd)
1959	Howard Hurt (2nd)
	Carroll Youngkin (2nd)
1960	Howard Hurt (1st)
	Doug Kistler (1st)
	John Frye (2nd)
	Carroll Youngkin (2nd)
1961	John Frye (1st)
	Art Heyman (1st)
	Carroll Youngkin (2nd)
1962	Art Heyman (1st)
	Jeff Mullins (1st)
1963	Art Heyman (1st)
	Jeff Mullins (1st)
	Jay Buckley (2nd)
	Buzzy Harrison (2nd)
1964	Jay Buckley (1st)
	Jeff Mullins (1st)
	Danny Ferguson (2nd)
	Hack Tison (2nd)
1965	Steve Vacendak (1st)
	Bob Verga (1st)
	Jack Marin (2nd)

1966	Mike Lewis (1st)
	Steve Vacendak (1st)
	Bob Verga (1st)
	Jack Marin (2nd)
	Bob Riedy (2nd)
1967	Bob Verga (1st)
	Mike Lewis (2nd)
1968	Mike Lewis (2nd)
1969	Dick DeVenzio (1st)
	Steve Vandenberg (1st)
	Dave Golden (2nd)
1972	Gary Melchionni (2nd)
1976	Tate Armstrong (1st)
1977	Mike Gminski (2nd)
	Jim Spanarkel (2nd)
1978	Gene Banks (1st)
	Mike Gminski (1st)
	Jim Spanarkel (1st)
	Kenny Dennard (2nd)
1979	Mike Gminski (1st)
	Jim Spanarkel (1st)
1980	Gene Banks (1st)
	Mike Gminski (1st)
	Vince Taylor (2nd)
1984	Mark Alarie (1st)
	Johnny Dawkins (1st)
1985	Johnny Dawkins (1st)
	Jay Bilas (2nd)
1986	Mark Alarie (1st)
	Johnny Dawkins (1st)
	David Henderson (1st)
1988	Robert Brickey (1st)
	Danny Ferry (1st)
	Quin Snyder (2nd)
1989	Danny Ferry (1st)
	Phil Henderson (1st)
	Christian Laettner (2nd)
1990	Phil Henderson (1st)
	Christian Laettner (2nd)
1991	Christian Laettner (1st)
	Grant Hill (2nd)
	Greg Koubek (2nd)
1992	Brian Davis (1st)
	Bobby Hurley (1st)
	Christian Laettner (1st)
	Grant Hill (2nd)
1994	Grant Hill (2nd)
	Cherokee Parks (2nd)
1998	Trajan Langdon (1st)
	Roshown McLeod (1st)
	Chris Carrawell (2nd)
1999	William Avery (1st)
	Elton Brand (1st)
	Shane Battier (2nd)
	Corey Maggette (2nd)
2000	Shane Battier (1st)
	Chris Carrawell (1st)

	Jason Williams (1st)
	Carlos Boozer (2nd)
	Mike Dunleavy (2nd)
	Nate James (2nd)
2001	Shane Battier (1st)
	Mike Dunleavy (1st)
	Jason Williams (1st)
	Nate James (2nd)
2002	Carlos Boozer (1st)
	Mike Dunleavy (1st)
	Jason Williams (1st)
	Chris Duhon (2nd)
2003	Daniel Ewing (1st)
	Dahntay Jones (2nd)
	J.J. Redick (2nd)
2004	Chris Duhon (1st)
	Daniel Ewing (1st)
	Shelden Williams (1st)
	Luol Deng (2nd)
2005	Daniel Ewing (1st)
	J.J. Redick (1st)
	Shelden Williams (1st)
2006	J.J. Redick
	Shelden Williams (1st)
	Josh McRoberts (2nd)
	Greg Paulus (2nd)
2009	Gerald Henderson (1st)
	Jon Scheyer (1st)
	Kyle Singler (1st)
2010	Jon Scheyer (1st)
	Nolan Smith (1st)
	Kyle Singler (1st)

NCAA Tournament AWARDS

All-NCAA Finals

1963	*Art Heyman
1964	Jeff Mullins
1966	Jack Marin
1978	Mike Gminski
	Jim Spanarkel
1986	Mark Alarie
	Tommy Amaker
	Johnny Dawkins
1989	Danny Ferry
1990	Phil Henderson
1991	Bobby Hurley
	*Christian Laettner
	Billy McCaffrey
1992	Grant Hill
	*Bobby Hurley
	Christian Laettner
1994	Grant Hill
	Antonio Lang
1999	Elton Brand
	Trajan Langdon

2001	*Shane Battier
	Mike Dunleavy
	Jason Williams
2010	*Kyle Singler
	Nolan Smith
	Jon Scheyer

All-East Regional

1963	Art Heyman
	Jeff Mullins
1964	*Jeff Mullins
	Steve Vacendak
1966	Jack Marin
	Steve Vacendak
	*Bob Verga
1978	Gene Banks
	Mike Gminski
	*Jim Spanarkel
1986	Mark Alarie
	*Johnny Dawkins
1988	*Danny Ferry
	Billy King
	Kevin Strickland
1989	*Danny Ferry
	Phil Henderson
	Christian Laettner
1990	Alaa Abdelnaby
	Phil Henderson
	*Christian Laettner
1992	Bobby Hurley
	*Christian Laettner
1999	William Avery
	Elton Brand
	*Trajan Langdon
2000	Shane Battier
2001	Shane Battier
	*Jason Williams

All-South Regional

1980	Mike Gminski
1994	Jeff Capel
	*Grant Hill
	Cherokee Parks
1998	Trajan Langdon
	Roshown McLeod
2004	*Luol Deng
	Shelden Williams
2010	Nolan Smith
	Jon Scheyer

All-Midwest Regional

1987	Tommy Amaker
1991	Thomas Hill
	*Bobby Hurley
	Christian Laettner

Named Most Outstanding Player

National Invitation Tournament

All-NIT

1971	Randy Denton

All-Preseason NIT

1986	Mark Alarie
	Johnny Dawkins
	David Henderson
1996	Trajan Langdon
2000	*Carlos Boozer
	Jason Williams
2005	J.J. Redick
	Shelden Williams
2010	Jon Scheyer
	Nolan Smith

Named Most Valuable Player

Swett-Baylin Award given to the most valuable player as selected by the team. Set up by Dr. George Baylin in memory of Dr. and Mrs. Francis Swett. Dr. Swett was a Duke faculty member and ardent basketball fan.

1952	Dick Groat
1953	Rudy D'Emilio
1954	Bernie Janicki
1955	Ronnie Mayer
1956	Joe Belmont
1957	Bobby Joe Harris
1958	Paul Schmidt
1959	Howard Hurt
1960	Doug Kistler
1961	Art Heyman
1962	Art Heyman
1963	Art Heyman
1964	Jeff Mullins
1965	Denny Ferguson
1966	Jack Marin
	Steve Vacendak
1967	Bob Verga
1968	Mike Lewis
1969	Fred Lind
1970	Randy Denton
1971	Randy Denton
1972	Alan Shaw
1973	Gary Melchionni
1974	Bob Fleischer
1975	Bob Fleischer
1976	Tate Armstrong
1977	Tate Armstrong
	Jim Spanarkel
1978	Gene Banks
	Mike Gminski
	Jim Spanarkel
1979	Mike Gminski
	Jim Spanarkel

1980	Gene Banks
	Mike Gminski
1981	Gene Banks
	Kenny Dennard
1982	Vince Taylor
1983	Johnny Dawkins
1984	Mark Alarie
	Johnny Dawkins
1985	Johnny Dawkins
1986	Johnny Dawkins
1987	Tommy Amaker
	Danny Ferry
1988	Danny Ferry
1989	Danny Ferry
1990	Phil Henderson
	Christian Laettner
1991	Bobby Hurley
	Christian Laettner
1992	Bobby Hurley
	Christian Laettner
1993	Bobby Hurley
1994	Grant Hill
1995	Erik Meek
	Cherokee Parks
1996	Chris Collins
1997	Steve Wojciechowski
1998	Roshown McLeod
1999	Elton Brand
	Trajan Langdon
2000	Shane Battier
	Chris Carrawell
2001	Shane Battier
	Jason Williams
2002	Jason Williams
	Mike Dunleavy
2003	Dahntay Jones
2004	Chris Duhon
2005	Daniel Ewing
	J.J. Redick
	Shelden Williams
2006	J.J. Redick
	Shelden Williams
2007	Josh McRoberts
	DeMarcus Nelson
2008	DeMarcus Nelson
2009	Gerald Henderson
	Jon Scheyer
	Kyle Singler
2010	Jon Scheyer
	Kyle Singler
	Nolan Smith
	Lance Thomas
	Brian Zoubek

Glenn E. "Ted" Mann Jr. Award presented by Kappa Sigma fraternity to the reserve voted by his teammates as contributing the most to team morale. The award is dedicated to the memory of Ted Mann Jr., a member of the Duke basketball team who died in a swimming accident on September 12, 1964, just prior to his senior year at Duke.

1965	Ron Herbster
1966	Jim Liccardo
1967	Stuart McKaig
1968	Tim Kolodziej
1969	Steve Vandenberg
1970	Don Blackman
1971	Alan Shaw
1972	Pat Doughty
1973	Pete Kramer
1974	Terry Chili
1975	Terry Chili
1976	Dave O'Connell
1977	Scott Goetsch
1978	Bruce Bell
1979	Scott Goetsch
1980	Jim Corrigan
1981	Jim Suddath
1982	Todd Anderson
1983	Mike Tissaw
1984	Richard Ford
1985	Todd Anderson
1986	Billy King
1987	Robert Brickey
1988	John Smith
1989	John Smith
1990	Brian Davis
1991	Brian Davis
1992	Antonio Lang
1993	Marty Clark
1994	Marty Clark
1995	Steve Wojciechowski
1996	Steve Wojciechowski
1997	Justin Caldbeck
	Jay Heaps
	Todd Singleton
1998	Todd Singleton
1999	Nate James
2000	Mike Dunleavy
2001	Dahntay Jones
	J.D. Simpson
2002	Daniel Ewing
2003	Andre Buckner
2004	Sean Dockery
2005	Lee Melchionni
2006	Patrick Johnson
2007	David McClure
2008	Jon Scheyer
2009	Elliot Williams
2010	Miles Plumlee

ALL-TIME LETTERWINNERS

- A -

Abdelnaby, Alaa 1987-90
Alarie, Mark 1983-86
Albert, Roy 1932
Albright, Doug 1959-61
Allen, Bucky 1956-58
Allen, Dayton 1950-51
Allen, J. Clyde 1940, 42
Allen, Phil 1964-66
Amaker, Tommy 1984-87
Anderson, Todd 1982-85
Armstrong, Tate 1974-77
Ashley, Larry 1950
Ast, Christian 1991-92
Ausbon, Doug 1946-48
Avery, William 1998-99

-B -

Bailey, William F. 1944
Balitsaris, George 1944
Banks, Eugene 1978-81
Barone, Tony 1966-68
Barrett, George 1958-59
Bateman, Larry 1958-60
Battier, Shane* 1998-01
Beal, Jay 1959-61
Beall, Curtis 1944
Beard, Joey 1994
Bell, Bruce 1976-78
Bell, Sam 1933-35
Belmont, Joe 1953-56
Bender, Bob 1978-80
Bennett, C.G. 1926-28
Bergman, Russell 1937-39
Berndt, Andy 1987
Bilas, Jay 1983-86
Billerman, Kevin 1973-75
Blackman, Don 1970
Blakeney, Kenny 1992-95
Bledsoe, Gene 1944
Boozer, Carlos 2000-02
Borman, Andy 2000-02, 2004
Bowman, James 1940
Boyd, Jack 1958-59
Boykin, Jamal 2006
Brand, Elton* 1998-99
Brand, Joe 1945
Brickey, Robert 1987-90
Brown, Kenney 1993
Brown, Ray 1941
Brummer, George 1945
Brunson, Stan 1993-96
Bryan, Jay 1982-85
Bryant, D. 1999
Bryson, Ed. 1957
Buckley, Clay 1988-91
Buckley, Dan 1945
Buckley, Jay 1962-64
Buckner, Andre 2000-03

Buhowsky, Tony 1956
Bullock, E.J. 1926
Burch, Edgar 1974
Burdette, Jeff 1972-74
Burgess, Chris 1998-99
Burgin, George 1987-89
Burt, Ron 1992
Butler, M.W. 1926-27

- C -

Caldbeck, Justin 1997, 99
Caldbeck, Ryan 1999-01
Candler, Coke 1927-29
Cantwell, John 1960-61
Capel, Jeff 1994-97
Capelli 1931
Carrawell, Chris 1997-00
Carter, Pete 1931-32
Carver, Gordon 1943-45
Cashman, Don 1956
Causey, Mark 2002
Chapman, Warren 1966-67, 69
Chappell, Mike 1997-98
Cheek, Herbert 1935-37
Cheek, James 1946
Chili, Terry 1973-76
Chinault, Neil 1973-74
Christensen, Matt 1996, 2000-02
Claiborne, C.B. 1967-69
Clark, D. 1933
Clark, Marty 1991-94
Clark, Robert 1942
Clement, Hayes 1957-58
Coleman, Jack 1943
Colley, Nelson 1931-32
Collins, Ben 1947-49
Collins, Chris 1993-96
Colonna, Dave 1987
Connelly, Tom 1939-41
Cook, Bob 1973-74
Cook, Joe 1988, 90
Cordell, Thomas 1946
Corrigan, Jim 1980
Councilor, Harry 1928-30
Cowdrick, Tom 1941
Cox, Ray 1962-64
Croson, Joe 1929-31
Crow, Mark 1974-77
Crowder, Dick 1950-52
Crowder, John 1945
Crump, Vince 1984
Curry, Seth 2010
Czyz, Olek 2009

- D -

Davidson, Patrick 2004
Davidson, Jordan 2006-10
Davis, Brian 1989-92
Davis, William 1935

Dawkins, Andre 2010
Dawkins, Johnny* 1983-86
Dawson, Jeff 1971
Decker, Marvin 1953-54
Deimling, Kes 1951-52
D'Emilio, Rudy 1952-54
Deng, Luol 2004
Dennard, Kenny 1978-81
Denton, Randy 1969-71
DeVenzio, Dick 1969-71
Dockery, Sean 2003-04
Doherty, Marty 1954-55
Domzalski, Taymon 1996-99
Doughty, Pat 1970-72
Driesell, Charles 1953-54
Duff, Bob 1948
Duhon, Chris 2001-04
Dunleavy, Mike 2000-02

- E -

Edwards, Fred 1936-38
Edwards, Zeno III 1972
Emma, Tom 1980-83
Engelland, Chip 1980-83
Essex, Rey 1987
Evans, Brad 1969-70
Ewing, Daniel 2002-05

- F -

Farley, Roland 1928-30
Ferguson, Dennis 1963-65
Ferguson, James 1934
Ferry, Danny* 1986-89
Fleischer, Bob 1972-74, 75
Fleming, Bill 1950-52
Flentye, William 1940
Ford, Richard 1982-84
Fox, Paul 1973-76
Franke, Ned 1982
Frye, John 1959-61

- G -

Gantt, Robert 1942-44
Garber 1930
Gilbert, Richard 1943-44
Glasgow, Carl 1952
Gminski, Mike* 1977-80
Godfrey, George 1948
Goetsch, Scott 1976-79
Golden, Dave 1967-69
Gomez, Rick 1975-76
Goodman, Jon 1987
Gordon, Richard 1946-49
Gray, Irving 1946
Gray, Steve 1976-79
Green, Ted 1945
Groat, Dick 1950-52

- H -

Hall, Cameron 1977
Hardy, Rob 1977-79
Harner, Harry 1944
Harrell, Hohn 1978-79
Harris, Bobby Joe 1956-58
Harrison, Buzzy 1962-64
Harscher, Frank 1964
Hartley, Howard 1944
Hartness, W.R. 1926
Hayes, C. 1933
Heaps, Jay 1996-99
Henderson, David 1983-86
Henderson, Gerald 2007-09
Henderson, Phil 1987-90
Hendrickson, Evan 1938
Hendrickson, Horace 1934
Herbster, Ron 1963-65
Herrick, Albert 1935-37
Heyman, Art* 1961-63
Hibbitts, Harold 1949
Hill, Grant* 1991-94
Hill, Thomas 1990-93
Hobgood, Langhorne 1938
Hodge, Willie 1973-76
Hoffman, John 1936-38
Holley, Charles 1939-41
Hollingsworth, Wright ... 1944
Horne, O.W. 1931-33
Horvath, Nick 2000-04
Hubbell, David 1942-43
Hughes, Thomas 1948-49
Huiskamp, William 1935-36
Hurley, Bobby* 1990-93
Hurt, Howard 1959-61
Hyde, Henry 1944

- J -

Jackman, Bill. 1983
Jackson, Doug 1968, 70
James, Nate 1997, 99-01
Jamieson, Bob 1962-63
Janicki, Bernie. 1952-54
Jankoski, John 1928-29
Johnson, Dick 1951-52
Johnson, Patrick 2003-06
Johnson, Steve. 2007-10
Jones, Dahntay 2001-03
Joyce, Marty 1958-59

- K -

Kalbfus, Jack 1955
Kast, Fred 1959-60, 62
Katherman, Rick 1969-71
Kelly, D.L. 1926-28
Kelly, Ryan 2010
Kennedy, Joe 1966-68
King, Billy 1985-88
Kistler, Doug 1959-61

Kitching, Brent............ 1963-65
Koffenberger, Ed.......... 1945-47
Kolodziej, Tim 1966-68
Koubek, Greg.............. 1988-91
Kramer, Pete................ 1973-75
Kuhlmeier, Ray 1968-70
Kulpan, Jim 1950-51
Kunkle, Charles............ 1934-36

- L -
Lacy, Rudy 1952-54
Laettner, Christian*...... 1989-92
Lakata, Bob 1955-56
Lamley, Herky............. 1953, 55
Lang, Antonio 1991-94
Langdon, Trajan 1995, 97-99
Latimer, Dick 1951-52
Lewis, Cliff 1945
Lewis, Henry.............. 1932-33
Lewis, Mike 1966-68
Liccardo, Jim 1966-67
Lind, Fred.................... 1968-69
Linney, Larry............... 1980-81
Litz, Steve 1970-71
Loftis, Cedric 1942-43
Loftis, Garland 1942-43, 47
Love, Reggie 2001-02
Lyons, Pat................... 1948

- M -
Maggette, Corey........... 1999
Mainwaring, Rick 1977
Mann, Ted Jr................ 1963-64
Marin, Jack.................. 1964-66
Martin, William............ 1947-49
May, Reynolds 1934-35
Mayer, Ronnie............. 1953-56
McCaffrey, Bill 1990-91
McCahan, William G. .. 1940-42
McClure, David............ 2005-09
McGillicuddy, Cornelius, Jr. .. 1934
McGrane, Arthur 1943
McKaig, Stuart............. 1965-67
McLeod, Roshown........ 1997-98
McNeely, Doug 1981-82, 84
McRoberts, Josh........... 2006-07
Meagher, Dan 1982-85
Means, Andy 2002-04
Meek, Erik................... 1992-95
Melchionni, Gary 1971-73
Melchionni, Lee 2003-06
Melchionni, Lee 2003-04
Metzler, Robert 1944
Mewhort, Buzzy........... 1960-62
Miller, Alex 1943
Miller, Don 1957
Minor, John 1938-39
Mock, William 1940-41
Moore, Tony................. 1993-95

Morgan, Junior 1954-56
Morgan, Merrill............. 1959-60
Morris, John 1959
Morrison, Harold........... 1976-79
Moses, George 1976
Moss, P.E..................... 1926
Moyer, Bob 1941
Mullen, Jack................. 1960, 62
Mullins, Jeff* 1962-64

- N -
Naktenis, Peter 1935
Nelson, DeMarcus........ 2005-08
Nessley, Martin 1984-87
Newcome, Jim.............. 1956-58
Newton, Greg.............. 1994-97
Northrop, Geoff........... 1977
Novick, Tom................ 2005

- O -
O'Connell, Dave 1973-74, 76
O'Connor, Richard....... 1971
O'Mara, Robert 1937-39

- P -
Pagliuca, Joe 2004-07
Palmer, Crawford 1989-91
Parker, Clarence 1936
Parks, Cherokee 1992-95
Parsons, William 1939-40
Paulus, Greg................ 2006-09
Pergerm, Ernest............ 1949
Perkins, Ross............... 2005-06
Peters, Casey 2010
Plumlee, Mason............ 2010
Plumlee, Miles 2009-10
Pocius, Martynas.......... 2006-09
Podger, Ken................. 1935-37
Polack, Ernest 1934-35
Pope, Warren 1946
Posen, John 1968-70
Price, Glenn................. 1939-41
Price, Ricky................. 1995-98

- R -
Ragens, W.S. 1928
Randolph, Shavlik........ 2003-05
Redding, Chris 1972-74
Redick, J.J................... 2003-06
Reigel, Bill 1953
Riedy, Bob.................. 1965-67
Righter, Ron 1972
Riley, Joe 1935-37
Robb, Spencer 1938
Robert, Shaw 1931
Robertson, Jerry 1957-59
Robinson, Jack 1946
Roellke, Bob 1945
Rogers, George............. 1929-31

Rothbaum, Samuel....... 1941-42, 47
Rowe, Sam 1927

- S -
Sanders, Casey 2000-03
Sapp, Bill..................... 1945
Sapp, Carl.................... 1947-49
Saunders, Larry 1970-71
Scarborough, David 1949-50
Scheyer, Jon 2007-10
Schmidt, Fred.............. 1961-63
Schmidt, Paul 1956-58
Seward, John 1942-47
Shabel, Fred 1953-54
Shaw, Alan 1971-73
Shaw, John 1930-32
Shokes, Eddie.............. 1940-41
Simpson, J.D. 1998-01
Singler, Klye 2008-10
Singleton, Todd 1995-98
Smiley, Glen................ 1968-70
Smith, John 1986-89
Smith, Nolan 2008-10
Snyder, Quin 1986-89
Spanarkel, Jim 1976-79
Spuhler, Raymond........ 1940-42
Stark, Bill 1942, 48
Steele, John 1945
Strickland, Kevin 1985-88
Suddath, Jim................ 1978-81
Suk, Bill 1973-75
Sutton, Nick 2007
Sweet, Andre................ 2001
Swindell, Ed................ 1937-39

- T -
Taylor, Vince 1979-82
Teer, Tim 1968-70
Thomas, James............. 1938-39
Thomas, Lance 2007-10
Thompson, Herb 1932-34
Thompson, James......... 1932-34
Thompson, Michael 2003
Thorne, Robert 1929-30
Tison, Hack 1963-65
Tissaw, Mike 1980-83
Tobin, Don 1954-55
Tormey, Griffin............. 2007
Turner, Harold.............. 1954-55
Turner, Kenneth 1944

- U -
Ulrich, Bill 1962

- V -
Vacendak, Steve 1964-66
Valasek, Cy 1939-41
Vandenberg, Steve........ 1967-69
Van Schoik, Dick 1945

Verga, Bob................... 1965-67
Vernon, Bob 1957-58

- W -
Wallace, Carmen 1994-97
Watson, Bill................. 1957-59
Wayand, Bob............... 1959
Weaver, C.C. 1926-28
Weaver, Phil 1932-34
Wendelin, Ron............. 1966-68
Wendt, Greg 1982-83
Wentz, William............ 1935
Werber, Bill 1928-30
West, Robby 1970-72
Whiting, Richard.......... 1946
Williams, Allen 1980-82
Williams, Elliot 2009
Williams, Jason* 2000-02
Williams, Shelden 2003-04
Williams, Weldon 1983-86
Williamson, Scott 1962-63
Winkin, John 1941
Wojciechowski, Steve .. 1995-98
Wood, Robert 1938
Wright, William 1944

- Y -
Yarbrough, Stuart 1970-72
York, Scotty 1949-51
Youmans, Corren.......... 1948-50
Young, Kenny 1975-76
Youngkin, Carroll......... 1959-61

- Z -
Zafirovski, Todd........... 2010
Zimmer, Bill................ 1965
Zoubek, Brian 2007-10

* selected as a member of the ACC
50th Anniversary Basketball Team

Years	Name	G	MIN	FG	FGA	PCT	3PT	3PA	PCT	FT	FTA	PCT	OR	TR	AVG	AST	TO	PF	ST	BL	PTS	AVG
87-90	Abdelnaby, Alaa	134	1989	448	748	.599	0	0	.000	241	331	.728	184	494	3.7	47	142	276	50	70	1137	8.5
83-86	Alarie, Mark	133	4042	828	1505	.550	0	2	.000	480	602	.797	0	833	6.3	152	268	387	121	104	2136	16.1
59-61	Albright, Doug	30	0	9	26	.346	0	0	.000	12	23	.522	0	31	1.0	0	0	7	0	0	30	1.0
56-58	Allen, Bucky	36	0	89	209	.426	0	0	.000	149	206	.723	0	91	2.5	0	0	54	0	0	327	9.1
50-51	Allen, Dayton	58	0	136	177	.768	0	0	.000	104	0	.000	0	0	0.0	0	0	118	0	0	376	6.5
40-42	Allen, J. Clyde	50	0	139	0	.000	0	0	.000	73	0	.000	0	0	0.0	0	0	0	0	0	351	7.0
64-66	Allen, Phil	27	0	17	37	.459	0	0	.000	11	13	.846	0	19	0.7	0	0	16	0	0	45	1.7
84-87	Amaker, Tommy	138	4666	456	990	.461	44	103	.427	212	268	.791	24	308	2.2	708	336	261	259	11	1168	8.5
82-85	Anderson, Todd	81	676	40	96	.417	0	0	.000	55	77	.714	0	117	1.4	6	33	99	11	8	135	1.7
48-48	Armour, Bill	11	0	4	0	.000	0	0	.000	1	0	.000	0	0	0.0	0	0	0	0	0	9	0.8
74-77	Armstrong, Tate	83	520	529	1020	.519	0	0	.000	246	306	.804	0	182	2.2	217	35	156	0	0	1304	15.7
37-37	Ashby	4	0	1	0	.000	0	0	.000	1	0	.000	0	0	0.0	0	0	0	0	0	3	0.8
91-92	Ast, Christian	31	95	17	30	.567	1	8	.125	9	13	.692	7	24	0.8	2	10	13	1	4	44	1.4
43-46	Ausbon, Doug	27	0	30	0	.000	0	0	.000	7	0	.000	0	0	0.0	0	0	0	0	0	67	2.5
98-99	Avery, William	74	1884	303	655	.463	108	293	.369	163	208	.784	49	206	2.8	283	162	141	91	2	877	11.9
40-44	Bailey, Bill	6	0	12	0	.000	0	0	.000	2	0	.000	0	0	0.0	0	0	0	0	0	26	4.3
44-44	Balitsaris, George	21	0	13	0	.000	0	0	.000	5	0	.000	0	0	0.0	0	0	0	0	0	31	1.5
78-81	Banks, Gene	124	4285	827	1558	.531	0	0	.000	425	589	.722	0	985	7.9	360	399	337	37	9	2079	16.8
66-68	Barone, Tony	46	0	20	45	.444	0	0	.000	29	44	.659	0	28	0.6	0	0	54	0	0	69	1.5
57-59	Barrett, George	13	0	3	9	.333	0	0	.000	6	9	.667	0	22	1.7	0	0	17	0	0	12	0.9
58-60	Bateman, Larry	36	0	20	67	.299	0	0	.000	10	29	.345	0	82	2.3	0	0	50	0	0	50	1.4
00-99	Battier, Shane	146	4337	651	1303	.500	246	592	.416	436	561	.777	338	887	6.1	239	161	296	266	254	1984	13.6
59-61	Beal, Jay	22	0	15	46	.326	0	0	.000	17	24	.708	0	15	0.7	0	0	7	0	0	47	2.1
44-44	Beall, Curtis	6	0	0	0	.000	0	0	.000	0	0	.000	0	0	0.0	0	0	0	0	0	0	0.0
94-94	Beard, Joey	16	64	7	14	.500	0	2	.000	7	10	.700	2	8	0.5	3	10	4	4	0	21	1.3
75-78	Bell, Bruce	42	302	23	62	.371	0	0	.000	12	23	.522	0	26	0.6	37	32	33	0	0	58	1.4
53-56	Belmont, Joe	103	0	471	1259	.374	0	0	.000	396	547	.724	0	420	4.1	0	0	259	0	0	1338	13.0
78-80	Bender, Bob	83	2377	196	380	.516	0	0	.000	122	158	.772	0	116	1.4	332	169	188	0	0	514	6.2
37-39	Bergman, Sparky	58	0	141	0	.000	0	0	.000	62	0	.000	0	0	0.0	0	0	0	0	0	344	5.9
87-87	Berndt, Andy	6	9	0	2	.000	0	0	.000	0	0	.000	1	3	0.5	0	1	1	0	0	0	0.0
83-86	Bilas, Jay	127	2864	365	655	.557	0	0	.000	332	511	.650	0	692	5.4	56	167	379	54	37	1062	8.4
73-75	Billerman, Kevin	78	0	291	659	.442	0	0	.000	211	264	.799	0	174	2.2	270	0	287	0	0	793	10.2
55-55	Blackburn, Tom	11	0	4	10	.400	0	0	.000	3	10	.300	0	1	0.1	0	0	1	0	0	11	1.0
70-70	Blackman, Don	25	0	53	111	.477	0	0	.000	50	70	.714	0	131	5.2	8	0	45	0	0	156	6.2
92-95	Blakeney, Kenny	93	1065	105	229	.459	20	59	.339	67	105	.638	42	124	1.3	110	108	96	33	4	297	3.2
44-44	Bledsoe, Gene	17	0	47	0	.000	0	0	.000	19	0	.000	0	0	0.0	0	0	0	0	0	113	6.6
06-06	Boateng, Eric	20	50	6	7	.857	0	0	.000	2	2	1.00	4	12	0.6	1	5	11	1	0	14	0.7
00-02	Boozer, Carlos	101	2620	554	878	.631	0	2	.000	398	537	.741	260	724	7.2	115	157	288	95	72	1506	14.9
00-04	Borman, Andy	40	78	5	9	.556	3	6	.500	4	7	.571	4	12	0.3	5	8	6	1	0	17	0.4
38-40	Bowman, Jim	11	0	4	0	.000	0	0	.000	2	0	.000	0	0	0.0	0	0	0	0	0	10	0.9
51-51	Boyce, Rod	8	0	3	9	.333	0	0	.000	1	5	.200	0	0	0.0	0	0	12	0	0	7	0.9
58-59	Boyd, Jack	27	0	42	142	.296	0	0	.000	21	37	.568	0	47	1.7	0	0	59	0	0	105	3.9
06-07	Boykin, Jamal	29	100	10	19	.526	0	0	.000	9	10	.900	11	32	1.1	2	8	21	4	7	29	1.0
98-99	Brand, Elton	60	1634	355	580	.612	0	0	.000	262	390	.672	215	536	8.9	51	101	150	81	113	972	16.2
46-46	Brand, Joe	6	0	6	0	.000	0	0	.000	2	0	.000	0	0	0.0	0	0	0	0	0	14	2.3
87-90	Brickey, Robert	134	3039	484	884	.548	2	9	.222	329	531	.620	268	649	4.8	146	274	334	115	90	1299	9.7
93-93	Brown, Kenney	15	31	0	5	.000	0	1	.000	4	9	.444	2	5	0.3	0	1	3	0	0	4	0.3
40-41	Brown, Ray	30	0	22	0	.000	0	0	.000	10	0	.000	0	0	0.0	0	0	0	0	0	54	1.8
44-44	Bruce	1	0	0	0	.000	0	0	.000	0	0	.000	0	0	0.0	0	0	0	0	0	0	0.0
46-46	Brunner, George	16	0	12	0	.000	0	0	.000	7	0	.000	0	0	0.0	0	0	0	0	0	31	1.9
93-96	Brunson, Stan	36	208	5	22	.227	0	0	.000	7	12	.583	25	50	1.4	4	13	37	3	0	17	0.5
82-85	Bryan, Jay	57	244	20	57	.351	0	1	.000	22	50	.440	0	44	0.8	9	19	57	9	0	62	1.1
99-99	Bryant, D.	13	30	3	9	.333	1	3	.333	1	4	.250	0	3	0.2	2	3	4	1	0	8	0.6
56-57	Bryson, Ed	13	0	2	20	.100	0	0	.000	0	0	.000	0	8	0.6	0	0	12	0	0	4	0.3
88-91	Buckley, Clay	86	439	51	85	.600	0	0	.000	46	79	.582	37	88	1.0	12	25	44	13	6	148	1.7
62-64	Buckley, Jay	85	0	352	617	.571	0	0	.000	222	391	.568	0	714	8.4	0	0	241	0	0	926	10.9
00-03	Buckner, Andre	84	260	16	48	.333	5	16	.313	18	35	.514	7	30	0.4	27	23	26	13	1	55	0.7
56-56	Buhowsky, Tony	15	0	10	39	.256	0	0	.000	7	14	.500	0	33	2.2	0	0	28	0	0	27	1.8
74-74	Burch, Edgar	23	0	72	180	.400	0	0	.000	13	20	.650	0	33	1.4	27	0	34	0	0	157	6.8
72-74	Burdette, Jeff	57	0	22	84	.262	0	0	.000	15	41	.366	0	35	0.6	66	0	92	0	0	59	1.0
98-99	Burgess, Chris	75	1061	150	266	.564	3	9	.333	64	147	.435	106	268	3.6	49	62	127	44	58	367	4.9
87-89	Burgin, George	38	93	11	19	.579	0	0	.000	6	21	.286	7	17	0.4	4	6	10	4	6	28	0.7
92-92	Burt, Ron	19	38	3	11	.273	0	0	.000	4	4	1.00	0	2	0.1	8	4	3	1	1	10	0.5

Years	Name	G	MIN	FG	FGA	PCT	3PT	3PA	PCT	FT	FTA	PCT	OR	TR	AVG	AST	TO	PF	ST	BL	PTS	AVG
97-99	Caldbeck, Justin	28	70	5	13	.385	0	0	.000	3	8	.375	5	15	0.5	3	5	5	1	1	13	0.5
00-99	Caldbeck, Ryan	33	73	2	15	.133	1	10	.100	3	7	.429	1	13	0.4	2	1	3	1	0	8	0.2
49-49	Campbell, Ray	1	0	0	0	.000	0	0	.000	0	0	.000	0	0	0.0	0	0	0	0	0	0	0.0
60-61	Cantwell, John	38	0	50	129	.388	0	0	.000	14	24	.583	0	24	0.6	0	0	35	0	0	114	3.0
94-97	Capel, Jeff	129	3775	580	1362	.426	220	553	.398	221	327	.676	124	390	3.0	433	328	269	110	18	1601	12.4
71-71	Carr, Judge	1	0	0	0	.000	0	0	.000	0	0	.000	0	1	1.0	0	0	0	0	0	0	0.0
00-99	Carrawell, Chris	136	3541	542	1115	.486	62	172	.360	309	463	.667	211	608	4.5	309	231	206	105	114	1455	10.7
43-45	Carver, Gordon	78	0	374	0	.000	0	0	.000	138	0	.000	0	0	0.0	0	0	0	0	0	886	11.4
53-56	Cashman, Don	30	0	26	95	.274	0	0	.000	17	27	.630	0	60	2.0	0	0	37	0	0	69	2.3
51-51	Caudle, Lloyd	1	0	0	0	.000	0	0	.000	0	0	.000	0	0	0.0	0	0	0	0	0	0	0.0
02-02	Causey, Mark	12	47	4	10	.400	2	3	.667	3	6	.500	2	8	0.7	3	5	8	3	1	13	1.1
66-69	Chapman, Warren	66	0	89	193	.461	0	0 .	.000	55	104	.529	0	216	3.3	0	0	116	0	0	233	3.5
97-98	Chappell, Mike	68	901	143	342	.418	60	156	.385	57	103	.553	45	125	1.8	37	52	110	27	6	403	5.9
46-50	Cheek, Buck	49	0	51	0	.000	0	0	.000	21	0	.000	0	0	0.0	0	0	1	0	0	123	2.5
37-37	Cheek, Herbert	19	0	44	0	.000	0	0	.000	26	0	.000	0	0	0.0	0	0	0	0	0	114	6.0
73-76	Chili, Terry	65	0	108	162	.667	0	0	.000	48	106	.453	0	177	2.7	17	0	89	0	0	264	4.1
73-74	Chinault, Neil	12	0	4	9	.444	0	0	.000	2	2	1.000	0	2	0.2	3	0	2	0	0	10	0.8
00-96	Christensen, Matt	97	751	54	116	.466	0	0	.000	54	102	.529	94	189	1.9	16	34	143	20	35	162	1.7
67-69	Claiborne, C.B.	53	0	88	241	.365	0	0	.000	42	61	.689	0	100	1.9	19	0	83	0	0	218	4.1
91-94	Clark, Marty	122	1668	224	465	.482	49	131	.374	150	187	.802	74	181	1.5	134	148	155	68	18	647	5.3
41-41	Clark, Robert	1	0	0	0	.000	0	0	.000	0	0	.000	0	0	0.0	0	0	0	0	0	0	0.0
56-58	Clement, Hayes	48	0	104	266	.391	0	0	.000	83	125	.664	0	224	4.7	0	0	111	0	0	291	6.1
43-43	Coleman, Jack	16	0	51	0	.000	0	0	.000	13	0	.000	0	0	0.0	0	0	0	0	0	115	7.2
47-49	Collins, Ben	77	0	259	0	.000	0	0	.000	154	0	.000	0	0	0.0	0	0	0	0	0	672	8.7
93-96	Collins, Chris	120	2874	357	867	.412	209	539	.388	168	236	.712	55	243	2.0	291	175	167	108	3	1091	9.1
87-87	Colonna, Dave	2	2	0	0	.000	0	0	.000	0	0	.000	0	0	0.0	0	0	1	0	0	0	0.0
39-41	Connelly, Tom	55	0	31	0	.000	0	0	.000	26	0	.000	0	0	0.0	0	0	0	0	0	88	1.6
73-74	Cook, Bob	16	0	9	22	.409	0	0	.000	0	0	.000	0	13	0.8	0	0	8	0	0	18	1.1
88-90	Cook, Joe	48	286	28	67	.418	3	7	.429	23	33	.697	12	36	0.8	35	37	25	19	1	82	1.7
46-46	Cordell, Tom	19	0	21	0	.000	0	0	.000	7	0	.000	0	0	0.0	0	0	0	0	0	49	2.6
80-80	Corrigan, Jim	9	22	1	1	1.00	0	0	.000	2	2	1.00	0	1	0.1	3	2	3	0	0	4	0.4
46-46	Corrington, Jim	6	0	0	0	.000	0	0	.000	0	0	.000	0	0	0.0	0	0	0	0	0	0	0.0
39-40	Cowdrick, Tom	3	0	0	0	.000	0	0	.000	1	0	.000	0	0	0.0	0	0	0	0	0	1	0.3
61-63	Cox, Fred	11	0	3	6	.500	0	0	.000	1	2	.500	0	3	0.3	0	0	6	0	0	7	0.6
62-64	Cox, Ray	39	0	13	31	.419	0	0	.000	7	14	.500	0	25	0.6	0	0	20	0	0	33	0.8
49-49	Crigler, Benner	1	0	0	0	.000	0	0	.000	0	0	.000	0	0	0.0	0	0	0	0	0	0	0.0
74-77	Crow, Mark	87	841	341	675	.505	0	0	.000	138	174	.793	0	346	4.0	116	63	225	0	0	820	9.4
50-52	Crowder, Dick	93	0	258	492	.524	0	0	.000	116	127	.913	0	220	2.4	28	0	264	0	0	632	6.8
84-84	Crump, Vince	7	12	0	0	.000	0	0	.000	1	3	.333	0	1	0.1	0	1	0	0	0	1	0.1
44-44	Curry, Pat	3	0	2	0	.000	0	0	.000	0	0	.000	0	0	0.0	0	0	0	0	0	4	1.3
09-10	Czyz, Olek	19	112	10	25	.400	1	7	.143	2	6	.333	10	24	1.3	8	11	6	2	1	23	1.2
52-54	D'Emilio, Rudy	80	0	393	1125	.349	0	0	.000	242	363	.667	0	330	4.1	100	0	227	0	0	1028	12.9
06-10	Davidson, Jordan	55	101	4	13	.308	2	5	.400	8	14	.571	3	9	0.2	6	8	9	3	0 1	8	0.3
04-05	Davidson, Patrick	29	51	0	5	.000	0	2	.000	4	4	1.00	0	5	0.2	1	1	4	1	0	4	0.1
89-92	Davis, Brian	141	2788	326	701	.465	9	44	.205	291	424	.686	175	434	3.1	181	178	258	119	24	952	6.8
10-10	Dawkins, Andre	38	477	54	136	.397	36	95	.379	25	34	.735	6	43	1.1	13	15	36	11	2	169	4.4
83-86	Dawkins, Johnny	133	4749	1026	2019	.508	19	54	.352	485	614	.790	0	536	4.0	555	414	270	168	24	2556	19.2
71-71	Dawson, Jeff	30	0	124	289	.429	0	0	.000	40	50	.800	0	53	1.8	29	0	45	0	0	288	9.6
52-54	Decker, Marv	60	0	112	244	.459	0	0	.000	88	121	.727	0	350	5.8	3	0	125	0	0	312	5.2
51-52	Deimling, Kes	60	0	101	271	.373	0	0	.000	94	129	.729	0	123	2.1	20	0	141	0	0	296	4.9
04-04	Deng, Luol	37	1149	210	442	.475	40	111	.360	98	138	.710	82	255	6.9	68	83	82	49	39	558	15.1
78-81	Dennard, Kenny	117	3514	452	881	.513	0	0	.000	153	260	.588	0	671	5.7	232	246	383	47	10	1057	9.0
69-71	Denton, Randy	84	0	693	1295	.535	0	0	.000	272	400	.680	0	1067	12.7	56	0	259	0	0	1658	19.7
69-71	DeVenzio, Dick	81	0	294	634	.464	0	0	.000	105	138	.761	0	170	2.1	388	0	218	0	0	693	8.6
03-06	Dockery, Sean	133	2705	230	514	.447	65	178	.365	121	182	.665	88	281	2.1	234	149	295	194	13	646	4.9
54-55	Doherty, Marty	52	0	113	260	.435	0	0	.000	63	96	.656	0	245	4.7	0	0	145	0	0	289	5.6
96-99	Domzalski, Taymon	100	1301	154	292	.527	0	0	.000	116	158	.734	143	336	3.4	16	82	239	42	64	424	4.2
70-72	Doughty, Pat	23	0	8	22	.364	0	0	.000	10	22	.455	0	9	0.4	11	0	20	0	0	26	1.1
51-51	Downing, Bill	7	0	1	8	.125	0	0	.000	1	1	1.00	0	0	0.0	0	0	4	0	0	3	0.4
53-54	Driesell, Charles	45	0	65	157	.414	0	0	.000	51	102	.500	0	107	2.4	0	0	76	0	0	181	4.0
40-40	Dubois, Lou	3	0	1	0	.000	0	0	.000	1	0	.000	0	0	0.0	0	0	0	0	0	3	1.0
48-49	Duff, Bob	20	0	24	0	.000	0	0	.000	16	0	.000	0	0	0.0	0	0	0	0	0	64	3.2
01-04	Duhon, Chris	144	4813	432	1033	.418	162	505	.321	242	349	.693	109	489	3.4	819	355	268	301	16	1268	8.8

Years	Name	G	MIN	FG	FGA	PCT	3PT	3PA	PCT	FT	FTA	PCT	OR	TR	AVG	AST	TO	PF	ST	BL	PTS	AVG
00-02	Dunleavy, Mike	104	2995	499	1050	.475	179	483	.371	194	278	.698	145	601	5.8	225	202	213	166	55	1371	13.2
81-81	Dyke, Mack	3	4	1	1	1.00	0	0	.000	0	0	.000	0	0	0.0	0	0	1	0	0	2	0.7
37-38	Edwards, Mouse	38	0	61	0	.000	0	0	.000	33	0	.000	0	0	0.0	0	0	0	0	0	155	4.1
72-72	Edwards, Zeno	9	0	0	2	.000	0	0	.000	4	4	1.00	0	3	0.3	3	0	2	0	0	4	0.4
80-83	Emma, Tom	110	2818	273	625	.437	24	55	.436	214	254	.843	0	196	1.8	245	159	259	57	7	784	7.1
50-51	Engberg, John	32	0	27	74	.365	0	0	.000	34	36	.944	0	0	0.0	0	0	56	0	0	88	2.8
80-83	Engelland, Chip	113	2472	411	793	.518	41	74	.554	162	191	.848	0	148	1.3	168	118	174	45	5	1025	9.1
87-87	Essex, Rey	6	8	1	2	.500	0	0	.000	1	4	.250	2	7	1.1	0	0	0	0	0	3	0.5
69-70	Evans, Brad	50	0	133	281	.473	0	0	.000	88	154	.571	0	120	2.4	105	0	86	0	0	354	7.1
02-05	Ewing, Daniel	138	3825	538	1246	.432	217	554	.392	302	405	.746	117	382	2.8	293	258	365	191	24	1595	11.6
49-49	Farinella, Don	2	0	1	0	.000	0	0	.000	0	0	.000	0	0	0.0	0	0	0	0	0	2	1.0
63-65	Ferguson, Denny	81	0	184	402	.458	0	0	.000	41	56	.732	0	136	1.7	0	0	124	0	0	409	5.0
86-89	Ferry, Danny	143	4308	810	1675	.484	108	278	.388	427	551	.775	236	1003	7.0	506	396	394	169	71	2155	15.1
65-65	Fitts, Burton	3	0	1	3	.333	0	0	.000	0	0	.000	0	1	0.3	0	0	3	0	0	2	0.7
73-75	Fleischer, Bob	78	0	441	789	.559	0	0	.000	257	333	.772	0	817	10.5	125	0	226	0	0	1139	14.6
50-52	Fleming, Bill	75	0	164	458	.358	0	0	.000	121	192	.630	0	291	3.9	65	0	210	0	0	449	6.0
38-40	Flentye, Bill	12	0	3	0	.000	0	0	.000	0	0	.000	0	0	0.0	0	0	0	0	0	6	0.5
82-84	Ford, Richard	21	39	0	16	.000	0	0	.000	4	4	1.00	0	4	0.2	4	6	6	1	0	4	0.2
73-76	Fox, Paul	68	0	58	121	.479	0	0	.000	34	57	.596	0	71	1.0	24	0	87	0	0	150	2.2
67-67	Francis, Bob	1	0	1	2	.500	0	0	.000	3	3	1.00	0	4	4.0	0	0	1	0	0	5	5.0
82-82	Franke, Ned	3	3	1	1	1.00	0	0	.000	0	0	.000	0	1	0.3	0	0	0	0	0	2	0.7
59-61	Frye, John	81	0	267	699	.382	0	0	.000	232	326	.712	0	211	2.6	0	0	172	0	0	766	9.5
42-44	Gantt, Bob	46	0	174	0	.000	0	0	.000	29	0	.000	0	0	0.0	0	0	0	0	0	377	8.2
43-44	Gantt, Samuel	11	0	6	0	.000	0	0	.000	2	0	.000	0	0	0.0	0	0	0	0	0	14	1.3
62-62	Gebbie, Tom	3	0	1	2	.500	0	0	.000	1	2	.500	0	0	0.0	0	0	0	0	0	3	1.0
43-44	Gilbert, Richard	40	0	38	0	.000	0	0	.000	4	0	.000	0	0	0.0	0	0	0	0	0	80	2.0
52-52	Glasow, Carl	20	0	29	71	.408	0	0	.000	17	29	.586	0	88	4.4	11	0	42	0	0	75	3.8
77-80	Gminski, Mike	122	4157	901	1697	.531	0	0	.000	521	658	.792	0	1242	10.2	128	275	240	0	345	2323	19.0
48-49	Godfrey, George	26	0	17	0	.000	0	0	.000	2	0	.000	0	0	0.0	0	0	0	0	0	36	1.4
76-79	Goetsch, Scott	94	732	79	136	.581	0	0	.000	27	42	.643	0	177	1.9	37	49	107	0	0	185	2.0
67-69	Golden, Dave	80	0	304	677	.449	0	0	.000	144	190	.758	0	150	1.9	56	0	178	0	0	752	9.4
75-76	Gomez, Rick	14	0	4	17	.235	0	0	.000	6	7	.857	0	4	0.3	2	0	11	0	0	14	1.0
87-87	Goodman, Jon	10	20	1	7	.143	0	3	.000	4	5	.800	1	2	0.2	3	7	3	0	0	6	0.6
46-49	Gordon, Dick	101	0	154	0	.000	0	0	.000	124	0	.000	0	0	0.0	0	0	0	0	0	432	4.3
42-42	Gotye	1	0	0	0	.000	0	0	.000	0	0	.000	0	0	0.0	0	0	0	0	0	0	0.0
46-47	Gray, Irving	25	0	12	0	.000	0	0	.000	6	0	.000	0	0	0.0	0	0	0	0	0	30	1.2
76-79	Gray, Steve	88	967	76	169	.450	0	0	.000	71	84	.845	0	64	0.7	119	132	124	0	0	223	2.5
50-52	Groat, Dick	82	0	682	1669	.409	0	0	.000	522	710	.735	0	229	2.8	229	0	290	0	0	1886	23.0
42-42	Gross	2	0	1	0	.000	0	0	.000	1	0	.000	0	0	0.0	0	0	0	0	0	3	1.5
46-46	Hackett	4	0	3	0	.000	0	0	.000	0	0	.000	0	0	0.0	0	0	0	0	0	6	1.5
77-77	Hall, Cameron	27	418	47	94	.500	0	0	.000	22	39	.564	0	56	2.1	20	30	71	0	0	116	4.3
96-96	Hall, Jeremy	10	14	1	2	.500	0	0	.000	2	2	1.00	1	1	0.1	1	0	6	0	0	4	0.4
62-62	Hamilton, Roger	3	0	1	3	.333	0	0	.000	0	0	.000	0	0	0.0	0	0	1	0	0	2	0.7
77-79	Hardy, Rob	28	79	10	21	.476	0	0	.000	2	5	.400	0	12	0.4	5	6	21	0	0	22	0.8
44-44	Harner, Harry	25	0	63	0	.000	0	0	.000	34	0	.000	0	0	0.0	0	0	0	0	0	160	6.4
78-79	Harrell, John	63	1206	92	185	.497	0	0	.000	47	62	.758	0	53	0.8	98	64	111	0	0	231	3.7
56-58	Harris, Bobby Joe	75	0	288	768	.375	0	0	.000	168	225	.747	0	253	3.4	0	0	200	0	0	744	9.9
62-64	Harrison, Buzzy	83	0	284	589	.482	0	0	.000	107	150	.713	0	267	3.2	0	0	137	0	0	675	8.1
64-64	Harscher, Frank	15	0	8	21	.381	0	0	.000	7	8	.875	0	5	0.3	0	0	5	0	0	23	1.5
96-99	Heaps, Jay	30	69	2	6	.333	1	2	.500	3	10	.300	2	7	0.2	13	9	14	4	1	8	0.3
40-40	Heath, John	1	0	0	0	.000	0	0	.000	0	0	.000	0	0	0.0	0	0	0	0	0	0	0.0
83-86	Henderson, David	128	3325	586	1208	.485	9	33	.273	389	554	.702	0	513	4.0	263	327	332	151	10	1570	12.3
07-09	Henderson, Gerald	103	2607	456	995	.458	69	210	.329	281	398	.706	124	435	4.2	182	191	179	101	69	1262	12.3
87-90	Henderson, Phil	115	2886	510	1053	.484	128	320	.400	249	320	.778	130	330	2.9	217	246	225	129	20	1397	12.1
38-38	Hendrickson, Abe	20	0	9	0	.000	0	0	.000	10	0	.000	0	0	0.0	0	0	0	0	0	28	1.4
63-65	Herbster, Ron	85	0	98	225	.436	0	0	.000	85	123	.691	0	105	1.2	0	0	79	0	0	281	3.3
37-37	Herrick, Albert	21	0	30	0	.000	0	0	.000	20	0	.000	0	0	0.0	0	0	0	0	0	80	3.8
61-63	Heyman, Art	79	0	713	1580	.451	0	0	.000	558	853	.654	0	865	10.9	0	0	214	0	0	1984	25.1
49-49	Hibbitts, Harold	18	0	19	0	.000	0	0	.000	9	0	.000	0	0	0.0	0	0	0	0	0	47	2.6
91-94	Hill, Grant	129	3922	745	1400	.532	44	117	.376	390	559	.698	203	769	6.0	461	319	316	218	133	1924	14.9
90-93	Hill, Thomas	141	3462	590	1137	.519	95	246	.386	319	443	.720	174	488	3.5	177	189	264	194	49	1594	11.3
38-40	Hobgood, Lang	18	0	7	0	.000	0	0	.000	5	0	.000	0	0	0.0	0	0	0	0	0	19	1.1
73-76	Hodge, Willie	102	0	463	906	.511	0	0	.000	191	263	.726	0	605	5.9	100	0	287	0	0	1117	11.0

Years	Name	G	MIN	FG	FGA	PCT	3PT	3PA	PCT	FT	FTA	PCT	OR	TR	AVG	AST	TO	PF	ST	BL	PTS	AVG
37-38	Hoffman, John	45	0	45	0	.000	0	0	.000	30	0	.000	0	0	0.0	0	0	0	0	0	120	2.7
39-41	Holley, Chuck	69	0	178	0	.000	0	0	.000	75	0	.000	0	0	0.0	0	0	0	0	0	431	6.2
44-44	Hollingsworth, Wright	11	0	6	0	.000	0	0	.000	0	0	.000	0	0	0.0	0	0	0	0	0	12	1.1
00-04	Horvath, Nick	133	1193	124	277	.448	30	124	.242	69	111	.622	105	276	2.1	44	66	179	42	45	347	2.6
41-43	Hubbell, David	20	0	6	0	.000	0	0	.000	1	0	.000	0	0	0.0	0	0	0	0	0	13	0.7
48-50	Hughes, Tommy	72	0	179	0	.000	0	0	.000	175	0	.000	0	0	0.0	0	0	58	0	0	533	7.4
90-93	Hurley, Bobby	140	4802	513	1252	.410	264	652	.405	441	568	.776	54	306	2.2	1076	534	320	202	5	1731	12.4
59-61	Hurt, Howard	80	0	420	1070	.393	0	0	.000	255	341	.748	0	575	7.2	0	0	205	0	0	1095	13.7
44-44	Hyde, Henry	25	0	25	0	.000	0	0	.000	3	0	.000	0	0	0.0	0	0	0	0	0	53	2.1
83-83	Jackman, Bill	27	286	36	91	.396	5	9	.556	10	10	1.00	0	44	1.6	9	19	31	8	1	87	3.2
68-70	Jackson, Doug	4	0	3	10	.300	0	0	.000	0	0	.000	0	4	1.0	0	0	4	0	0	6	1.5
00-99	James, Nate	135	2813	387	818	.473	111	331	.335	231	315	.733	221	500	3.7	147	199	222	147	27	1116	8.3
62-63	Jamieson, Bob	30	0	19	32	.594	0	0	.000	12	24	.500	0	53	1.8	0	0	48	0	0	50	1.7
52-54	Janicki, Bernie	83	0	480	1283	.374	0	0	.000	287	429	.669	0	923	11.1	42	0	255	0	0	1247	15.0
42-43	Jarvis	3	0	0	0	.000	0	0	.000	1	0	.000	0	0	0.0	0	0	0	0	0	1	0.3
60-60	Johnson, C.B.	1	0	0	0	.000	0	0	.000	0	0	.000	0	0	0.0	0	0	1	0	0	0	0.0
51-52	Johnson, Dick	58	0	81	238	.340	0	0	.000	34	54	.630	0	38	0.7	58	0	112	0	0	196	3.4
03-06	Johnson, Patrick	53	147	10	12	.833	0	0	.000	6	10	.600	13	35	0.7	6	5	27	1	5	26	0.5
07-10	Johnson, Steve	21	39	2	4	.500	0	0	.000	3	5	.600	1	4	0.2	0	0	2	2	1	7	0.3
02-03	Jones, Dahntay	68	2026	351	724	.485	59	170	.347	214	289	.740	101	326	4.8	69	121	202	66	35	975	14.3
58-59	Joyce, Marty	18	0	6	32	.188	0	0	.000	6	12	.500	0	14	0.8	0	0	13	0	0	18	1.0
55-56	Kalbfus, Jack	38	0	112	260	.431	0	0	.000	67	124	.540	0	116	3.1	0	0	68	0	0	291	7.7
59-62	Kast, Fred	57	0	102	295	.346	0	0	.000	39	60	.650	0	167	2.9	0	0	66	0	0	243	4.3
69-71	Katherman, Rick	82	0	447	965	.463	0	0	.000	111	144	.771	0	362	4.4	65	0	186	0	0	1005	12.3
46-46	Kaufman,	2	0	1	0	.000	0	0	.000	1	0	.000	0	0	0.0	0	0	0	0	0	3	1.5
10-10	Kelly, Ryan	35	227	16	45	.356	5	19	.263	4	6	.667	6	38	1.1	13	8	34	8	14	41	1.2
66-68	Kennedy, Joe	62	0	177	429	.413	0	0	.000	100	130	.769	0	265	4.3	0	0	119	0	0	454	7.3
85-88	King, Billy	135	2825	234	464	.504	0	1	.000	134	280	.479	75	390	2.9	251	180	292	140	45	602	4.5
08-08	King, Taylor	34	330	63	152	.414	43	114	.377	17	29	.586	23	68	2.0	14	19	32	11	14	186	5.5
59-61	Kistler, Doug	81	0	388	864	.449	0	0	.000	156	240	.650	0	756	9.3	0	0	223	0	0	932	11.5
63-65	Kitching, Brent	61	0	91	210	.433	0	0	.000	53	74	.716	0	103	1.7	0	0	62	0	0	235	3.9
46-47	Koffenberger, Ed	54	0	280	0	.000	0	0	.000	173	0	.000	0	0	0.0	0	0	0	0	0	733	13.6
66-68	Kolodziej, Tim	60	0	130	300	.433	0	0	.000	157	207	.758	0	230	3.8	0	0	131	0	0	417	7.0
88-91	Koubek, Greg	147	2064	252	591	.426	80	214	.374	133	183	.727	125	364	2.5	104	134	213	68	12	717	4.9
73-75	Kramer, Pete	76	0	338	697	.485	0	0	.000	110	145	.759	0	253	3.3	117	0	166	0	0	786	10.3
68-70	Kuhlmeier, Ray	29	0	38	91	.418	0	0	.000	15	19	.789	0	30	1.0	17	0	25	0	0	91	3.1
50-51	Kulpan, Red	58	0	79	130	.608	0	0	.000	69	0	.000	0	0	0.0	0	0	170	0	0	227	3.9
52-54	Lacy, Rudy	70	0	158	337	.469	0	0	.000	132	194	.680	0	264	3.8	9	0	136	0	0	448	6.4
89-92	Laettner, Christian	148	4049	834	1452	.574	79	163	.485	713	885	.806	374	1149	7.8	273	398	425	243	145	2460	16.6
55-58	Lakata, Bob	68	0	156	397	.393	0	0	.000	119	181	.657	0	394	5.8	0	0	155	0	0	431	6.3
53-55	Lamley, Herky	47	0	91	275	.331	0	0	.000	64	90	.711	0	212	4.5	0	0	76	0	0	246	5.2
43-43	Landesberg,	7	0	2	0	.000	0	0	.000	1	0	.000	0	0	0.0	0	0	0	0	0	5	0.7
91-94	Lang, Antonio	135	3020	367	644	.570	0	3	.000	278	422	.659	273	586	4.3	90	198	305	68	106	1012	7.5
95-99	Langdon, Trajan	136	3922	623	1380	.451	342	802	.426	386	448	.862	106	389	2.9	255	210	282	120	25	1974	14.5
45-45	Lapp, Bob	1	0	0	0	.000	0	0	.000	0	0	.000	0	0	0.0	0	0	0	0	0	0	0.0
43-44	Larkin, Sidney	10	0	5	0	.000	0	0	.000	0	0	.000	0	0	0.0	0	0	0	0	0	10	1.0
51-51	Lasseter, Jack	1	0	0	1	.000	0	0	.000	0	0	.000	0	0	0.0	0	0	0	0	0	0	0.0
50-52	Latimer, Dick	66	0	50	193	.259	0	0	.000	25	49	.510	0	39	0.6	13	0	71	0	0	125	1.9
39-39	Lauteres	1	0	0	0	.000	0	0	.000	1	0	.000	0	0	0.0	0	0	0	0	0	1	1.0
66-68	Lewis, Mike	84	0	543	974	.557	0	0	.000	331	435	.761	0	1051	12.5	0	0	281	0	0	1417	16.9
65-67	Liccardo, Jim	58	0	49	119	.412	0	0	.000	23	33	.697	0	118	2.0	0	0	27	0	0	121	2.1
67-69	Lind, Fred	52	0	138	270	.511	0	0	.000	81	114	.711	0	281	5.4	13	0	87	0	0	357	6.9
80-81	Linney, Larry	39	298	24	74	.324	0	0	.000	31	43	.721	0	49	1.3	4	20	38	22	3	79	2.0
70-71	Litz, Steve	17	0	13	19	.684	0	0	.000	10	14	.714	0	25	1.5	1	0	13	0	0	36	2.1
42-43	Loftis, Cedric	49	0	210	0	.000	0	0	.000	73	0	.000	0	0	0.0	0	0	0	0	0	493	10.1
42-47	Loftis, Garland	67	0	169	0	.000	0	0	.000	52	0	.000	0	0	0.0	0	0	0	0	0	390	5.8
01-05	Love, Reggie	58	404	28	59	.475	0	2	.000	19	36	.528	55	108	1.9	15	19	68	18	13	75	1.3
49-49	Lynch, Hal	1	0	0	0	.000	0	0	.000	0	0	.000	0	0	0.0	0	0	0	0	0	0	0.0
48-48	Lyons, Pat	21	0	13	0	.000	0	0	.000	6	0	.000	0	0	0.0	0	0	0	0	0	32	1.5
99-99	Maggette, Corey	39	691	137	261	.525	29	84	.345	111	155	.716	56	151	3.9	59	80	99	29	15	414	10.6
77-77	Mainwaring, Rick	8	20	0	1	.000	0	0	.000	3	4	.750	0	3	0.4	1	3	0	0	0	3	0.4
46-46	Major	4	0	2	0	.000	0	0	.000	1	0	.000	0	0	0.0	0	0	0	0	0	5	1.3
63-64	Mann, Ted	29	0	6	30	.200	0	0	.000	8	15	.533	0	29	1.0	0	0	17	0	0	20	0.7

Years	Name	G	MIN	FG	FGA	PCT	3PT	3PA	PCT	FT	FTA	PCT	OR	TR	AVG	AST	TO	PF	ST	BL	PTS	AVG
57-57	Marcovecchio, Joe	2	0	0	3	.000	0	0	.000	0	2	.000	0	1	0.5	0	0	3	0	0	0	0.0
64-66	Marin, Jack	86	0	513	1027	.500	0	0	.000	253	336	.753	0	695	8.1	0	0	219	0	0	1279	14.9
47-50	Martin, Bill	76	0	85	0	.000	0	0	.000	28	0	.000	0	0	0.0	0	0	9	0	0	198	2.6
53-56	Mayer, Ronnie	105	0	566	1342	.422	0	0	.000	515	673	.765	0	954	9.1	0	0	347	0	0	1647	15.7
65-65	McBride, Elliott	4	0	2	2	1.00	0	0	.000	3	3	1.00	0	0	0.0	0	0	1	0	0	7	1.8
90-91	McCaffrey, Bill	76	1471	253	538	.470	32	95	.337	153	188	.814	21	95	1.3	105	104	95	59	5	691	9.1
40-42	McCahan, Bill	58	0	85	0	.000	0	0	.000	49	0	.000	0	0	0.0	0	0	0	0	0	219	3.8
05-09	McClure, Dave	124	1736	113	235	.481	6	18	.333	46	86	.535	123	379	3.1	79	76	157	86	57	278	2.2
42-43	McGrane, Arthur	21	0	5	0	.000	0	0	.000	11	0	.000	0	0	0.0	0	0	0	0	0	21	1.0
65-67	McKaig, Stuart	49	0	23	55	.418	0	0	.000	14	29	.483	0	41	0.8	0	0	37	0	0	60	1.2
97-98	McLeod, Roshown	69	1649	338	687	.492	71	179	.397	194	262	.740	135	376	5.4	78	125	207	72	60	941	13.6
81-84	McNeely, Doug	85	1103	88	202	.436	0	0	.000	55	82	.671	0	163	1.9	46	81	166	47	3	231	2.7
06-07	McRoberts, Josh	69	2047	279	517	.540	10	36	.278	174	262	.664	130	449	6.5	167	131	190	80	128	742	10.8
82-85	Meagher, Dan	118	2583	275	596	.461	0	0	.000	206	323	.638	0	476	4.0	137	189	334	74	14	756	6.4
02-03	Means, Andy	17	47	4	9	.444	2	2	1.00	2	4	.500	5	14	0.8	2	3	3	3	0	12	0.7
92-95	Meek, Erik	121	1877	214	358	.598	0	0	.000	185	322	.575	222	520	4.3	49	100	241	55	73	613	5.1
71-73	Melchionni, Gary	77	0	305	685	.445	0	0	.000	193	231	.835	0	207	2.7	184	0	127	0	0	803	10.4
03-06	Melchionni, Lee	117	1649	165	426	.387	111	309	.359	80	121	.661	66	260	2.2	68	67	168	63	14	521	4.5
43-44	Metzler, Robert	18	0	4	0	.000	0	0	.000	2	0	.000	0	0	0.0	0	0	0	0	0	10	0.6
60-62	Mewhort, Buzz	71	0	128	274	.467	0	0	.000	90	141	.638	0	225	3.2	0	0	110	0	0	346	4.9
42-43	Miller, Alex	19	0	9	0	.000	0	0	.000	0	0	.000	0	0	0.0	0	0	0	0	0	18	0.9
57-58	Miller, Don	39	0	45	121	.372	0	0	.000	27	40	.675	0	63	1.6	0	0	36	0	0	117	3.0
37-39	Minor, Stoop	37	0	36	0	.000	0	0	.000	20	0	.000	0	0	0.0	0	0	0	0	0	92	2.5
40-41	Mock, Bill	48	0	125	0	.000	0	0	.000	40	0	.000	0	0	0.0	0	0	0	0	0	290	6.0
93-96	Moore, Tony	56	456	55	90	.611	0	0	.000	32	47	.681	49	106	1.9	24	34	61	11	26	142	2.5
54-56	Morgan, Junior 7	9	0	249	611	.408	0	0	.000	215	330	.652	0	643	8.1	0	0	260	0	0	713	9.0
59-61	Morgan, Merrill	29	0	30	87	.345	0	0	.000	10	17	.588	0	26	0.9	0	0	31	0	0	70	2.4
59-59	Morris, Johnny	1	0	0	1	.000	0	0	.000	0	0	.000	0	0	0.0	0	0	2	0	0	0	0.0
76-79	Morrison, Harold	93	929	89	230	.387	0	0	.000	62	94	.660	0	193	2.1	45	66	136	0	0	240	2.6
75-76	Moses, George	35	0	122	226	.540	0	0	.000	35	77	.455	0	316	9.0	90	0	113	61	0	279	8.0
44-44	Mote, Kelly	2	0	0	0	.000	0	0	.000	0	0	.000	0	0	0.0	0	0	0	0	0	0	0.0
44-44	Mott	4	0	1	0	.000	0	0	.000	0	0	.000	0	0	0.0	0	0	0	0	0	2	0.5
39-41	Moyer, Bob	16	0	5	0	.000	0	0	.000	2	0	.000	0	0	0.0	0	0	0	0	0	12	0.8
60-62	Mullen, Jack	56	0	107	248	.431	0	0	.000	49	99	.495	0	187	3.3	0	0	88	0	0	263	4.7
62-64	Mullins, Jeff	86	0	770	1495	.515	0	0	.000	344	452	.761	0	776	9.0	0	0	190	0	0	1884	21.9
64-64	Murray, Terry	1	0	0	1	.000	0	0	.000	0	0	.000	0	2	2.0	0	0	1	0	0	0	0.0
42-42	Nauman	2	0	1	0	.000	0	0	.000	0	0	.000	0	0	0.0	0	0	0	0	0	2	1.0
46-46	Neighborgall,	4	0	0	0	.000	0	0	.000	0	0	.000	0	0	0.0	0	0	0	0	0	0	0.0
05-08	Nelson, DeMarcus	124	3254	473	1015	.466	124	332	.373	266	454	.586	177	606	4.9	222	255	265	145	40	1336	10.8
84-87	Nessley, Martin	92	731	86	180	.478	0	0	.000	52	83	.627	35	191	2.1	30	55	144	17	53	224	2.4
56-58	Newcome, Jim	75	0	335	836	.401	0	0	.000	156	256	.609	0	600	8.0	0	0	179	0	0	826	11.0
94-97	Newton, Greg	107	2006	310	545	.569	0	0	.000	192	315	.610	195	550	5.1	48	118	233	68	98	812	7.6
77-77	Northrop, Geoff	12	44	6	14	.429	0	0	.000	5	7	.714	0	8	0.7	2	6	12	0	0	17	1.4
05-05	Novick, Tom	2	0	0	0	.000	0	0	.000	0	0	.000	0	0	0.0	0	0	1	0	0	0	0.0
73-76	O'Connell, Dave	64	0	74	169	.438	0	0	.000	35	67	.522	0	78	1.2	23	0	79	0	0	183	2.9
71-72	O'Connor, Richie	47	0	237	543	.436	0	0	.000	170	232	.733	0	236	5.0	90	0	95	0	0	644	13.7
37-39	O'Mara, Bob	53	0	93	0	.000	0	0	.000	35	0	.000	0	0	0.0	0	0	0	0	0	221	4.2
43-43	Osborn,	1	0	1	0	.000	0	0	.000	0	0	.000	0	0	0.0	0	0	0	0	0	2	2.0
04-07	Pagliuca, Joe	13	21	0	3	.000	0	1	.000	0	0	.000	0	1	1.0	0	0	2	0	0	0	0.0
89-91	Palmer, Crawford	82	670	75	126	.595	0	0	.000	45	70	.643	51	151	1.8	13	48	115	19	32	195	2.4
37-37	Parker, Ace	2	0	0	0	.000	0	0	.000	0	0	.000	0	0	0.0	0	0	0	0	0	0	0.0
92-95	Parks, Cherokee	131	3464	629	1142	.551	34	102	.333	351	465	.755	263	874	6.7	103	206	270	93	230	1643	12.5
38-40	Parsons, Bill	66	0	87	0	.000	0	0	.000	52	0	.000	0	0	0.0	0	0	0	0	0	226	3.4
06-09	Paulus, Greg	139	3752	376	907	.415	210	527	.398	231	298	.775	55	293	2.1	468	303	310	172	5	1193	8.6
49-49	Pergerm, Ernest	16	0	8	0	.000	0	0	.000	8	0	.000	0	0	0.0	0	0	0	0	0	24	1.5
05-06	Perkins, Ross	11	17	1	3	.333	1	1	1.00	0	0	.000	0	2	0.2	0	1	2	0	0	3	0.3
96-96	Perry, Baker	5	5	2	2	1.00	1	1	1.00	1	1	1.00	0	1	0.2	0	0	2	0	0	6	1.2
10-10	Peters, Casey	7	8	0	0	.000	0	0	.000	0	0	.000	0	1	0.2	0	1	0	0	0	0	0.0
53-53	Peters, Tommy	9	0	3	6	.500	0	0	.000	4	6	.667	0	2	0.2	0	0	9	0	0	10	1.1
10-10	Plumlee, Mason	34	480	49	106	.462	2	8	.250	25	46	.543	39	104	3.1	30	32	73	18	30	125	3.7
09-10	Plumlee, Miles	64	819	101	186	.543	1	1	1.000	45	70	.643	78	231	3.6	13	63	140	24	38	248	3.9
06-09	Pocius, Martynas	81	532	51	129	.395	19	76	.250	21	26	.808	16	45	0.6	32	43	59	19	1	142	1.8
37-37	Podger, Ken	21	0	75	0	.000	0	0	.000	28	0	.000	0	0	0.0	0	0	0	0	0	178	8.5

Years	Name	G	MIN	FG	FGA	PCT	3PT	3PA	PCT	FT	FTA	PCT	OR	TR	AVG	AST	TO	PF	ST	BL	PTS	AVG
48-48	Poplin, Walt	14	0	31	0	.000	0	0	.000	6	0	.000	0	0	0.0	0	0	0	0	0	68	4.9
68-70	Posen, John	29	0	28	59	.475	0	0	.000	19	26	.731	0	35	1.2	23	0	26	0	0	75	2.6
39-41	Price, Glenn	58	0	170	0	.000	0	0	.000	59	0	.000	0	0	0.0	0	0	0	0	0	399	6.9
95-98	Price, Ricky	112	2509	382	895	.427	90	273	.330	172	252	.683	105	310	2.8	112	174	202	72	18	1026	9.2
61-61	Raksnis, Charlie	2	0	1	1	1.00	0	0	.000	1	1	1.00	0	1	0.5	0	0	2	0	0	3	1.5
03-05	Randolph, Shavlik	92	1608	205	405	.506	12	42	.286	158	247	.640	174	394	4.3	56	97	257	70	129	580	6.3
42-42	Rauch,	2	0	1	0	.000	0	0	.000	0	0	.000	0	0	0.0	0	0	0	0	0	2	1.0
72-74	Redding, Chris	78	0	399	813	.491	0	0	.000	343	425	.807	0	473	6.1	44	0	216	0	0	1141	14.6
03-06	Redick, J.J.	139	4732	825	1906	.433	457	1126	.406	662	726	.912	66	375	2.7	306	296	226	152	9	2769	19.9
65-67	Riedy, Bob	79	0	288	627	.459	0	0	.000	165	233	.708	0	535	6.8	0	0	197	0	0	741	9.4
53-53	Riegel, Bill	26	0	147	361	.407	0	0	.000	131	213	.615	0	189	2.4	0	0	93	0	0	425	16.3
72-72	Righter, Ron	25	0	59	128	.461	0	0	.000	44	59	.746	0	78	3.1	5	0	36	0	0	162	6.5
37-37	Riley, Joe	17	0	17	0	.000	0	0	.000	5	0	.000	0	0	0.0	0	0	0	0	0	39	2.3
38-38	Robb, Spencer	18	0	8	0	.000	0	0	.000	2	0	.000	0	0	0.0	0	0	0	0	0	18	1.0
57-59	Robertson, Jerry	68	0	103	285	.361	0	0	.000	64	122	.525	0	255	3.8	0	0	125	0	0	270	4.0
46-46	Robinson, Jack	20	0	17	0	.000	0	0	.000	3	0	.000	0	0	0.0	0	0	0	0	0	37	1.9
46-46	Roellke, Bob	22	0	14	0	.000	0	0	.000	9	0	.000	0	0	0.0	0	0	0	0	0	37	1.7
55-56	Rosenthal, Dick	23	0	20	50	.400	0	0	.000	9	18	.500	0	23	1.0	0	0	5	0	0	49	2.1
41-47	Rothbaum, Sammy	71	0	123	0	.000	0	0	.000	43	0	.000	0	0	0.0	0	0	0	0	0	289	4.1
62-62	Salisbury, Steve	2	0	1	2	.500	0	0	.000	0	1	.000	0	0	0.0	0	0	0	0	0	2	1.0
00-03	Sanders, Casey	124	1348	117	221	.529	0	0	.000	102	197	.518	150	316	2.5	27	85	238	29	120	336	2.7
47-49	Sapp, Carl	74	0	94	0	.000	0	0	.000	51	0	.000	0	0	0.0	0	0	0	0	0	239	3.2
70-71	Saunders, Larry	56	0	191	319	.599	0	0	.000	123	176	.699	0	406	7.3	24	0	145	0	0	505	9.0
47-50	Scarborough, Dave	70	0	151	0	.000	0	0	.000	94	0	.000	0	0	0.0	0	0	90	0	0	396	5.7
07-10	Scheyer, Jon	144	4759	586	1442	.406	297	780	.381	608	706	.861	148	522	3.6	440	211	229	208	30	2077	14.4
61-63	Schmidt, Fred	64	0	176	371	.474	0	0	.000	61	73	.836	0	106	1.7	0	0	71	0	0	413	6.5
56-58	Schmidt, Paul	67	0	193	425	.454	0	0	.000	173	273	.634	0	409	6.1	0	0	168	0	0	559	8.3
42-47	Seward, John	100	0	354	0	.000	0	0	.000	188	0	.000	0	0	0.0	0	0	0	0	0	896	9.0
52-54	Shabel, Fred	61	0	79	181	.436	0	0	.000	56	78	.718	0	76	1.2	10	0	115	0	0	214	3.5
71-73	Shaw, Alan	82	0	263	480	.548	0	0	.000	218	300	.727	0	673	8.2	104	0	215	0	0	744	9.1
39-41	Shokes, Eddie	40	0	65	0	.000	0	0	.000	16	0	.000	0	0	0.0	0	0	0	0	0	146	3.7
44-44	Shy	13	0	11	0	.000	0	0	.000	2	0	.000	0	0	0.0	0	0	0	0	0	24	1.8
49-49	Simmons, Buck	3	0	1	0	.000	0	0	.000	0	0	.000	0	0	0.0	0	0	0	0	0	2	0.7
00-99	Simpson, J.D.	80	186	11	46	.239	4	25	.160	15	24	.625	6	27	0.3	14	22	13	9	0	41	0.5
08-10	Singler, Kyle	111	3601	595	1370	.434	205	543	.378	372	488	.762	272	762	6.9	233	246	289	134	95	1767	15.9
95-98	Singleton, Todd	42	100	13	26	.500	0	0	.000	10	17	.588	5	15	0.4	5	5	12	1	4	36	0.9
47-50	Skibstead, Wes	32	0	30	0	.000	0	0	.000	14	0	.000	0	0	0.0	0	0	13	0	0	74	2.3
68-70	Smiley, Glen	8	0	6	13	.462	0	0	.000	2	5	.400	0	6	0.8	1	0	6	0	0	14	1.8
86-89	Smith, John	120	2061	338	619	.546	26	54	.481	243	320	.759	118	358	3.0	54	160	219	67	21	945	7.9
08-10	Smith, Nolan	106	2583	407	922	.441	109	288	.378	224	284	.789	70	232	2.2	217	173	194	95	16	1147	10.8
86-89	Snyder, Quin	136	3178	292	682	.428	108	303	.356	156	223	.700	44	260	1.9	575	316	341	185	59	848	6.2
76-79	Spanarkel, Jim	114	3298	724	1374	.527	0	0	.000	564	700	.806	0	454	4.0	399	309	305	253	0	2012	17.6
40-42	Spuhler, Raymond	64	0	103	0	.000	0	0	.000	29	0	.000	0	0	0.0	0	0	0	0	0	235	3.7
42-48	Stark, Bill	35	0	33	0	.000	0	0	.000	7	0	.000	0	0	0.0	0	0	0	0	0	73	2.1
43-43	Stough,	9	0	17	0	.000	0	0	.000	11	0	.000	0	0	0.0	0	0	0	0	0	45	5.0
51-51	Strauss, Bob	3	0	1	6	.167	0	0	.000	0	2	.000	0	0	0.0	0	0	4	0	0	2	0.7
85-88	Strickland, Kevin	125	2337	411	827	.497	91	241	.378	182	231	.788	115	374	3.0	119	155	222	84	52	1095	8.8
78-81	Suddath, Jim	113	1076	105	214	.491	0	0	.000	57	81	.704	0	148	1.3	73	81	132	13	2	267	2.4
73-75	Suk, Bill	70	0	73	177	.412	0	0	.000	47	66	.712	0	140	2.0	42	0	142	0	0	193	2.8
07-07	Sutton, Nick	1	2	0	0	.000	0	0	.000	0	0	.000	0	0	0.0	0	0	0	0	0	0	0.0
01-01	Sweet, Andre	7	79	13	27	.481	1	5	.200	2	6	.333	8	18	2.6	4	4	6	6	1	29	4.1
37-39	Swindell, Ed	67	0	207	0	.000	0	0	.000	79	0	.000	0	0	0.0	0	0	0	0	0	493	7.4
79-82	Taylor, Vince	120	3530	573	1112	.515	0	0	.000	309	479	.645	0	343	2.9	212	264	326	89	9	1455	12.1
68-70	Teer, Tim	40	0	53	150	.353	0	0	.000	13	19	.684	0	54	1.4	4	0	35	0	0	119	3.0
37-39	Thomas, Jim	47	0	45	0	.000	0	0	.000	30	0	.000	0	0	0.0	0	0	0	0	0	120	2.6
07-10	Thomas, Lance	140	2758	235	448	.525	0	0	.000	177	295	.600	255	508	3.6	64	166	397	77	33	647	4.6
03-04	Thompson, Michael	19	70	9	16	.563	0	0	.000	9	11	.818	6	9	0.5	0	4	12	1	6	27	1.4
55-55	Thuemmel, Bob	18	0	6	25	.240	0	0	.000	1	9	.111	0	5	0.3	0	0	20	0	0	13	0.7
63-65	Tison, Hack	85	0	315	617	.511	0	0	.000	169	258	.655	0	583	6.9	0	0	202	0	0	799	9.4
80-83	Tissaw, Mike	94	1525	75	178	.421	0	0	.000	85	160	.531	0	244	2.6	39	97	166	20	12	235	2.5
54-55	Tobin, Don	36	0	67	193	.347	0	0	.000	46	82	.561	0	121	3.4	0	0	93	0	0	180	5.0
07-07	Tormey, Griffin	0	0	0	0	.000	0	0	.000	0	0	.000	0	0	0.0	0	0	0	0	0	0	0.0
53-55	Turner, Hal	58	0	117	337	.347	0	0	.000	24	39	.615	0	52	0.9	0	0	67	0	0	258	4.4

Years	Name	G	MIN	FG	FGA	PCT	3PT	3PA	PCT	FT	FTA	PCT	OR	TR	AVG	AST	TO	PF	ST	BL	PTS	AVG
43-44	Turner, Kenny	25	0	14	0	.000	0	0	.000	7	0	.000	0	0	0.0	0	0	0	0	0	35	1.4
62-62	Ulrich, Bill	21	0	34	86	.395	0	0	.000	10	18	.556	0	31	1.5	0	0	35	0	0	78	3.7
64-66	Vacendak, Steve	84	0	378	877	.431	0	0	.000	197	289	.682	0	358	4.3	0	0	199	0	0	953	11.3
39-41	Valasek, Cy	66	0	136	0	.000	0	0	.000	65	0	.000	0	0	0.0	0	0	0	0	0	337	5.1
67-69	Vandenberg, Steve	76	0	239	443	.540	0	0	.000	160	214	.748	0	458	6.0	13	0	178	0	0	638	8.4
65-67	Verga, Bob	80	0	728	1486	.490	0	0	.000	302	414	.729	0	299	3.7	0	0	195	0	0	1758	22.0
57-58	Vernon, Bob	49	0	222	540	.411	0	0	.000	94	132	.712	0	156	3.2	0	0	61	0	0	538	11.0
94-97	Wallace, Carmen	81	927	97	218	.445	29	67	.433	57	78	.731	67	138	1.7	29	46	115	37	27	280	3.5
47-49	Wallingford, Tom	30	0	15	0	.000	0	0	.000	5	0	.000	0	0	0.0	0	0	0	0	0	35	1.2
66-66	Warren, Dick	5	0	0	3	.000	0	0	.000	1	2	.500	0	3	0.6	0	0	1	0	0	1	0.2
57-59	Watson, Bill	32	0	27	79	.342	0	0	.000	18	29	.621	0	34	1.1	0	0	37	0	0	72	2.3
59-59	Wayand, Bob	1	0	0	2	.000	0	0	.000	1	2	.500	0	2	2.0	0	0	1	0	0	1	1.0
81-81	Weingart, Jon	6	10	1	4	.250	0	0	.000	0	0	.000	0	1	0.2	1	0	1	0	0	2	0.3
66-68	Wendelin, Ron	81	0	118	312	.378	0	0	.000	59	98	.602	0	154	1.9	0	0	171	0	0	295	3.6
82-83	Wendt, Greg	44	366	41	102	.402	0	2	.000	21	36	.583	0	71	1.6	14	22	54	13	0	103	2.3
70-72	West, Robby	37	0	62	157	.395	0	0	.000	18	28	.643	0	49	1.3	40	0	43	0	0	142	3.8
41-41	Wetmore,	4	0	3	0	.000	0	0	.000	0	0	.000	0	0	0.0	0	0	0	0	0	6	1.5
46-46	Whiting, Dick	29	0	80	0	.000	0	0	.000	62	0	.000	0	0	0.0	0	0	0	0	0	222	7.7
81-81	Whitted, Gordon	11	17	0	1	.000	0	0	.000	0	2	.000	0	2	0.2	1	4	2	3	0	0	0.0
46-46	Williams	3	0	1	0	.000	0	0	.000	1	0	.000	0	0	0.0	0	0	0	0	0	3	1.0
80-82	Williams, Allen	73	833	85	174	.489	0	0	.000	47	75	.627	0	128	1.8	16	52	107	7	16	217	3.0
09-09	Williams, Elloit	34	563	56	127	.441	9	36	.250	23	46	.500	29	77	2.3	23	29	58	21	1	144	4.2
00-02	Williams, Jason	108	3572	713	1575	.453	313	797	.393	340	507	.671	89	395	3.7	644	424	253	235	14	2079	19.3
03-06	Williams, Shelden	139	3903	687	1202	.572	4	12	.333	550	796	.691	447	1262	9.1	119	321	432	161	422	1928	13.9
83-86	Williams, Weldon	73	369	52	97	.536	0	0	.000	22	37	.595	0	81	1.1	11	28	54	7	4	126	1.7
62-63	Williamson, Scott	18	0	3	13	.231	0	0	.000	5	6	.833	0	15	0.8	0	0	3	0	0	11	0.6
40-41	Winkin, John	2	0	0	0	.000	0	0	.000	0	0	.000	0	0	0.0	0	0	0	0	0	0	0.0
95-98	Wojciechowski, Steve	128	3263	198	517	.383	141	387	.364	150	205	.732	74	291	2.3	505	202	287	203	0	687	5.4
38-38	Wood, Bob	2	0	0	0	.000	0	0	.000	1	0	.000	0	0	0.0	0	0	0	0	0	1	0.5
44-44	Wright, Bill	26	0	129	0	.000	0	0	.000	38	0	.000	0	0	0.0	0	0	0	0	0	296	11.4
70-72	Yarbrough, Stu	51	0	93	175	.531	0	0	.000	91	125	.728	0	116	2.3	21	0	71	0	0	277	5.4
48-51	York, Scotty	98	0	154	328	.470	0	0	.000	103	83	1.241	0	0	0.0	0	0	96	0	0	411	4.2
47-50	Youmans, Corren	99	0	390	0	.000	0	0	.000	193	0	.000	0	0	0.0	0	0	62	0	0	973	9.8
75-76	Young, Kenny	43	0	79	200	.395	0	0	.000	32	48	.667	0	24	0.6	45	0	70	0	0	190	4.4
59-61	Youngkin, Carroll	81	0	413	765	.540	0	0	.000	328	572	.573	0	829	10.2	0	0	232	0	0	1154	14.2
10-10	Zafirovski, Todd	0	0	0	0	.000	0	0	.000	0	0	.000	0	0	0.0	0	0	0	0	0	0	0.0
38-38	Zavlaris	11	0	4	0	.000	0	0	.000	1	0	.000	0	0	0.0	0	0	0	0	0	9	0.8
65-66	Zimmer, Bill	9	0	4	16	.250	0	0	.000	8	12	.667	0	6	0.7	0	0	0	0	0	16	1.8
07-10	Zoubek, Brian	133	1670	225	379	.594	0	0	.000	112	184	.609	276	599	4.5	73	130	289	55	86	562	4.2

CAREER SCORING LEADERS

#	Player	Points	#	Player	Points	#	Player	Points	#	Player	Points
1.	J.J. Redick, 2003-06	2,769	16.	Dick Groat, 1950-52	1,886	31.	Mike Lewis, 1966-68	1,416	46.	Chris Redding, 1972-74	1,141
2.	Johnny Dawkins, 1983-86	2,556	17.	Jeff Mullins, 1962-64	1,884	32.	Phil Henderson, 1987-90	1,397	47.	Bob Fleischer, 1973-75	1,139
3.	Christian Laettner, 1989-92	2,460	18.	Kyle Singler, 2008-p	1,767	33.	Mike Dunleavy, 2000-02	1,371	48.	Alaa Abdelnaby, 1987-90	1,137
4.	Mike Gminski, 1977-80	2,323	19.	Bob Verga, 1965-67	1,758	34.	Joe Belmont, 1953-56	1,338	49.	Nate James, 1997-01	1,116
5.	Danny Ferry, 1986-89	2,155	20.	Bobby Hurley, 1990-93	1,731	35.	DeMarcus Nelson, 2004-08	1,336	50.	Willie Hodge, 1973-76	1,115
6.	Mark Alarie, 1983-86	2,136	21.	Randy Denton, 1969-71	1,658	36.	Tate Armstrong, 1974-77	1,304	51.	Kevin Strickland, 1985-88	1,095
7.	Jason Williams, 2000-02	2,079	22.	Ronnie Mayer, 1953-56	1,647	37.	Robert Brickey, 1987-90	1,299		Howard Hurt, 1959-61	1,095
	Gene Banks, 1978-81	2,079	23.	Cherokee Parks, 1992-95	1,643	38.	Jack Marin, 1964-66	1,279	53.	Chris Collins, 1993-96	1,091
9.	Jon Scheyer, 2007-10	2,077	24.	Jeff Capel, 1994-97	1,601	39.	Chris Duhon, 2001-04	1,268	54.	Jay Bilas, 1983-86	1,062
10.	Jim Spanarkel, 1976-79	2,012	25.	Daniel Ewing, 2002-05	1,596	40.	Gerald Henderson, 2007-09	1,262	55.	Kenny Dennard, 1978-81	1,057
11.	Shane Battier, 1998-01	1,984	26.	Thomas Hill, 1990-93	1,594	41.	Bernie Janicki, 1952-54	1,247	56.	Rudy D'Emilio, 1952-54	1,028
	Art Heyman, 1961-63	1,984	27.	David Henderson, 1983-86	1,570	42.	Greg Paulus, 2006-08	1,193	57.	Ricky Price, 1995-98	1,026
13.	Trajan Langdon, 1995-99	1,974	28.	Carlos Boozer, 2000-02	1,506	43.	Tommy Amaker, 1984-87	1,168	58.	Chip Engelland, 1980-83	1,025
14.	Shelden Williams, 2003-06	1,928	29.	Chris Carrawell, 1996-00	1,455	44.	Carroll Youngkin, 1959-61	1,156	59.	Antonio Lang, 1991-94	1,012
15.	Grant Hill, 1991-94	1,924		Vince Taylor, 1979-82	1,455	45.	Nolan Smith, 2008-p	1,147	60.	Rick Katherman, 1969-71	1,005

BIBLIOGRAPHY

Duke Basketball: An Illustrated History, Taylor Publishing Company, By Bill Brill, 1986

A Season is a Lifetime, Simon & Schuster, By Bill Brill and Mike Krzyzewski, 1992

If Gargoyles Could Talk, Carolina Academic Press, By William E. King, 1997

Leading with the Heart, Warner Books, By Mike Krzyzewski with Donald T. Phillips, 2000

Duke Men's Basketball 2010-2011 Media Guide, Duke University, 2011